D1231456

THE ZERO TO 100 MILLION
SALES BLUEPRINT

Advance Praise

"As a partner with Microsoft Advertising, Gary helped put a region on the map. He did nothing short of shifting mindsets. He was key in marrying a near-shore business model and offering best-in-class digital marketing services. His determination and passion changed the way we think about winning business. He didn't just win new business; he built a playbook that extended customer lifetime value. Gary is the type of person who knows how to find opportunity, attract the right people, and win partnerships for the long haul."

—**Mauricio Orantes**, Director of Partner Development: Americas at Microsoft

"Gary is a truly legendary sales leader! He embodies all of the traits of a highly capable salesperson, yet he remains humble and respectful. He is consultative in his approach whilse still being able to hold his own during negotiations, all the while being charming and charismatic. I find myself walking away from every conversation with Gary a better salesperson, and his wisdom in sales is unmatched. When I found out Gary was writing a step-by-step guide to sales excellence, I immediately requested a copy because I knew that I would gain tremendous value from it."

—**Christian Moore**, Commercial Account Executive II at Salesloft

"Despite my fifteen years of sales experience, I've never ever seen a leader be so passionate and engaged when it comes to sales. Even when we were growing like crazy with over 200 employees and Gary was in the boardroom or corner office, he'd always make time almost every day to come down and sit with the sales team, take phone calls with us, and close deals! I can say with certainty that this is the book we have all been waiting years for Gary to write to reveal some of his methods, tactics, and secret sauce!"

—**Will Peralta**, Senior Digital Marketing Consultant at First Rank Digital

"This blueprint is a perfect distillation of Gary's strengths as a sales leader in the tech industry: a deep understanding of how to quickly identify a market's needs, technology's role as a force multiplier, and pathways to scale the business to realize profits. An excellent toolkit for tech and sales leaders out there."

—**Patrick Tam**, Strategic Partner Manager at Google

"As an early reader, I'm excited to see this hit the bookshelves soon and recommend it to anyone who needs to crack the code with their sales and revenue. Gary shares tangible and actionable recommendations on how to assess your sales tech stack (new or existing), a thorough list of considerations and priorities before change/implementation, and how to get buy-in and adoption from everyone to secure success. There are too many fluffy sales books out there with little to zero value. This book is an exception and will yield significant returns if you implement just 10 percent of Gary's proven blueprint!"

—**H. Rodnie Silva**, Manager of Growth at Republix

"It was impressive to see how Gary managed to build a strong reseller business from scratch, growing his sales team and keeping performance and operational excellence throughout the journey. He became one of Google's strongest partners while I was managing the program due to his ability to see and make things happen."

—**Marcela Tonello**, Program Manager at Meta (Facebook)

"When big thinking meets fundamental execution, amazing things are possible. People from all organizations can learn from Gary's experience and approach to business. Build a great team. Develop mutual partnerships, and most importantly, drive sales. This book can be an effective resource for anyone who wants to start a business or be successful as an individual contributor."

—**Brett Klee**, Account Executive at Salesforce

"I will always remember my time working with Gary in sales as one of the best learning experiences in my career. His drive allows him to think outside the box and set audacious goals. His discipline is the key component of his success. He's an advocate for hard work and team effort. This book will be an excellent toolkit for tech and sales leaders out there."

—**Karen Hite**, Co-Founder of Hite Digital

THE

ZERO

TO 100

MILLION

SALES BLUEPRINT

GARY GARTH

WITH A FOREWORD BY BEN TYSON

LIONCREST

PUBLISHING

The Zero to 100 Million Sales Blueprint

ISBN 978-1-5445-3916-4 Hardcover

978-1-5445-3915-7 Paperback

978-1-5445-3914-0 Ebook

978-1-5445-3917-1 Audiobook

CONTENTS

FOREWORD

By Ben Tyson, Global Head of Sales Enablement at Google

Gary has a story to tell that's unique in the world of sales. I've witnessed it firsthand. I've had the real pleasure to know him personally as we worked closely together during my time as Head of Sales Enablement at Google empowering our marketing agency partners. The first time I met Gary I was surprised to see the CEO walking around the sales floor taking customer calls instead of sitting in the corner office.

Rarely have I seen such a customer-centric CEO. Gary wasn't shy to get right in the trenches with his team and make sales calls. All kinds of calls. His hands-on approach to sales process optimization stood out. Gary didn't hide out in the boardroom talking about strategy and KPIs. Instead, we would write sales scripts, rebuttals, and email templates together to better enable his team to succeed.

I believe that's why his sales teams have such respect for him and have followed his leadership through thick and thin. Over the years I've trained tens of thousands of sales reps. In that time I've identified a big gap between what sales leadership talks about rolling out and the actual needs felt by the sales reps themselves.

Whether it's hard-core outbound sales, media advertising programs, inside sales, or channel sales, Gary has walked the walk and always as a top performer in the game! This is where Gary shines. And it's why, for many years, I've encouraged him to write this book. Finally, this is it. From the heart.

That's why this book belongs (opened) in the library of every founder, sales leader, and even marketing manager. Gary set out to define the complete blueprint for successful practical sales strategy, tactics, and processes in the B2B, SaaS, and tech markets. But beyond that focus, Gary has paid special attention to providing guidance for entrepreneurs creating their business plans from scratch. Having worked with many founders, I know this is something critical for survival in today's competitive economy.

There's no silver bullet for succeeding in today's B2B or SaaS sales environment. This book stands out because it's jammed with nitty-gritty wisdom, hardened through 20+ years of experience. I'm a big fan of Gary's multifaceted sales strategy. He has successfully incorporated core psychological principles and proven sales best practices together with today's tech-dominated digital trends and tools.

This blueprint covers the entire range of what it takes to be successful in B2B and SaaS sales. Some of the topics that particularly stand out for me include a summary of the classic principles of persuasion, how to create a company's sales playbook, and methods to develop a lean, mean lead-generation machine. The book lays out how to expand your share of wallet by driving cross-sells and upsells, the specifics of building a metrics-driven culture, and how to develop a winning sales team. Gary then provides practical guidance to improve the integration between sales and marketing. The book concludes with an overview of today's sales tech stack and how to leverage it for winning results.

You can't afford to not read and absorb the lessons in this outstanding book. It's also chock-full of great stories illustrating Gary's failures and successes along the way. He clearly lays it all out and with no fluff. This is the real deal.

Everyone who has worked closely with Gary has nothing but respect and admiration for him. It's no surprise to see the success that Gary has had and continues to have with his current endeavors. I feel blessed to have had the opportunity to have a mentor like Gary. I trust you'll benefit from this masterful sales blueprint as much as I have.

INTRODUCTION

I had just spent twenty minutes circling the little hotel room in Palo Alto, California, sweating like crazy and hyperventilating. A few weeks back, I had been speaking with the Google Account Manager assigned to our marketing agency who asked whether we selected Nicaragua as our HQ to also target the fastest growing demographic in the United States—the 55 million US Hispanics. My response: "Of course!"

Fast forward a few weeks, and here I was, invited to talk with Google's Channel Sales team to discuss our experience in targeting US Hispanics with campaigns and selling this approach with Google Ads to business owners.

I gladly accepted the invite, and just hours before driving to Google's massive HQ in Mountain View, California, my Google point of contact told me where to meet and that I could send my presentation to a certain email address.

My presentation? I didn't have one. Not even another boilerplate I could haul out and quickly repurpose. I thought we were going to have a conversation! I can't recall ever before being so stressed out—we finally get an opportunity to get on the radar with Google, establish some authority for our agency, and potentially scale our revenue—only for me to f**k it up like this!

So I calmed myself down and repeated over and over to the mirror, "*Gary, you got this... You got this! You've done this a thousand times before. This is just like a prospect throwing you a curveball. Just stay cool, think on your feet, and adapt."*

Two hours later, still tremendously nervous, I went on stage at Google HQ in front of a team of forty to fifty Googlers—right after another invited agency speaker who had blown away the room with a great presentation and a PowerPoint full of statistics, research, and formulas for US Hispanic marketing.

So I spent a few seconds assessing the audience. Then I walked down from the speaker stand where my computer was supposed to be connected to the projector, stood in front of the first table, and instead said, as I then circled the room:

"I've chosen not to put together a deck for you all today. Why? You're Google for Christ's sake! You have more data, statistics, and research in front of you than I could ever dig up and show to you. Instead, I'm going to tell you, straight from the horse's mouth, the real-life business war stories, after managing a forty-person sales team that cold-calls 20,000 to 30,000 new SMB business owners every single month, and let you know how they react to our pitch on Google Ads, our experiences with US Hispanic business owners, and where we have success pitching a multilanguage targeted campaign. Hopefully, you can draw some conclusions from our last two years of calling on 500,000+ businesses, and together we can figure out how to pitch this audience bilingual campaign strategies and capture more market share."

A couple of months later we were awarded the "Google AdWords Premier SMB Partnership" contract as Partner #22 in the United States among tens of thousands of other agencies. It was at that point an elite group of companies who were all with either publicly traded companies, huge media conglomerates, or at least 100x our size in both clients, employees, and revenue.

I can by no means take credit alone for the above-mentioned accomplishment since behind the scenes were supportive partners and an amazing team. But the opportunity would never have been triggered in the first place or realized for that matter, if it wasn't for a series of applied sales learnings accumulated over the years prior. This book tells that story. Welcome aboard!

WHY I WROTE THIS BOOK

Having worked with tens of thousands of companies over the last twenty years in my own businesses, I've witnessed firsthand how a great idea, a superior product, or a groundbreaking new concept can go completely unnoticed and ultimately fail if lacking a proper sales strategy and execution.

I've had friends close to me who banked *everything* they owned into their startups, only to shut them down when failing with sales, running out of cash, and causing them great suffering as a result.

I've painfully witnessed from the sidelines how that can lead to personal bankruptcy, losing one's home, broken relationships, divorce, affecting kids and family, developing bad habits such as drug and alcohol addictions, and even committing suicide because of the emotional pain and shame of failure.

Well, news flash! Failure should be expected, especially with business and sales. Failure is a good thing as long as you just learn from it. That's why this book also could have been labeled "101 Things to Avoid in Sales and Business" because it's an accumulation of my personal mistakes and learnings over the last decades.

According to *Forbes* and Bloomberg, eight out of ten new businesses go under within eighteen months or less. By writing this book, I aim to help you avoid the mistakes I made in sales and business, not fall into the 80 percent failure category, and instead attain success with *your* purpose and passion so that you can change the world with your great ideas.

This may sound fluffy and like kumbaya for you, but seriously, if you want your solutions and services to gain any traction, create a massive reach, make an impact the world notices, or change the status quo, then you *must* become profitable. Only sustainable companies and solutions survive and get the opportunity to make a difference in the end. And all of that starts with sales, which is why I wrote this book.

At least fifty or more of my former employees today now run their own successful companies. I like to think that my daily sales huddles, live coaching sessions, motivation, and mentoring has played a little role in their success.

Many of them are also my good friends today, and I experience great joy when hearing from them that I am their original mentor who helped them get to where they are today.

By writing this book, I have compiled all of my business learnings and sales lessons forged together with those former employees into one Sales Blueprint in hopes of also helping you become successful and make my résumé of "Successful Entrepreneur Mentor" go from fifty-plus to 50,000 or more.

I have spent *many* years writing this book because I wanted to guarantee every single reader that if you apply the lessons from these learnings acquired through blood, sweat, tears, stress, ulcers, a divorce, depression, financial struggles, and ultimately costing me many millions of dollars, then you won't have to make the same mistakes I did. Instead you can climb to the mountaintop of success *without* encountering the unnecessary obstacles I did on my way.

WHAT TO EXPECT FROM THIS BOOK

Most sales books in the market are subject-specific. How can you close more deals? How to become a better sales leader? What tools or processes do you need? How to coach your sales reps? How to hire salespeople?

And since I am 100 percent autodidact in sales and business, with only a high school degree, rest assured that I've read every single sales and business book I could get my hands on over the last two decades.

There are a lot of *great* books out there, but during my reading journey I have never come across any that began with the end goal of your business in mind and provided me with all the pieces of the puzzle required to build a successful sales organization and thereby create a thriving business.

And if you're like me, you may find that most books you read touch on one or two core concepts, and after reading the first couple of chapters, you get it! Time to move on. There's little value in continuing reading the rest of that book and you might as well put it back on your bookshelf and forget all about it.

This book is the complete opposite. This is full of 100 percent end-to-end practical tangible concepts that you can apply to your business tomorrow. Zero fluff, unnecessary fillers, or expanded stories. I only share stories as context and evidence for what strategies worked for me or others and what didn't!

Additionally, I frankly don't want to read more books from sales leaders at big organizations with a ton of resources, market capital, and a strong brand behind them. When you are at that point you are already at the top of the mountain. How difficult is it then to build out a sales team and processes?

Instead, I wanted to write a book targeting the vast majority that don't have a reputable brand yet. Who, like me, were bootstrapped and didn't have a limitless marketing machine behind them flooding them with leads every day. It's intended for readers who need to make every single penny count, every hire impactful, and develop winning strategies that you, as David, can best use in your slingshot to beat Goliath.

You can also navigate straight to a chapter depending on where you are in your company's journey. If you haven't launched sales effectively yet, perhaps you need to start with Chapter 1 and begin with the end in mind—understanding whom to target, their problems, the pain points you solve, who your actual customers are, where they are to be found, how to cut through the noise, and how to pitch them.

But maybe you already have all that locked down to a science and instead are struggling with scaling. You can't afford superstar reps, you have a hard time hiring good salespeople within your budget limitations, and you need to crack the code on how to add inexperienced salespeople to the process who meet their quotas and can grow within your organization. For that, check out Chapter 7.

Then come questions such as what processes and framework to implement, what to measure, or which tools to use to make all of that happen. Or even what marketing knowledge and methods do I need to be an effective sales leader? Each has a chapter. Every single principle, process, and best practice you need to build a successful sales machine for your company is covered in these pages.

Last, feel free to assess where you are in your journey, and begin by reading the most pertinent chapters if you don't want to read the entire book from beginning to end but just want to get some immediate wins for your business. Either way works for me. As long as you extract value, shorten your learning curve, and crush your goals, then I'm happy! Mission accomplished.

WHO IS THIS BOOK *NOT* FOR AND WHO CAN BENEFIT

This is not a "Sales 101" book or intended for a B2C-focused company or retail concept.

People who aren't prepared to put in hard work and practice patience with regard to the outcome should put down this book. I hate to burst your illusion, but 99 percent of the sponsored posts you see on social media with hacks and shortcuts are get-rich-quick schemes and won't work. You need to study, try, fail, then try again, and work twelve to sixteen hours a day. Then my recommendations can work.

And don't expect a conventional book with subject-matter expertise on some fresh new concept on how to sell easier and better.

This is an entire *sales blueprint*—a bible, if you will—on what's required to take your startup to the next level by working through a framework for scale from A to Z. In other words, how to go from $0 to $100 million.

This book has a strong focus on B2B, SaaS, and tech sales and is *especially* written for the startup entrepreneurs behind the scenes of these companies —the founders of the next successful startup that no one saw coming.

The inexperienced sales leader looking to elevate his or her game into the big leagues can also find value in this book, with learnings, proven concepts, and applicable examples on how to scale your team. Finally, some marketing folks may pick up a few insights that help them create Smarketing nirvana—a close integration of sales *with* marketing.

A Quick Overview of the Contents

This book delves into a wide-ranging set of topics. And it's very content-rich with many practical examples. I begin with strategy and the importance of always having the end in mind. The book then dives into the sales trenches and emerges with some key marketing first principles before engaging again with the main aspects of sales strategy.

One of the key themes of the book is then explored, and that is to focus on your strengths and delegate the rest. This is followed by an in-depth walk-through of sales metrics—why they are critical to your lifeblood and growth and which ones to track.

Great salespeople are made, not born. Chapter 7 illustrates why this is so true and what to look for in your hiring and onboarding processes. I then set out for you my formula for superstar sales management and related best practices to foster this.

Messaging and execution, although often thought of as activities "owned" by marketing, are shown to be just the opposite—sales involvement is critical to success.

Chapter 10 is rich with information and guidance on sales demos, collateral, testimonials, proposals, and negotiation.

I firmly believe that customer satisfaction is the key to revenue growth and show why this sets the stage for successful cross-selling and upselling. Sales organization is one of my favorite topics and should be yours too. Here I dig into sales operations, effective sales meetings, and the critical role of your Customer Relationship Management (CRM) system.

I've devoted a lot of time and research into the role of the sales technology stack for successful scaling and provide recommendations of my top picks as well as an extensive resource list of many more in the landscape. Outsourcing is a strategic decision and so I devote an entire chapter to that important topic.

Finally, I wish you well as you adopt some of these concepts, practices, and technologies in your own growth journey—from zero to 100 million!

Scan the QR code below to access our YouTube channel with video trailers for each chapter of the book.

1

BEGIN WITH THE END IN MIND

Stephen R. Covey reminded us of a saying often (wrongly) attributed to Abraham Lincoln: "Give me six hours to chop down a tree and I spend the first four sharpening the ax."

So here I was at 1:00 a.m. in the pitch dark doing it again. I tossed back my second espresso, squeezed my 6' 5" frame into a tiny Suzuki Alto and raced along torturous jungle roads to my office in Managua, Nicaragua, all the while asking myself, "What the hell did I sign up for here?" A few months earlier I had just celebrated at a blowout farewell party in Copenhagen, Denmark, this time driving my white BMW Cabriolet to a fancy 2-star Michelin restaurant with my family, friends, and business associates. All of them wished me good luck on my promising next business adventure in Nicaragua, with special funding support from the Danish government!

And then third world reality hit hard—unexpectedly of course. Only a few months after arriving, I was thrown directly into what everyone had warned about. But I was convinced it wouldn't happen to me—massive political unrest. President

Daniel Ortega was reelected for the third term and due to an international dispute, all funding from Nordic countries was immediately stopped and embassies were shut down. I found myself banging my head asking how could I be so stupid.

Everyone had advised me against coming with my grand plan to help the Nicaraguan economy. My partner Alexander and I were going to invest millions of dollars to hire, train, and convert bilingual underemployed call center employees into digital marketing professionals. If only I had followed the risk assessment reports where reputable investors rated Nicaragua as the 186th least desirable country in the world to invest in. I could have just stayed in my comfort zone maintaining my luxurious lifestyle with a penthouse apartment on Strandvejen, at the time the most upscale street in Copenhagen. Instead, I jumped into this black hole, forcing myself every day to get up at midnight only to pound the phones to Denmark until dawn, upselling advertising campaigns to radio clients so I could fund our harebrained project in Nicaragua. A project now with a very grim outlook.

If I'd begun with a realistic end in mind, I probably never would have jumped on a plane and relocated to Nicaragua in 2010 because that year was undoubtedly one of the hardest years in my life—ever. Almost nine months with no sleep, grabbing a few hours whenever I could during the day after pulling a double shift selling to clients back home all night. Then, seven espressos later, welcoming the Nicaraguan staff at 9:00 a.m. to the morning huddle. I struggled to maintain a positive outlook to inspire my team for the next eight hours before going home to crash, only to start all over again. That's where I got my first gray hair! Worse, I felt like I was destroying my body and my mind. "What a fool," I thought.

So why is this story instructive? Especially so, during these times where entrepreneurship has become a glorified aspirational occupation and social media is filled with get-rich-quick schemes and hacks. It seems everyone wants to be a digital nomad working from the beach or aspires to be the next Elon Musk.

The truth of the matter is that the statistics are very, very grim for aspiring entrepreneurs. The vast majority—80 percent—cease to exist within the first eighteen months of operation. In fact, only 4 percent of all companies make it beyond the ten-year mark. That doesn't mean they're successful. In many cases they're just surviving as a family-owned or life-style business, often still struggling to become profitable. Ninety-five percent of these companies won't even reach $1 million in annual sales.

So how did I beat the stats to survive and then thrive in the most challenging of circumstances?

Grit, determination, and fear of the failure that could force my return back home, only to look my friends and family in the eyes and admit I was wrong—and worse, they were right!

This is why it's so important to begin with the end in mind. Stop and ask yourself if you're really up for the journey. Are you ready to face the unexpected and go above and beyond to realize your vision? Is it that important to you that you're going to make sacrifices for what you actually want to do, because let me assure you, your motivation to make money isn't going to be enough—far from it, my friend.

That's why I wrote this book: *To save you some of the pain.*

DON'T FORCE A SQUARE PEG INTO A ROUND HOLE

Begin with the end in mind. That's one of the most important lessons I share with my sales and marketing clients and budding entrepreneurs. Many tend to focus on preparing an elaborate business plan and feature-rich product launch only to become mired in analysis paralysis. Or they quickly go to market because *their* family and friends love the idea. So they decide to launch without knowing whether their offering has product market fit.

I've learned my lessons the hard way. I was nineteen and still in high school when I started my very first business venture. I visited my brother

Pax in Mansfield, Texas, back when DVD players were the hot new thing. There was still a regional system determining when a movie was released, typically first in the United States. When I boldly walked into the Block-buster video store and saw all these movies that were already available in the States but not back home in Denmark, my eyes lit up. I spent every bit of my small savings and filled three suitcases with DVDs, certain I would have a booming business when I returned home.

When I got back to Copenhagen, I discovered they were unusable without a localized DVD player programmed with a unique code for Denmark. Simply put, my seat-of-the-pants marketing strategy was not aligned with the current industry distribution model. Although this may seem obvious to many, as a novice entrepreneur I made a classic mistake that cost me all my available hard-earned capital. So it's important to do your homework and create a proper base of market research to understand what your pro-spective customers need and then map that to your resources and strategy. Even for a teenager hustling DVDs!

When my partners and I launched my last digital marketing agency, White Shark Media (WSM), we specialized in Paid Search, pitching basic low-cost Pay Per Click (PPC) management packages to small and medium-sized businesses. After selling for a couple of months, we discovered that when executing a campaign strategy, despite having the right structure and exe-cution, if the client's website was not up to scratch we were just sending a lot of qualified traffic to a website that would never convert. And that was a failing recipe. It became obvious to us that we needed to train our entire sales staff on how to sell websites *first* to our Small and Medium-sized Busi-ness (SMB) clients, so we could sustain the relationship, avoid cancellations, and *then* upsell to a PPC management solution. In other words, *"Never let ads write checks your website can't cash."*

Despite what we were convinced was a brilliant idea, we failed to acknowledge that a few major players in the market such as Wix.com and Web.com had very compelling low-cost high-quality SMB website solutions superior to ours. We had pivoted the whole company and then nearly went bankrupt because we couldn't effectively sell these solutions. Worse still, our sales staff were frustrated about having to stop selling what they had finally mastered. Instead, we instructed them to pitch websites as a tactical step to sell a low-cost PPC package—without our unique value proposition. So now we were selling a mediocre product at a higher cost than the competition and up against established popular big brands with deep pockets—a recipe for disaster.

It's lessons like these that gave rise to the development of my Accelerator Platform. Successful entrepreneurs spend weeks or even months investigating and conducting competitive research to define their go-to-market strategy. My recommendation to any entrepreneur is that the founder should be the Chief Sales Officer as well. It doesn't matter if you're a software engineer or a chef, go out in the market early and start pitching. Personally survey and sell, gathering direct prospect and customer feedback. Then adjust your offering *before* you start hiring other people and assuming they can sell your solution. They usually can't until you can. And perish the thought that they can and you can't!

My angel investing firm, Great Dane Ventures, is pitched every single day by hopeful entrepreneurs trying to sell me the vision of why I should invest in their business or help them market their product. Yet they've failed to answer even the most fundamental questions needed to create a successful venture.

As one of my favorite authors, Jim Collins, writer of *Great by Choice*, emphasizes one should fire bullets (low-cost, low-risk, low-distraction experiments) to figure out what works, then cannonballs (concentrating resources into a big bet).

> *"My greatest learning as a serial entrepreneur is to never ever remove yourself from the sales equation—sales is the lifeblood of your organization, and you should always be in control of this."*

HAVE YOU BUILT YOUR MINIMUM VIABLE PRODUCT?

One of the best methods for beginning with the end in mind is with the well-established concept of Minimum Viable Product (MVP), articulated in Eric Ries's book *The Lean Startup*.

The MVP approach can be viewed as a seven-step process:

1. **Identify your target customer.** For a consumer good, this involves every detail of their life and creating an avatar (or persona, in marketing lingo). It summarizes where they live, their household income, recreational preferences, education, geographical location, age, and so forth.

2. **Understand your customers.** And more importantly, their needs, their pain, and what they gain with your product. It's important to include their emotional needs, not just their rational expectations. Remember that everything we do in life is typically to avoid pain or to gain pleasure. As a marketer, your goal is to leverage this.

3. **Know your offer.** In other words, define the value proposition. Find out what problem you are solving for your customers. Equally important is learning what underserved needs there may be within the existing solutions. It's not enough to just have a slightly better price or new tweak to an existing solution for an otherwise happy customer.

4. **Specify the MVP feature set.** In other words, as the founder,

what basic solution features you build as your prototype to test with real customers.

5. **Create your MVP prototype.** String together the solution and the most cost-effective way possible to go out and sell, knowing it's not a complete solution.

6. **Test by selling the MVP prototype to prospective customers (shooting bullets).** Equally important is getting their honest opinions and product feedback after they have *paid* for the value of your solution. This form of market research is essential.

7. **Launch your product. Fire cannonballs.** Assuming your prototype worked and you had a reasonable success rate. Else review your MVP feature set (step 4).

Never assume what you don't know about your prospective customers.

There are a variety of ways to get to know your prospective customers depending on your style, preference, resources, and timeline. A couple of different methods have proven effective:

- Conduct surveys at scale using tools like Google Survey.
- Interview employees at competing companies within your domain.
- Talk with subject matter experts in the industry you're entering.
- Explore online forums such as Quora, Meta (Facebook), and LinkedIn groups.
- My personal preference is to craft and personally validate a stellar offer.

In year six at WSM, we again struggled financially. Our direct sales growth model had stagnated, bleeding money with high overhead expenses, requiring continued growth and profitability. Once more, necessity forced me to walk through the seven-step process with a new market offer to save our nearly bankrupt company.

I recall it as clear as day. And luck was on my side. I was at a premier Google partnership conference in Mountain View, California, with an exclusive group of preferred partners. I showed up late to the meeting. I opened the door and interrupted the head of the Google channel sales program who was speaking. He said to the crowd, *"Oh, thank you for joining us, Gary."* Then he expanded on that by saying, *"Well, Gary is excused as he commuted a long way from Nicaragua to come join us today."*

My lateness turned out to be a blessing in disguise as the entire room turned around and saw me standing in the doorway—late! During the next break, several participants—all marketing agency owners—approached me, keen to ask whether we could create a partnership. Select partners were in a fortunate situation exceeding their sales projections but stretched on fulfillment capacity. Instead of hiring and training more full-time staff, they could engage with us in a white label model to immediately fulfill their clients' needs and at an attractive markup, given our low-cost structure in Nicaragua.

On my return to the office, I excitedly shared this great idea with my partners, executive team, and board of directors. Fueled by more espressos, we brainstormed an idea we'd flirted with for a long time. As with any struggling sales organization looking to pivot, they asked a million questions about the concerns and obstacles we had to address financially. These included:

- How could I expect the company to pivot, put together an entirely new solution, and go to market with rapidly diminishing cash reserves?
- How would we deal with the fact that we didn't have sufficient time to retrain our staff and acquire the needed tools and technologies?
- How about the fact that a channel sales model instead of our direct sales model would entail letting go of 50 percent of our existing highly loyal staff?
- Who was going to take the lead in executing this great idea?

Plus, we had a very short time span before we would cease to exist.

So being the type of person who would rather ask for forgiveness than beg for permission, a few weeks later I walked into our fulfillment department with a signed contract from another agency for us to provide them with white label managed services for twenty of their clients. Hell, yeah!

Now, in the secrecy of my corner office, I followed the 7-step process to specify, create, and test our MVP with potential customers. And I negotiated a signed agreement for us to fulfill without having yet built the solution! Obviously this created a lot of tension internally. Several senior people left the company. Top performers were now challenged with this change in solution and process.

THE CRITICAL PIVOT

So we pivoted our entire focus with a new strategy—becoming a reseller to other marketing agencies. Our plan was to sell PPC management solutions in a white label format to resellers to offer their clientele under their brand and with a high markup.

In this process, I stepped down from the CEO role to take the lead on this company-saving initiative to launch our white label PPC partner program. And Alexander, our newly appointed CEO at the time, had to juggle expenses exceeding income, ultimately with no choice but to let go of more than 50 percent of the company staff. Pivoting and changing our culture in a company with 200+ employees was certainly easier said than done.

One of the hardest things was to let go of thirty-five loyal, hardworking appointment setters whom, as a leader for many years, I had grown very fond of. Our new strategy required a more sophisticated sales approach with an entirely different positioning statement, outreach strategy, and lead nurturing process, using a variety of new tools and technology not previously needed.

Because I chose to fake it until we made it, we also got very valuable customer feedback from our prospective partners during the sales process. This helped us craft an innovative solution as the renewed foundation for the company's very successful subsequent growth.

The lessons from these days of blood, sweat, and tears were invaluable. I learned to always begin with the end in mind. Now every single client call, investor meeting, or key employee hiring process *always* begins with defining our desired outcome and then reverse engineering the process step by step until we can meet our overarching objective—profitable, sustainable growth.

In summary, here are some critical lessons that may help you too:

- As an entrepreneur and CEO, *always* stay close to your sales process and team.
- As an entrepreneur, never hide in your corner office and solely rely on your team to identify your customers' pain and needs. Continuously keep your finger on the pulse.
- The best market research money can buy is to pick up the phone and speak directly with your prospective customers about your fantastic new idea. Then let the outcome of those calls dictate whether to move forward.
- Write your sales pitch and test it *before* developing your product or solutions.
- Always begin with the end in mind. Worry later on about how to reverse engineer the process and get there.

In Chapter 2, I'll walk you through my roller coaster of sales experiences: the hard knocks of pounding the phones for over two decades and the lessons I've picked up along that long and bumpy road.

2

I GOT 99 PROBLEMS BUT SALES AIN'T ONE

*I'll give you the missing ingredient that nine
out of ten entrepreneurs fail to consider and that is:
How the heck am I going to get my customers?*

I remember it as if it was yesterday. I was seventeen years old, on summer vacation, and just got a break to enter the adult workforce. Despite not yet being eighteen years old, I joined a sales boiler room pitching a phone directory selling business advertising listings. The truth of the matter was that the phone book was unknown. It was printed and published in low volume in comparison to the highly familiar Yellow Pages.

The company had one thing going for it and that was sales. The owners of this publication had established a hard-core outbound telemarketing sales environment where young studs and hardworking girls would be hustling day in and day out selling. Everyone was very aggressive striving to earn the 30–50 percent levels of possible commission.

I'd been on the phone for about two weeks and was the only one who hadn't produced a single sale. Fortunately, three rows over from me sat another young kid only four years older who was killing it sales- and commission-wise, drove a big car, sported all the flashy clothes, got the attention of all the girls, and had the lifestyle I aspired to. I wanted to be just like him.

My blessing with this entire experience was that at a young age, by sheer coincidence, I began my journey learning how to sell. And in this book, I share many painful lessons learned on that winding road—hopefully so you don't have to.

Despite a rocky start, I stayed with that first sales role because of the promise of such lucrative commissions. I learned to ask the right questions, sugarcoat things, and leverage the aspirations and dreams of my prospective customers to get a signature on the dotted line. And, of course, handsome payouts.

What astonishes me now is just how many entrepreneurs spend tens of thousands of dollars developing their product or company, without having *any idea whatsoever* whether there's an actual market for their product, or how the hell they're going to sell it at scale and with profitability!

And to this day, I've yet to find a company that gets this right out of the gate.

So why do so many founders fail to tackle this crucial element of launching a business that becomes profitable? Psychologically, it's far more comforting for an entrepreneur to remain in their comfort zone rather than navigate the unpredictable stormy seas required to develop new customers. The truth of the matter is that you're not doing yourself a favor. On the contrary.

As an entrepreneur, when looking at the bottom line, your number one responsibility is to generate sales and acquire customers. Yet sales is arguably the most underappreciated skill. In fact it's often the last ingredient in the business growth equation instead of being the first to tackle head-on.

> *The fate of your business, its survival, your profitability levels,*
> *and overall growth trajectory, doesn't rely on whether*
> *your product or solution is superior to the competition's*
> *but rather in your ability to market it better!*

REVENUE PAIN?
UP YOUR SALES GAME!

What most business owners prioritize is to design the solution considering the features that go into a product instead of asking the central question *"Will this produce revenue and how?"*

I'm most often solicited by early stage founders who have left this to the end of the equation. Believing they're ready to go to market, they are now interviewing marketing agencies expecting them to do all the heavy lifting for their brand and the company's future, hoping the agency creates a winning go-to-market strategy that produces revenue and profits right away.

On the contrary, the common thread I've identified working with many business owners, is that no matter which profession they operate in, whether they are architects, engineers, house builders, or app developers, when they prioritize sales and revenue-producing activities, they usually don't have a cash flow or profitability problem.

My question to you as an entrepreneur is where are you spending the majority of your 80-hour workweek? Do you keep track of your activities? Are you constantly in react mode putting out fires? Or are you taking a proactive approach to prioritize where you get the biggest bang for your buck? And thereby ensure the livelihood of your business, with revenue-generating strategies that make an impact tomorrow and over the next decades.

Let me be more specific. No matter which field you're in, a powerful way to consider your weekly or monthly planning as an entrepreneur is to adopt the popular concept of the Pareto principle, commonly known as the 80-20 rule. Simply put, 80 percent of your activities and tasks should be focused on the 20 percent of initiatives that produce 80 percent of your revenue.

So it's critical to consider these key questions:

- Are you continuously working on your sales pitch and optimizing it based on market trends, new competition entering the market, or the needs or knowledge gaps of your sales reps?
- Are you working on pitch decks or product explainers that could increase the conversion rates for your client-facing staff, whether that's by acquiring a new customer or upselling to generate more revenue in the customer life cycle?
- Do you have a complete rebuttal library in alphabetical and chronological order that enables both existing and new sales reps to quickly combat challenging questions from your prospective customers? (By the way, this should be thicker than an old-school phone book if you're running your business correctly.)
- Are you spending your time building out an extensive FAQ section that can answer the unasked questions from your prospective clients? This is an immediate way to improve your sales process and move leads down the funnel who might otherwise have concerns but not bother to ask questions—and then leave you for another better prepared competitor.
- Have you built out an extensive library of sales sequences (also referred to as cadences) for yourself and your sales representatives that can save time with continuous repetitive emails to increase personalization? And have you created a snippet library that can

easily be accessed by your team to explain a feature, a process, or quickly answer next-steps questions from a prospect?

- Have you put yourself in front of your prospective clients and then shot short promotional YouTube or TikTok videos? This can be a very effective investment of your time. Not only can they inspire your sales reps, but they also create authority and credibility, influencing your prospects to choose you over the competition based on your presence and the conviction in your tone of voice. Additionally, by leveraging these social media channels, you can pitch to an audience of hundreds of thousands instead of only on a one-to-one basis.

- How about networking, a skillset that has almost been forgotten in today's remote-working age? In my last Business-to-Business (B2B)-focused company the most cost-effective customer acquisition source was LinkedIn. Connecting with industry thought leaders, participating in subject matter expert groups, answering questions from prospective clients, or just voicing my expertise on a trending topic has often yielded 10x returns for the time invested. Could you do something similar? And if you have a B2C focus, you could explore Facebook Groups.

- Or what about "simple" things such as brainstorming promotional offers related to trending topics or seasonality? If you want more than just a cookie-cutter approach to promotional copy, you need to get creative and take the initiative. Don't expect your marketing agency to handle everything from A to Z.

- Are you implementing high-impact activities such as recruiting and onboarding the right team members? More importantly, are you training and then coaching them for success so you have an army of winning sales reps instead of just a lone-wolf all-star?

- Have you assessed your entire customer journey to determine metrics for every single activity throughout that process? And are you taking a rigorous approach to consistently monitor these metrics? You always get what you measure.

These are just some of the critical factors to consider in your execution strategy.

In fact, I would even take it to the next level and challenge my team to break down the sales process using the 80-20 rule to then focus on the 20 percent. Prioritize which of the 20 percent activities can produce the best return. For example, allocate your limited time by helping your sales representatives close large deals. Make yourself available and communicate the significance of working with a prospective client by attending meetings or calls, thereby earning trust—the single most important asset you have, yet the hardest to achieve.

And a key factor that characterizes top entrepreneurs is whether *after* the contract is signed they remain highly engaged in those client relationships that have significant growth potential. Allocate time and prioritize resources to focus on your VIP clients, giving them the attention they deserve and more importantly, growing your top and bottom line exponentially.

LESSONS FROM THE TRENCHES: TWENTY YEARS OF SALES AND HUNDREDS OF MILLIONS INVESTED IN ADVERTISING LATER

What clicked for me was when I discovered how to apply universal sales and marketing fundamentals in use for decades. Still relevant today, they also will work in years to come. These are fundamentals of human psychology applied to influencing buying behavior. Psychologist Robert Cialdini was the first to codify these into six principles set out in his 1984 bestseller *Influence: The Psychology of Persuasion* and summarized nicely as follows by Roger Dooley, author of *Brainfluence: 100 Ways to Persuade and Convince Consumers with Neuromarketing*.

1. Reciprocity

Do something for a person with no conditions or expectation of a return favor, and they are more likely to do something for you.

2. Commitment/Consistency

People unconsciously want to behave in a manner that is consistent with past behavior.

3. Social Proof

People pay attention to what other people are doing, both consciously and unconsciously.

4. Authority

People defer to those in authority—officials, professors, doctors, and experts in a field.

5. Liking (How to Win Friends and Influence People)

People we like more easily persuade us. Although some liking feelings are conscious, as with a friend, often they are so subtle we aren't aware of them.

6. Scarcity (and a Sense of Urgency)

The fewer there are of something, the more people like and want them. Examples include:

- Time-limited (e.g., holiday sales or seasonal offerings)
- Quantity limited (limited supply, etc.)
- Access limited (e.g., freemium models, limiting features, etc. Good to get your foot in the door and then upsell)

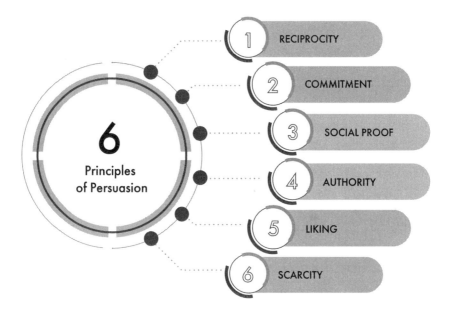

Through blood, sweat, and tears, a few ulcers, a lot of gray hair, and one divorce later, I've been very successful in a wide variety of sales environments: outbound call centers, media advertising programs, enterprise sales, inside sales, and channel sales. And very often the products and solutions I sold were subpar, compared with other players in the market.

Throughout my career I've learned to apply these fundamental psycho-logical sales principles that can make the difference between struggling to hit quota or driving in lots of new profitable customers.

What follows are snapshots of that journey.

The Boiler Room: Commitment/Consistency

Let me rewind the clock to one of my very first business ventures in outbound sales—about as hardcore as it gets. Back in the mid-2000s in Copenhagen, Denmark, we were selling advertising in a "free" online business directory, which we created ourselves, with hundreds of thousands of listings. It was during this venture I earned my first million by the age of twenty-three. Now, I'm not proud to say that I was selling high volumes of mostly ineffective directory listings, but I learned the *power of sales* and that *having a superior product is not the most important ingredient in the mix.*

This was an early call center boiler room environment where I employed hundreds of young sales agents working on a straight high commission-based compensation structure. Each rep was calling on 200–300 small business owners *daily.*

For the directory, after earning the customers' initial trust, we pitched an upsell to the "free" first-year basic business listing. Often these might be a better page placement or listed in multiple categories. Our sales team sold millions of dollars' worth of online advertising based on pure hustle, high-volume call frequency, and leveraging all the psychological persuasion tricks we could dream up.

Our business directory listings strategy was focused on using the technique of Commitment/Consistency. Assuming that most companies would naturally extend the subscription to year two, we offered the first year free. However, we deliberately "forgot" to underline this, anticipating most businesses would keep the listing for the subsequent year because it meant keeping consistency—a psychological fact we highly leveraged with outstanding results. We grew that business from zero revenue to US $1 million (all currency in USD) in just a few months. And I got rich enough to own a cool penthouse, drive fancy cars, and travel around Europe.

In truth, despite earning millions of dollars sellings these listings, we had to give up the business and move on due to too much heat in the media—because we weren't exactly acquiring happy customers. But I sure learned how to sell ice to Eskimos!

Smart Outbound Calling: Reciprocity

I started my next venture with the best of that very same crew. We began cold-calling the same business audience as with the directory. But this time we added a twist to our approach. Our cold-calling strategy was disguised as a follow-up call after we had sent them a complimentary box of chocolates, together with a sample ink cartridge and an introductory offer for our environmentally friendly cartridges (these were low-cost used ones we refilled and recycled with cheap ink and resold at a 1,000 percent profit margin).

Both business models are clear-cut examples of how you can very successfully leverage Reciprocity in addition to Commitment/Consistency approaches. In both cases we gave out a little bit for free, apparently expecting nothing in return. But with the power of persuasion and the laws of influence, combined with plenty of manipulative, pushy, high-pressure sales techniques, we managed to convert a great percentage of these prospects into customers.

Despite a heavy up-front cost on free listings, chocolates, and sample ink cartridges, we built a booming business within a year, enabling me to earn millions for several years running while still in my early twenties. And this was no dot-com blowout. This was a hard-core, tried-and-true, outbound sales process informed by the classic psychology of persuasion.

Radio Ads on Steroids: Scarcity, Urgency, and Social Proof

From here I transitioned to the broadcast media industry, selling radio advertising for the largest network in Europe, Radio NRJ. They had a franchise-based business model. We engaged with the Danish franchisee who had launched the radio station some six years prior, never really getting it off the ground in a profitable fashion.

How I got on the radio station's radar is quite a funny story and somewhat of a coincidence. During my boiler room outbound sales days, my sales manager and I were having our usual Friday afternoon ritual celebrating the top sales performers of the week with some heavy cash payouts to spend during the weekend. All while downing shots of vodka as we waited for the limousines full of strippers to pull up at our office door. So safe to say the energy was at its peak! Exactly like the film *Boiler Room*, released in 2000, just around this time!

My thirty-minute sales huddle rants were usually about committing to the cause of making money and putting forth an extraordinary effort (of course to the benefit of our company). One Friday, I was at peak speed delivering yet another motivational pep talk. Suddenly, during the heat of the moment, one of the sales reps, in his wild excitement, yanked off his wedding band, tossed it out the window, and loudly shouted he was now getting married to the cause of making money and to the company, instead of having his wife hold him back!

Let me be the first to say that, of course, I obviously no longer condone this behavior! However, in hindsight it turned out to be a blessing because across the street from our offices, peeking out the window during all this excitement, was a very curious CEO of the radio station who was struggling with poor sales and high operational losses for six straight years.

Just a few days after this episode, my secretary knocked on my office door only to tell me that the radio station CEO was outside wondering if I could take a few minutes out of my schedule. After a few conversations with him, I moved forward with yet another business initiative and became the exclusive sales partner for the radio station.

My excitement was at an all-time high since I would be pivoting from selling my own homegrown products that, despite having high profitability, were not ones I was particularly proud of. I was now about to sell for the leading radio network in Europe with exclusive rights for Denmark. Hey, Ma, I made it!

But my enthusiasm quickly diminished once we learned that being fifth in the market in terms of audience share and with subpar coverage in the major Danish cities posed a serious challenge selling-wise. Once again I had to get really creative. Now more than ever. So, together with my young crew of commission-only hungry sales reps, we brainstormed a strategy to sell available airtime for radio ads.

We had tons of advertisement airtime to sell—our advertisement slots were embarrassingly empty—and there was not a high demand to buy airtime on this struggling, far-less-popular radio station.

So we had to create a different narrative to sell it!

Our pitch, somewhat improvised each time, was based on an actual scenario. One of our existing large advertisers (a major hotel) who had an annual agreement with us, needed to cancel his booked airtime for the following week because they were maxed out at full capacity with customers.

This narrative, when pitched in a cold call to a new prospective advertiser, communicated a high degree of *social proof* since they would indirectly assume that the ads on our station had caused an existing customer to sell out—whether that was a hotel or restaurant now fully booked for the following weeks, or a store selling out its inventory and waiting for a new supply before they should run ads again.

The follow-up ask was then whether they would like to buy this canceled airtime, which because of the annual agreement, we could sell them at an introductory rate with a 50–60 percent discount. A perfect *scarcity*-based model. Our "logic" was that we had handpicked them for this offer, because we wanted to help them take advantage of this special promotion. We justified this due to the potential of later engaging them with a larger scale agreement once we had proven the concept and value of our ads. As a result, whereas the average revenue per rep had been $10,000–$20,000 per month, I was soon selling over $75,000 per month.

This is when things really took off. In three years we drove 5x growth in annual sales for the radio station. How? It wasn't about the product, our competition, or the market situation—we just needed to create a better story. A classic example of the techniques of social proof and scarcity/urgency.

Welcome to the Channel

During this venture with radio ads I learned a lot, to say the least, besides making a lot of money. After getting some success and becoming a little cocky trying to directly sell to the bigger brands such as Coca-Cola, McDonald's, Burger King, Lego, and so forth, I was introduced to the subject of Channel Sales when I tried to sell my airtime to them directly. Safe to say, they weren't eager to buy airtime from the fifth-largest radio station. They abruptly interrupted my eloquent pitch and referred me to the established Danish media houses for large advertisers.

So I decided to go after them and invested in personal relationships with these folks through attentive listening and detailed follow-through. And they began to like and trust me and my offering. The best part of establishing these relationships was the occasional, yet consistent, bluebird order. This was a classic example of how the principle of *liking* (first popularized in Dale Carnegie's bestseller *How to Win Friends and Influence People*) can be a key persuasive strategy for success.

My Crazy Move to Nicaragua: Authority

It was due to our success that led me to my next venture—crossing the Atlantic Ocean to set up an operation in Nicaragua but targeting advertisers in the United States. I'll never forget this story because I've told it to a lot of people when they ask, *"How the heck did you end up in Nicaragua?"*

My then-partner Alexander and I were at a Michelin-star restaurant in Copenhagen having dinner with his brother Morten. He was a highly successful entrepreneur and consultant for the Danish government helping to set up innovative businesses that could export their services to third world countries such as Nicaragua. The objective was to create new jobs, innovation, and fuel the economy indirectly.

Well, due to our success selling radio advertising, and just as I was about to order a steak cordon bleu, Morten asked me, *"Gary, you guys are doing a phenomenal job with sales and marketing. Have you ever considered taking your skillset to the United States by creating a salesforce in Nicaragua at a dramatically lower cost?"* I choked on my pre-dinner gin and tonic, looked at him incredulously, and said, *"What the f**k am I going to do in Africa?"*

About a year later, in 2011, I was all-in, setting up an inside sales team for a company my partner and I formed, with support from the Danish government. And I now knew where Nicaragua was! Initially we were going to market under the commercial name US PPC Consultants—what to us sounded like a really legit business name. Within a few months we decided it was a horrible choice. So we switched to White Shark Media—the best choice to reflect our ambition to become the biggest, baddest player in the industry. It's still the brand today.

Our business focused on selling digital marketing services—in particular, Google AdWords (as Google Ads was then known) management services but also website creation and search engine optimization. In the US target market we acquired more than 5,000 small to medium-sized business customers and ultimately managed a media spend of over $300 million.

But the journey was brutal and so was the learning curve. It turned out that cold-calling SMBs in the United States was a completely different game than cold-calling in Denmark. An average small business in the United States gets two or more phone calls every single day from some company concerning their Google rankings or Google AdWords performance, or lack thereof. Once again we were up against the wall and had to go through plenty of experiments and failures. We had no choice. It was that or go home, an utterly unacceptable option.

What turned out to become the winning formula, after countless trial-and-error approaches, was calling out and offering a "free, no-strings-attached, guaranteed-to-provide-value" complimentary Google AdWords account audit. And we warranted to find some degree of mismanaged ad spend or areas of improvement that could result in a high ROI—all performed by a Google Certified Specialist. This was anchored by an *appeal to authority* persuasion technique.

So we implemented a classic "Fronter" and "Closer" setup. The Appointment Setters would call suspects and pitch the perceived high value of speaking with the Google Certified Specialist (who was our in-house Closer and had taken the necessary certifications).

The Closer would then perform an account audit and start earning trust with the prospect. By building up enough value for them to realize they needed help with the account, he was highly successful in moving the prospect forward to become a new customer with our paid search managed services.

This setup turned out to work like a charm and we closed these audits with a 35–40 percent success rate—far higher than a traditional rate of ~25 percent. At our peak we onboarded more than 200 new customers every single month. This approach led us to become the 22nd Google Ads Premier SMB Partner out of 30,000+ established existing digital marketing agencies in the United States. And what's more, we were the only one based out of Nicaragua and without a single employee in the United States.

The key takeaway was that we cracked the code by creating *authority* and building up the value of speaking with a certified specialist (trained of course to get under the skin of the prospect). They asked all the right questions, identified opportunities for improvement, and then focused on closing the customer. So we went from near bankruptcy to a high-growth company in the United States.

Five years later, after taking this approach with inside sales, we hit the glass ceiling as far as growth potential. At our peak, we had 40+ appointment setters using predictive dialer software and 10 closers calling on 40,000+ small business owners every month in a highly competitive environment. However, by 2017 our success rate began to decline due to changing telephone behaviors by our prospects who were no longer picking up the phone. Our growth rates had stagnated like many other mature businesses.

Pivot to the Channel Again: Sales Enablement and Loss Leaders

I'd found myself in another critical position in 2017. By now I had a beautiful little daughter with my Nicaraguan ex-wife. Returning to Denmark, and with a failed business, was out of the question. After extensive soul searching, brainstorming, and some internal conflict, I was able to convince my partners of our next strategy.

So we pivoted from a direct sales focus to building out a channel sales company. A couple of years later, as the head of channel sales, I had now sold partnership agreements to more than 200 marketing agencies: all partners of ours reselling white label PPC management services to their clients under their brand.

Until now, I had drawn on all my accumulated sales experience and business learnings with great success. But for what I faced at this point, it just wasn't enough. Doing channel sales and establishing partnerships with savvy and rather successful digital marketing agencies turned out to be a whole different level than selling inside sales to SMBs.

Besides having to leverage a whole stack of sales technologies for success in this venture, the biggest challenge turned out to be how to get our partners' sales reps to sell our solutions—easier said than done!

What I learned this time was how powerful sales enablement can be in fueling partnership program growth. The winning approach was a multi-faceted sales enablement strategy. This included providing our partners' reps with the creation of white labeled proposals. We offered them at no cost, enabling the reps to easily pitch their clients a paid search campaign solution as a revenue expansion initiative. An easy sell. By making it almost effortless for them to pitch additional value to their existing clientele, we created a true partnership model—one built on win-win-win.

After having some success with this sales enablement initiative, we quickly fueled this strategy by also creating free pitch decks, audits, and even sales training for high-potential resellers. And in many cases, myself, or some of our sales reps, would even jump on phone calls with our partners, disguised as team members of their agency, pitching our solution to their clients.

Another trick I learned during this venture was the value of having a *loss leader* during the sales cycle. This is, of course, not a new concept, as you often see big supermarket chains promote two gallons of milk at the store entrance with the objective to get you in the door and buy other products.

In our case, we chose to partner with a leading dashboard platform provider and bundle it into our solution. We offered this complete white label reporting setup at a minor loss. This small investment allowed us to get a foot in the door with many new resellers, making it even easier for them to sell our white label PPC Management Solutions to their existing customer base.

This turned out to be a powerful differentiator and account entry strategy. Now our account managers would have access to a partner's customer base via the shared client dashboards they used. On an ad hoc basis, we could easily identify high-potential prospects within their pipeline.

Then via a sophisticated solicitation, we put together a one-pager with some insights about their competition and how they were already leveraging Google AdWords to dominate the search result page. Using *social proof*, we also very effectively deployed ROI calculators to provide a breakdown of the expected return from our proposed solution for paid search management. In other words, we demonstrated *how to* before asking for the opportunity or sale.

Best Product, Service, or Market Position Does Not Secure Success

Throughout my business ventures over the last twenty years, in no case did I have a superior product, solution, or market position. I learned how, with a well-executed *sales strategy* and the principles of *persuasion*, I could often overcome the significant challenges of an inferior product.

As you read this book, you may still have 99 problems, but sales won't be one of them! In this chapter I've shared with you some powerful, painful lessons I've had to learn selling a wide range of services and products. And you've seen how they've been applicable in Europe, Central America, and the United States, in fact pretty well anywhere. Most importantly, you've seen powerful examples of the critical impact sales strategy *and* execution, drawing on appropriate uses of the psychology of *persuasion*, had on my journey. Hopefully it can inspire yours!

Now let's get to the meat and potatoes. In the rest of this book, I'll share how you can deeply leverage sales strategy to go to market effectively—and significantly increase your chance of extreme success.

I'll provide you with:

1) An invaluable **playbook** that any entrepreneur or sales leader can leverage to architect a predictable, programmatic, and profit-oriented sales process.

Why is this so important?

- According to Gartner research, only one out of three sales reps make it and 57 percent consistently miss their quota! And since the cost of employee attrition is dreadful for your bottom line, you want to do everything in your power to increase the success ratio of your reps.
- Because a whopping 95 percent of sales leaders are unable to forecast revenue within 5 percent accuracy due to a lack of consistency in revenue acquisition.
- The average sales rep's tenure is only eighteen months. Extending this can make a massive impact in your growth trajectory and profits.

2) My deep **insights** after working with hundreds of marketing agencies and tech giants like Google and Microsoft, where I learned how to navigate today's Wild West digital marketing ecosystem so you can supercharge your sales team with a high-velocity lead-generation machine.

Why is this so important?

- Finding a good marketing agency is like finding a needle in a haystack. Did you know there are more than 165,000 agencies in the United States alone?
- Fifty-nine percent of marketers outsource a good portion of their scope of service overseas to subcontracted marketing services providers in countries like India, the Philippines, and Nicaragua.
- Research shows that B2B-focused organizations that achieve cross-functional alignment between their marketing and sales teams, are 57 percent more efficient at closing deals. In return, this justifies 208 percent incremental growth in marketing revenue, resulting in 20 percent higher annual revenue growth than their industry peers.

3) A comprehensive **overview** of today's fragmented sales technology marketplace and automation tools, along with recommendations that are imperative for your scale, performance, and ROI.

Why is this so important?

- Sixty-one percent of businesses leveraging sales tech and automation reported exceeding their revenue targets in 2021.
- Forty-four percent of sales leaders who expected to exceed their revenue targets in 2022 use competitive intelligence and market data.
- More than 30 percent of sales-related activities can be automated— that is, enable your sales team to spend more time selling.

3

FAILING TO PREPARE
IS PREPARING
TO FAIL

*I'll make sure you're not entering a gunfight with a knife
by enabling you to understand who your actual customers
are and where to find them. So you can send the right
message to the right people at the right time.*

CUSTOMER JOURNEY AND ENHANCED B2B
CUSTOMER BUYING EXPERIENCE

There was one month at WSM I'll never forget: May 2016. Our churn rate was up to nearly 20 percent. Despite bringing on nearly 150 new customers that month, our growth had declined. God knows there were a million reasons for the spike in cancellations, but one thing was evident: we hadn't prepared! Despite being years into the operation, we didn't have a detailed customer journey mapped out. So we didn't really understand our customers.

Why is this so important? Because companies that usually hire me to help boost their sales ask me questions like:

1. *What should our lead conversion rate be?*
2. *How many emails should I include in my email sequences?*
3. *How many new customers do you think your company can help us get every month?*

All legit questions. I can give you answers or you can just do a simple Google search to reveal some. But I refuse to answer this before understanding your *entire* customer journey, its activities, amount of touch points, and how it's measured, managed, and optimized.

Sales is more than just landing new customers. I learned this the hard way. Treating each customer like a one-night stand gives you a bad rep, limited attractiveness to new customers, and ultimately significantly limits your growth potential. If, instead, you treat your prospects and soon-to-be-acquired new customers like your future partner, and not just with the aim of getting the signature, your revenue can be expanded to a higher lifetime value per new customer (more on this in Chapter 11). Here are five key ways to do this:

1. **Increasing Initial Deal Value Size:** Immediately reduce the time to break even and immediately impact your bottom line. The better you understand your customer and explain the perceived value of your solution compared with the competition, the better suited you are to comfortably increase the overall pricing for your solution without diminishing your returns.
2. **Upselling:** One of the most impactful ways to grow your business. Statistically speaking, upselling is 20x more effective than cross-selling and, according to Marketing Metrics, 50 percent more

likely to be successful when compared to acquiring a new customer (besides the reduction of a typically high Cost Per Acquisition (CPA)). Another interesting element about upselling is the "preventive churn reduction" strategic element behind the initiative. You see, a client who is planning to up their budget or retainer with you is presumably not unsatisfied with your solution. This is why using your ability to upsell the customer as an indicator to detect potential churn can be very insightful.

3. **Cross-selling:** Depending on your offering, this can be a very strong revenue optimization strategy, especially with B2C. In fact, it can be so powerful that Amazon once claimed up to 35 percent of its revenue came from cross-selling. However, I've learned from personal experience that cross-selling should be done cautiously. If, for example, you're offering a B2B subscription-based solution, you need to be cautious about the value-add of your new added product offering. If you pitch it to your client but they don't deem it as valuable as expected, you can trigger cancellation clauses due to frustration from the client with your entire solution.

4. **Boosting Referrals:** For many companies this is usually an untapped gold mine waiting to be exploited, yet only 30 percent of B2B companies have a referral business program. And for the B2B sector it's extremely valuable to continuously revamp your referral marketing strategy, especially because research shows that referrals experience a 70 percent higher conversion rate than regular leads! And the CPA is usually pennies on the dollar compared with regular paid sourced leads.

5. **Extending Client Relationships:** Arguably one of the most significant revenue optimization drivers your organization can implement and expect a strong ROI on efforts invested. In fact, a study

from Bain & Company (the inventors of the Net Promoter Score) showed that increasing your customer retention rates by only 5 percent can yield increases in your profits by 25–95 percent.

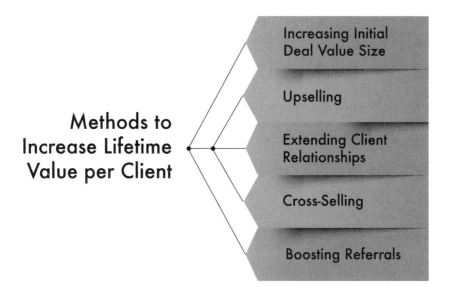

Of course, the better you know your customer, the market, the competition, and the trends, the better you can influence the emotional triggers of your prospective buyers and lead them through their search, purchase, and decision-making process to select your company and your solutions!

On the following page is a high-level overview of what that looks like. Fundamentally there are three core processes: Demand-Generation Marketing, Sales Cycle and Lead Nurturing, and Customer Lifetime Journey. Within each are many tasks to consider and define an implementation plan for. As the wise saying goes, "*Seek first to understand, then to be understood.*"

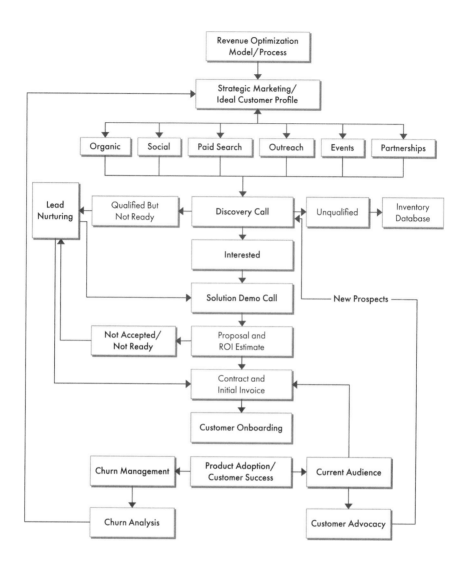

Looking back at my previous companies, if we had mapped out a detailed Customer Journey like this, our growth would have skyrocketed.

And no successful company, despite defining thorough Customer Journey mapping, can succeed without also placing a high value on better cross-departmental collaboration (especially with sales, marketing, and operations/fulfillment teams), high employee engagement, and a genuine customer-centric approach from their teams.

When mapping out your Customer Journey in such detail, you can ask probing questions such as:

- In order to hit our sales goals, how many MQLs (Marketing Qualified Leads) do we need?
- Which sectors and market segments should we focus on to more effectively realize our targets?
- Through which channels can we cost-effectively reach our target audience and move them down the funnel?

Admittedly, most of my companies have been hard-core sales fueled, leveraging only a few cylinders sales- and marketing-wise. Nowadays, especially post-COVID, it's even more complex, since today's B2B buyer can do their vendor research and preliminary assessments online to create a short list in which you're either on or off. And all without ever contacting you or giving you the chance to pitch. In fact, research shows that today's B2B buyer already has done 57 percent of their research before landing on your website and taking an action.

Phenomenal Customer Experience (CX) is typically linked with incremental revenue gains for companies. However, I've come to learn that most companies in the B2B sector are severely lacking an adequate CX when compared with the B2C sector.

By comparison, most B2C companies' typical CX scores are between 65 percent and 85 percent, while B2B companies average 50 percent. Just let that sink in for a second or two! According to McKinsey & Company, B2B companies can expect:

- A 10–15 percent reduction in customer churn as a result of an elevated CX
- A 40 percent increase in deal win rates
- Upward of 50 percent reduction in your cost-to-serve model via better CX
- A 3x likelihood of hitting your revenue targets if the CX is sublime

The *why*? Pretty obvious, right? I rest my case. The big question is *how* and *who* can help you elevate your CX experience so you're three times more likely to exceed your revenue targets.

Gartner announced in 2018 that the marketing-to-sales handoff should no longer exist. They identified six jobs that buyers perform in a purchase process. The study showed that most B2B buyers revisit nearly every "buying job" at least once before they make a purchase. The result: a customer buying journey that resembles more of a maze than a linear path. As Brian Adamson of Gartner wrote, *"Unfortunately, the current commercial process today is not built to support this new world of B2B buying...The organizations that succeed going forward will be those that materially simplify the purchase process for customers. It's on marketing and sales teams to take the customer by the hand and guide them through the purchase, from start to end."*

The graphic on the following page, adapted from Gartner 2018, highlights the complexity of the B2B buying experience.

A Long, Hard Slog
Illustrative B2B Buying Journey

Bold is indicative of always-on "validation" and "consensus-creation" activities.

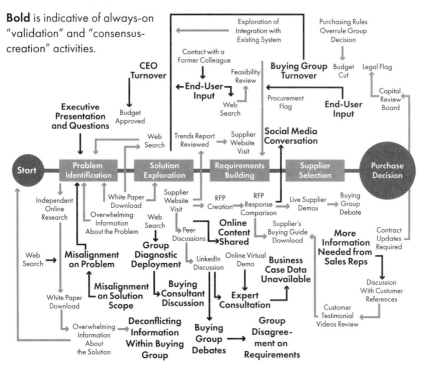

Source: Gartner

Why is understanding the B2B buying cycle and consumer attributes so important? Well, if we always want to begin with the end in mind, we need to:

- Ask the right questions
- Conduct proper research to understand the customer fully and know what they truly care about
- Learn where to find them (online and offline)
- Know how to speak to them
- Understand how to influence them

- "Get" how to win them over
- And ultimately, successfully enter into a marriage with them

Looking back at our critical mistake in my last company, when we initially had a 20 percent cancellation rate, we were boiling the ocean by selling to all types of verticals and sizes of companies. When our new client acquisition approach really became effective was after we pivoted to focus on channel sales and sold to other marketing agencies. You see, I had just spent nearly six years as CEO for our own reputable and "successful" agency, so when we began selling to other marketing agencies, I truly understood my prospective customers, their pains, challenges, pleasures, and what kept them up at night—in *great, great* detail. So selling to them became easier than ever, without any brute force, purely by quickly identifying their pain points and positioning our solution as the answer to that!

In comparison, when we pivoted to this approach with a small team of salespeople, we managed to bring the same volume of revenue as we did previously with a salesforce 20x bigger and with a 10x higher marketing budget! That's how powerful truly understanding the Customer Journey can be.

STRATEGIC MARKETING AND IDEAL
CUSTOMER PROFILING

> *Never assume what you don't know about*
> *your prospective customers.*

If you want to create a truly predictable, programmatic, and profit-oriented sales process that can scale, it all starts with conducting a *robust* strategic marketing process. With this invaluable intel, you can then more concisely and realistically establish your goals, objectives, and process to maximize the effectiveness of your new client acquisition strategy and overall revenue optimization!

I once told my Chief Revenue Officer an analogy. I said, "Think of seeing your dream girl at a bar or at the supermarket. How lucky will you be if you throw out a tired pickup line like 'Excuse me, beautiful...There's something wrong with my cell phone. It doesn't have your number in it.' Now, imagine instead you'd done a little bit of digging. You knew this dream girl of yours was a social worker for the city, who loved to travel—Europe in particular—and cooks a lot. She also spends a lot of her spare time working for NGOs, aiming to create awareness for climate change and reverse its impact over the next decades."

He raised his eyebrows as I continued, "With this intel, instead you might try saying: 'Excuse me, do you happen to know where I can find organic flour to bake a Danish bread recipe. I'm volunteering in an after-school program for disadvantaged kids, trying to teach them about European culture and food while stimulating their awareness of the health and environmental benefits of eating organic food.'" With a skeptical look, my CRO nodded and said, "I think you're likely right. But it won't do me much good. I've been married seventeen years."

Choice one presents you as another cheesy lifelong bachelor with "lead conversion rates" in the low single digits, and attracting less-than-ideal partners (or clients in the case of business), or

Choice two quickly adds you to the short list of ideal-spouse-candidate material (or in business language, becoming a customer for life!)

Firmographics

So how do you truly understand and market to your customer base? First, you have to gather the following intel by researching:

- **Company Size and Tenure:** How many employees do they have? Years in business? Annual revenue?
- **Revenue Growth Factors:** What moves the needle both revenue- and profit-wise? What are their core service offerings?
- **Geography/Market:** Where are they based, and are they local, regional, or national?
- **Industries:** Are you catering to only one or select verticals?
- **Market Objectives:** What do they aim to achieve as a business?
- **Budget:** Do they have the budget allocated (or can they find it) for a product like yours?
- **Purchasing Patterns:** When do they acquire products like yours? Do they do long-term agreements? Are there any growth-dependent factors, or are they open to business at any given time?
- **Decision Makers:** Who's usually in charge or can make decisions regarding purchasing from you?
- **KPIs:** What Key Performance Indicator (KPI) metrics of theirs, if you can demonstrate how to improve them, can land you the deal?
- **Benchmarks:** What are the industry standards, benchmarks, and factors you need to align yourself with and aim to improve with your solution?
- **Competitor Landscape:** Who are your potential competitors in this domain? What are they offering? What are their USPs?

Customer Firmographic Data

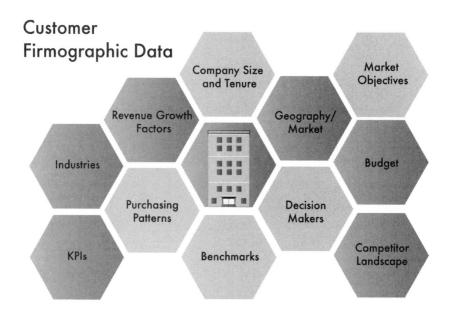

Demographics

With this in mind, you want to dive even deeper to understand *who* you'd be selling to in an organization and then create your buyer persona (or avatar):

- **Demographics:** Age, gender, education
- **Career:** Their job title, success criteria for their job (what do they get measured on), place in organizational chart (whom do they report to, if any), and so on
- **Job Responsibilities:** Client facing, sales, finance, management, operations, and so on
- **Objectives:** What are their main KPIs or Objectives and Key Results (OKRs)?
- **Pain Points:** What are their biggest challenges you can help them solve?

- **Systems and Software:** What tools or technology do they use to execute on their objectives?
- **Knowledge and Trends:** What resources do they consult or conferences do they attend to seek industry knowledge?
- **Communication Preferences:** Email, face-to-face, calls, social media (and which channels)?

Customer Demographic Data

Psychographics

Although buyer personas are powerful ways to express general characteristics of groups of buyer types, at an individual level during the sales process, I like to take things a step further. To be truly able to influence a prospect's decisions is to understand their psychographics—that is, what drives them. In conventional marketing terms, this can be identified in the following eight key ways:

1. **Interest:** This varies from one person to another, but generally speaking, your target audience should share common interests, and if understood properly, this can be highly leveraged during your sales cycle.
2. **Lifestyle:** Helps you gauge how your prospect sees themself in society. It's often influenced by their choice of relationships (or lack thereof), occupation, hobbies, and other recreational choices.

3. **Values:** I use this on almost every large deal I'm hunting since I've learned through my coaching work with Tony Robbins that we are all driven by six emotional needs. Whichever one drives you the most influences your decisions (and purchases):

   a. **Certainty/Security:** Assurance you can avoid pain and gain pleasure. People scoring high in this category are less risk averse, an important fact to consider when trying to land a big complex contract with them!

   b. **Uncertainty/Variety:** The need for the unknown, change, and new stimuli. These prospects can be intrigued by new shifts in the market, trends, and so forth, which you can leverage to grasp their attention and purchasing consideration.

   c. **Significance:** Feeling unique, important, special, or needed. For example, in such scenarios, I'd mention and subconsciously have them visualize their success and significance by reporting increased profits, leads, sales, or whichever metrics they would want highlighted to their superiors or shareholders. Make them the hero and feel significant.

   d. **Love/Connection:** A strong feeling of closeness or union with someone or something. Personally, I double down on the rapport-building process when facing such prospects. Not in a fake way but genuinely try to bond and explore common ground and interests.

   e. **Growth:** An expansion of capacity, capability, or understanding. Whether this is translated into their own career development and learning or the growth of their organization, understanding and influencing this need can be a very effective deal-closing technique!

f. **Contribution:** A sense of service and focus on helping, giving to, or supporting others. For example, in events where the founders of a company are looking to transform lives, an industry, or make another significant impact, understanding their objectives and tying your solution into the mix is almost a surefire way to get the signature on the dotted line.

4. **Social Status:** Conventional theory is centered on the constructs of low, middle, and upper classes. However, this can be segmented even further by a variety of demographic factors, which ultimately largely determine a prospect's product choices, acceptable price ranges, and niche markets.

5. **Behaviors:** This can help you identify how your prospect's purchasing patterns, their level of product adoption, and frequency of purchase or customer life cycle impact the sales process.

6. **Activities:** Learning whether your prospect is into sports, music, or social activities, for example, is lethal information to favor you as a candidate in their purchasing decisions because you have some shared interests or values to anchor your relationships.

7. **Attitudes:** Whether shaped by cultural background, upbringing, religion, or education, these traits reveal your prospect's nature. But because they are intangible, you need to carefully consider what and how to use them when crafting your marketing and sales copy.

8. **Opinions:** Whether political, religious, sports, or other, these factors are highly important to understand in order to establish rapport and then most effectively convey your message.

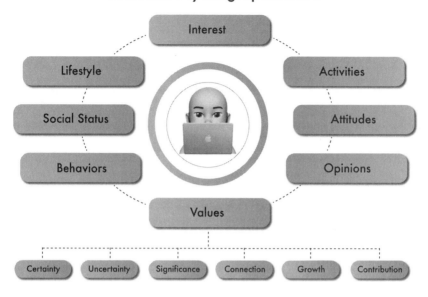

Customer Psychographic Data

Interest

Lifestyle

Activities

Social Status

Attitudes

Behaviors

Opinions

Values

Certainty | Uncertainty | Significance | Connection | Growth | Contribution

When you *truly* understand your customer segment at this level of granularity is the time to begin investing a much bigger budget in advertising and crank up your outbound sequences. This allows you to write emotionally compelling copy and scale things exponentially (more on this in Chapter 9). Otherwise you might as well donate your cash to charity instead of donating it to Google, TikTok, Meta, or Microsoft. Why? Because you'll be yet another generic voice trying to cut through the noise to grab the incredibly low attention span that both B2C and B2B buyers have nowadays. I have seen firsthand how marketing and sales campaigns can achieve 10x performance because of the targeting capabilities that today's Sales Tech and Mar Tech offer (more on this in Chapter 13).

For me this is a science. Breaking these processes down granularly into their components and then leveraging the right systems and technology allows you to not only meet your overall sales targets effectively and consistently but, equally important, further optimize all pertinent revenue-driving metrics such as:

- Shortening your sales cycle
- Lowering your customer acquisition cost
- Increasing customer satisfaction levels
- Increasing your renewal rates (if contracts)
- Boosting your upsells and cross-sells
- Amplifying your number of referrals

COMPETITOR RESEARCH AND FINDING GAPS IN THE MARKET

You don't want to enter a gunfight with a knife. And now that we have a strong grasp of our prospective customers, how they interact, what they prioritize, etc., the next and missing ingredient in the mix is to make your Go-to-Market strategy a winning formula.

And then to get to know who you are about to enter the ring against! Just as an athlete or a boxer about to go 12 rounds in a heavyweight fight prepares, or how Kobe Bryant and Michael Jordan always studied films of the leading players on opposite teams before a game, you want to study your business competition in an equal fashion.

I've failed at this many times over, whenever I just did a quick analysis before entering the market, only to get my ass whooped in royal fashion. Then I had to quickly pivot and adjust—painfully and tens of thousands of dollars later—because of the lack of understanding my competition. A classic scenario is the case back in 2012 when I tried to sell websites up against Web.com, Wix, and Squarespace.

The right way to do a competitive analysis is *not* with a quick two-day process involving a few calls and skimming your competitors' websites. It's researching the dominant companies in your industry that you face to gather a complete oversight of their solutions, sales tactics, processes, marketing channels, messaging, and value propositions. Understanding their overall business strategy and market approach helps you find competitive differentiators for your company which trickle all the way down to your sales, marketing, and operational execution.

Your analysis should reveal the pros and cons of your competitors' solutions and where they're falling short (gaps in the market you can attack). Furthermore, you'll uncover market trends during the process, and ultimately develop your solutions to create a greater impact, enabling you to then market and sell to them more effectively.

Mystery Shopping Process

With origins in the financial services industry and later widely adopted in the consumer packaged goods industry, mystery shopping has been relatively little used in the B2B sector, given its focus on end-customer surveys. I learned of the power and benefits that mystery shopping could play in B2B when Google introduced me to the concept.

Mystery shopping is an efficient way to gain direct firsthand intel on a competitor, ideally before you go to market with your product or service. In B2B it is primarily conducted in an interview format, where you have a legitimate reason to gain such an interview. The process can be conducted virtually, which makes it easier to simultaneously conduct an interview and collect the data of what was said. Another more traditional way is through face-to-face meetings at trade show booths, although the quality of the information is often filtered through the other party's "booth sales talk."

I've developed a process that has proven effective and with an accompanying set of questions and spreadsheets. Typically there are three phases to a mystery shopping exercise: (1) Research, (2) Interview, and (3) Analysis.

Research Phase:
- Research and select the top competitors in your category. Create a short list. I recommend ten to twenty companies.
- Study their websites, published information, and press releases.
- Study their social media presence, strategies, and customer reviews.
- Gather a complete firmographic overview, including size, locations, results, awards, etc.
- Determine what solutions they offer and how they price them.
- Identify which tools and tech stack they use, especially at a client-facing level.
- Uncover their marketing and sales tactics (this is where it gets tricky).
- Identify channels they market themselves via keywords and where they dominate using paid search.
- Assess their content creation and distribution networks.
- Study their pitch, USPs, and promotional offers.

Interview Phase:
- For each company, decide on a valid premise to obtain an interview and a reciprocal offer of value to them as an incentive.
- It's best to have two people conduct each interview to better triangulate notes and memories.
- Prepare a set of questions for a semistructured conversational interview.
- Topics may include (some are harder to elicit than others):
  - » About
  - » Founded

- » Amount of customers
- » Team size
- » Location
- » USPs
- » Services offered
- » Exclusivity with clients (per GEO)
- » Core competencies
- » Team structure
- » Communication/process
- » Reporting
- » Technology
- » Pricing
- » Contract terms/length
- » Promotions
- » Reviews
- » Testimonials
- » Pros (best features)
- » Cons
- Record or take detailed notes during the interview.

Analysis Phase:

It's helpful to track this information in a summary spreadsheet. This requires transcribing or copying the notes taken by each participant during the interview. Transcription tools or direct note-taking in an app can make this more efficient. Otherwise this can be time consuming.

The primary fields I use in a summary sheet include:

- Company and website
- Point of contact
- Role

- Notes (with link to the file)
- Proposal (with link to the file)
- LinkedIn page
- Instagram page
- TikTok page
- Facebook page
- Overview (main notes summary)
- Comments (secondary notes)
- Product/Service functions (as many columns as needed)
- Package pricing
- Options pricing
- Contract length/terms
- Differentiators

> *You can download a mystery shopping template along*
> *with other resources at www.0to100million.com.*

With the summary sheet, you can relatively easily do a comparative analysis of the competitors interviewed. It can be the basis for a living document that marketing owns and has responsibility to maintain. The mystery shopping analysis can be a powerful tool to:

- Craft winning solutions with compelling differentiating factors based on data
- Quickly and effectively educate sales staff and new hires
- Rapidly create winning proposals
- Create alignment on interdepartmental priorities (what do we need to agree and do collectively to beat the competition)
- Contribute to the competitor scorecard on the following page

Competitor Scorecard

The results and analysis from your study will likely be massive. And although very beneficial, it can be overwhelming for your average employee to decipher. Instead, extrapolate the key insights from your analysis and put them into bite-size, easy-to-view chunks. With this comparative data, you can equip all your client-facing staff to identify which competitor(s) they are up against when conducting sales calls.

Competitor Scorecard

	Competitor 1	Competitor 2	Competitor 3	Competitor 4	Competitor 5	Competitor 6
Packages						
Pricing						
Contract Terms						
USPs						
Customer Reviews						
Strengths						
Weaknesses						
Differentiators						

I learned this by coincidence years back as a Google Premier Partner. They conducted a mystery shopping process with us using both an inbound call and submitting a contact form with a fictitious SMB. They later scored our approach from A to Z and stacked us up against our peers (anonymously). This lightbulb moment led me to always create similar scorecards for myself and my reps that I continuously update so they're always at our fingertips when needed. As we undergo our sales process, we usually discover who we are competing against for the deal. This allows us to at least engage the competition well armed with all the arguments in our arsenal to tilt the scale in our favor.

Values or information for my Competitor Scorecards vary from project to project but usually include the following, informed in part by the Mystery Shopping Summary:

- Name of business, website(s), social media (so your staff can keep tabs)
- Solution overview. Top products they focus on
- Markets or verticals that they are stronger and weaker in (choose your battles carefully)
- Pricing and perks
- Contract terms
- Differentiating factors
- Promotional strategy and offers
- Their USPs and how (message) and where (channels) they market themselves
- Pros (what they are really good at)
- Cons (what they are less good at)
- Gaps (where your solution makes a positive difference for your prospect)
- SLA (Service Level Agreement) details worth highlighting

DEFINING MARKET OBJECTIVES
(SOLVING CUSTOMERS' PROBLEMS)

Sales is all about solving problems with your solutions. Once you understand that and can uncover the needs of your prospects (without them perhaps even knowing yet), that's when you'll never ever again have a sales problem! People will *want to* buy from you.

And since we now have a complete understanding of their Ideal Customer Profile (ICP)—the firmographics, demographics, and psychographics (I'll dive deeper into this)—we are now one step closer to being able to draft killer sales and marketing copy and pitch decks that convert, since they'll now be highly tailored and effective.

With all this information in mind, it's time to crystallize the concepts so that we can focus on the pains and gains of our prospects.

I like this simple but powerful way of thinking about markets called the Blue Ocean strategy, coined by Chan Kim and Renée Mauborgne in 2005. Essentially the traditional approach is the Red Ocean strategy where competition is fierce in known (and finite) market spaces. This is a zero-sum game in which one company's gain is achieved at another company's loss.

Blue Ocean strategy shifts attention from supply to demand, from a focus on competing to a focus on creating innovative value to unlock new demand. By expanding the demand side of the economy, new wealth is created. The diagram below compares the key elements of each. It's obviously easier said than done to create a true Blue Ocean approach. I would highly recommend fully exploring a go-to-market approach that attempts to define a Blue Ocean strategy. The upside potential benefits can be extreme despite the risks involved in successfully positioning and executing, given the unknowns of market readiness.

Blue Ocean vs Red Ocean Business Strategies

Instead of competing in overcrowded industries ("Red Oceans"), strategize how to compete by creating "Blue Oceans"

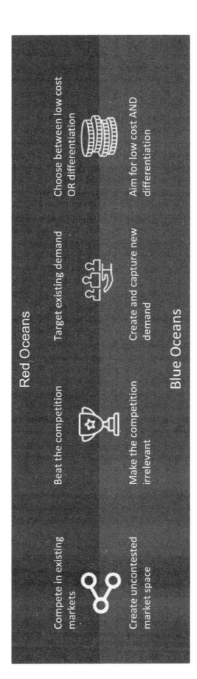

Red Oceans

- Compete in existing markets
- Beat the competition
- Target existing demand
- Choose between low cost OR differentiation

Blue Oceans

- Create uncontested market space
- Make the competition irrelevant
- Create and capture new demand
- Aim for low cost AND differentiation

⟩ The underlying technology usually already exists for blue oceans. The trick is finding innovative ways to link it with what customers value

⟩ Most blue oceans are created from within existing industries. It's not necessary to create entirely new industries

Source: Blue Ocean Strategy (2004), W. Chan Kim & Renee Mauborgne. More info here.

DEFINE YOUR UNIQUE SELLING PROPOSITION, VALUE PROP, AND ELEVATOR PITCH

After weeks of research, you're now ready to attack the whiteboard with your fellow founders to craft a USP that knocks the legs out from under your competition. This is critical to get 100 percent right, because your USP is the holy grail of all the market research you've conducted, your business vision, and what makes you *unique* compared with your competition.

But a USP is not to be confused with a Value Proposition or Elevator Pitch. Your USP should be one to two sentences that demonstrates the uniqueness of your company and communicates to your prospective customers why they should do business with you over your competition.

If you invest time in developing a compelling USP that does the trick, it will be your unified communications statement across all mediums, interactions, and marketing communications—why it's important to get it right and do all the necessary legwork in this chapter. Many new startups tend to skip the market research process and go straight to trying to write sexy marketing copy. But without the right foundation, it's like designing a slick-looking race car only without an engine! Get it right, even though it may take a few attempts to do so, because you can use it across all of your digital marketing communications, interactions, and business branding. Your USP, when paired with your mission statement, can provide a lot of clarity to your business model, what you do, and why you do it.

Here are a few examples of USPs from well-known companies:

- **Stripe:** The new standard in online payments
- **Tiffany:** The right one is worth waiting for
- **Slack:** Be more productive at work with less effort
- **HubSpot:** There's a better way to grow

- **Accelerator:** Secure the success of your startup
- **Evernote:** Remember everything
- **Unbounce:** A/B testing without tech headaches
- **Emirates:** Don't just fly, fly better
- **Airbnb:** Book unique places to stay and things to do

Your Elevator Pitch—
Know It like the Back of Your Hand

Although I was familiar with the concept of an Elevator Pitch, it was not until 2014 during a sales training meeting with Ben Tyson, then Head of Sales Enablement at Google, that it really clicked for me just how important it is. I recall it clearly as I considered myself quite a sales professional back then. We had a staff of sixty sales reps whom Ben was training on-site in Nicaragua on behalf of Google's Channel Sales Program initiative. At one point during Ben's two-day training session, a heated exchange took place where the Business Development Reps were challenging him with all the customer objections they received on a daily basis and how difficult it was to overcome them, especially since we were cold-calling businesses regarding their Google AdWords account (or lack thereof) and offering free account audits and new account strategy sessions.

Typical frequent rebuttals from prospects just a few seconds into the call included:

- Where are you calling from again? I never requested a Google AdWords audit.
- Stop calling us about Google this and Google that—we're not interested!
- We already spoke with a Google rep once and we're all set!

The takeaway from Ben's session, and a lightbulb moment for me, was that very few reps, and especially at scale with sixty reps, could be expected to effectively answer all these immediate objections. Ben called me out as the founder of the business and asked me how I'd tackle these rebuttals. I can't remember exactly what I said, but I can assure you it was inconsistent and somewhat vague. I'm pretty sure that nine out of ten prospects would also have hung up on me if I'd replied like that during a live prospecting call.

Instead, Ben helped craft a compelling Elevator Pitch that became the universal reply for each interruption when cold-calling, regardless of industry. Every single one of my sixty reps, including myself, quickly familiarized ourselves to an extent that we could wake up any of them at 2:00 a.m., and they could recite it verbatim with the right mix of tonality, body language, and excitement. Out of all the valuable training and sales methodologies Ben taught my team during these sessions, this was one of the more remarkable results-wise because it enabled immediate impact and could be used regardless of sales role and in any stage of the sales cycle.

Today I always exhort my fellow entrepreneurs to get this right down to the penny. Isn't it evident as a business owner that you're always selling your company? Whether to prospective customers, potential investors, new hires, or partners, your Elevator Pitch should do the trick each time.

Here's the Elevator Pitch for my Accelerator Program, in eighty-four words, and can be said in under a minute. What would you improve?

"We help companies launch, scale, and become profitable by providing a comprehensive playbook—tested and curated by subject matter experts across multiple industries. You see, a commonly known fact is that about 80 percent of startups cease to exist within eighteen months. Our platform significantly mitigates that risk of failure. Furthermore, it streamlines the execution of all tasks required to

become profitable. We have helped many companies become a success by providing

them with everything they need in one place so they can launch, scale, and succeed!"

A simple way to get started is to use a template such as this one:

Elevator Pitch Template

Who?	
Who is your audience?	
What are their problems?	
What?	
What do you do?	
What is your unique selling point?	
What value do you bring to the customer?	
What are you running your business for?	
How?	
How can you solve the customer's problem?	
Why?	
Why should the customer choose you?	
What is your product differentiation?	

Your Value Proposition

USPs and Elevator Pitches are cousins of the value proposition, but there is one critical difference to consider: they lack the same effectiveness when selling to the corporate or enterprise market as your Value Proposition does. Whereas your USP can get you the initial attention in your marketing copy, your Value Proposition does the heavy lifting. In a few sentences, while being specific (often citing statistics, values, numbers, or position), it clearly conveys the unique benefits that your prospect gains from using your company's solutions.

In other words, it's not a slogan, a glowing description, or eloquent marketing copy. Instead, it's a *promise* of the outcome to be expected if they move forward with you!

Here are a few examples of good Value Propositions:

- **Stripe:** "Millions of companies of all sizes—from startups to Fortune 500s—use Stripe's software and APIs to accept payments, send payouts, and manage their businesses online."
- **Accelerator Platform:** "Our Accelerator Platform helps companies go to market, scale and become profitable via a comprehensive playbook tested and curated by subject-matter experts across multiple industries."
- **Freshbooks:** "The all-new FreshBooks is accounting software that makes running your small business easy, fast and secure. Spend less time on accounting and more time doing the work you love."
- **Great Dane Ventures:** "GDV is an angel investment and accelerator firm that helps Tech and Software as a Service (SaaS) startups with 100x potential go to market via 360 degrees marketing and sales support, incubator programs, and hands-on advisory services."
- **Apple:** "iOS 15 is packed with new features that help you connect with others, be more present and in the moment, explore the world, and use the power of intelligence to do more with iPhone than ever before."

Financing Is Not for Everyone

The work you invest to develop a focused and effective USP, Elevator Pitch, and Value Proposition sets the groundwork if you decide you need to raise financing. However, there are three key questions to consider before looking for outside capital:

1. Are you running a "lifestyle business" with no chance of scale?
2. Can you bootstrap (self-fund) with no need for external investors?
3. Do you have extreme passion for your business?

Then ask yourself *why* you need outside financing investment. Here are the top three reasons:

1. To seize an opportunity to grow you may otherwise lose
2. If what you do requires lots of capital (e.g., machinery or clinical studies)
3. Strategic/"smart" money

If the answers lead you to decide to seek external investment, then consider these key success factors beforehand:

- Have you clearly identified your "secret sauce" and an IP strategy behind it?
- Do you have a clear initial product vision? And for the next two to three years?
- Is there demonstrated growth potential?
- Have you defined and tested your MVP with early customers?
- Have you tested your business model with early customers?
- Do you understand your cash flow and key milestones for growth?
- Do you clearly know what you'll use the investment funds for?
- Are all material facts about your company understood and disclosed?

Honest answers to these, and other questions specific to your business, should provide you with the ability to make an informed clear decision.

Your Corporate Pitch Deck

So you've decided seeking investment is for you. Now the infamous pitch deck. It's your twelve minutes on the mic to tell the story about what very well might be your life's work. A powerful pitch deck is your one-way ticket to securing funding. But founders often struggle to create a pitch deck that's compelling in both factual and emotional terms—one that tells a story with cold hard facts backing your narrative every step of the way.

Having developed a clear Elevator Pitch, Value Proposition, and USPs positions you to create a concise, effective pitch deck. And you can use it not only when looking for potential investors but also for presenting to key hires or strategic partners. And you may also adapt parts as a section in your sales pitch deck.

Pitch decks are close to an art form, but there are some common core elements and the best follow a certain sequence to communicate complex messages quickly. So we've set out an eleven-part structure that does your venture justice. Dive into each step and allow it to become the foundation you use to build your pitch deck. I've highlighted some key points to consider as you prepare.

Create Pitch Deck

Tell a coherent story to convince potential investors and other relevant stakeholder of your business model

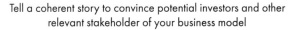

Standardized '11 Slide' Pitch Deck

1 Title Slide

- Present your company's name, logo, and one-liner describing what your company does

2 Problem / Opportunity

- Indicate the problem your business idea solves
- Remember: the solution arises } from the problem, not vice versa

3 Solution / Value Proposition

- Explain how your business solves this problem
- Make it clear how the value is delivered and experienced

4 Traction / Business Model

- Spell out your business model
- Represent a unit economics that is associated with product units
- Show the numbers (turnover, growth, etc.)

5 Customer / Market

- Illustrate a sufficiently large market out there
- Suggest how the market will develop in the future
- Specify who your customer is

6 Marketing Plan / Go-To-Market

- Outline how you reach out to your customer
- Define your Marketing/Sales campaign

7 Competition

- Touch on your competitors
- Differentiate your business idea from others'

8 Financial Projections

- Take a 'Look into a crystal ball' with the help of the financial model
- Prove the possibility for exponential growth

9 Use of Funds

- Describe your status quo
- Share your plan on financial resources for the next 3-4 years

10 Team

- Convince them you are the right person/team for the business model and domain
- Stress on the Founder-Market-Fit

11 Closing / Call-to-action

- Short call-to-action depending on the addressee of the pitch (e.g., for planned equity financing x $ for y %)

> Each slide should have one sentence as heading, which summarizes the whole slide. All slide headings together form the storyline of your pitch deck.

Remember the research we did earlier in this chapter? Now it's time for you to boil down the essentials of all this work and explain it as concisely as possible. Know your audience and keep them in mind. Think of your deck (and presentation when you deliver the pitch) as a play or Netflix drama in three acts.

Act 1:

Hook them with the inciting incident. A reason to learn more.

Slide 1 Title: Include a brief statement or visual of what your company does so they "get" it before you begin... or at least, are very curious.

Slide 2 Problem/Opportunity: Hook their interest here. Summarize the problem you solve. Succinctly state the opportunity this represents for your customers and company.

Slide 3 Value Proposition/Solution: Summarize your value proposition. Focus only on how it solves the problem and how you deliver value. Don't go into functional/technical details here. That's later in the Q&A.

Act 2:

Build the confrontation, then release with the climax

Slide 4 Business Model: Illustrate the business model. Show the key numbers. Explain the "secret sauce" and how this fulfills the Value Proposition.

Slide 5 Customer and Market: Clearly define who your customer is. Show the market size now and in the future.

Slide 6 Marketing and Sales: Define how you reach your market. Summarize your go-to-market strategy and sales plan.

Slide 7 Competition: Outline your key competitors. Clearly explain how you differentiate from them.

Slide 8 Team: Focus on Founder/Market fit. Convince them you and your core team have what it takes.

Act 3:

Climax with the ask, pose a decision, then provide resolution

Slide 9 Financials and *the Ask*: Show your key projections with assumptions. Prove the potential for exponential growth. Clearly *ask* what investment resources you are seeking.

Slide 10 Use of Funds and *the Ask*: What is your current status? State your plan and timeline over three to five years. Repeat the *Ask*, reinforced by your plan.

Slide 11 Summary and Call to Action: Very briefly repeat how your Value Proposition meets the market opportunity and you are the right team. Restate the *Ask* in a different way that's clear.

Optional Slides: Backup Notes

Market, product, technical, financial details. Use *only* if necessary and when asked. Resist the temptation to volunteer these now. Provide later as needed.

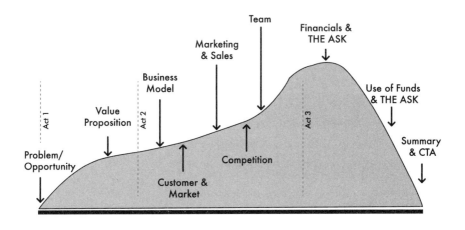

B2B/SAAS PRICING MODELS
AND STRATEGIES

So now you've done your homework for your B2B or SaaS product/service offering. You've researched the market, your prospective customers, your competition, the gaps in the market, their pain, and the gains they'll experience with your solutions. Finally you're in a better position to structure an appropriate pricing strategy that ensures you're paid adequately for your work but doesn't devalue your level of expertise. It does this by portraying the correct perceived value as accurately as possible and establishing a price range that correlates with market conditions, your competitor's pricing, and most critically, positions you as the most favorable solution from a pricing *and* value perspective.

Back in 2011, I made all the mistakes in the book when it came to the above exercise, or rather lack thereof. The end result was that we went to market with a PPC management solution for US advertisers starting at $129/month under the notion that at that price (significantly cheaper than anyone else in the market at that point), our solution would be the best thing since sliced bread. We thought we would sell our PPC management solutions at such a pace that I'd be up there along with Elon Musk and Jeff Bezos on the *Forbes* list of wealthiest people!

The truth, however, was the complete opposite and financially brutal. Because of the perceived value of our solutions, after we had stripped away fundamental core service offerings in order to reduce the price (e.g., email only instead of phone support), prospects went running in the opposite direction when we pitched them. They believed either (a) there had to be a catch since we were so inexpensive, or (b) the price portrayed a discounted cheap solution that was not worth the value compared with a significantly higher priced solution (despite them being identical).

Much is written about B2B pricing, but it's important to understand the basic elements involved. In summary, you need to define your pricing model *and* your pricing strategy. A B2B pricing model is the framework within which you set your pricing strategy. A B2B pricing strategy is the way you decide the final cost and price point for your product or service. This may be dynamic in response to market conditions.

B2B pricing models typically fall into four categories: (1) user-based, (2) usage-based, (3) flat rate, and (4) tiered. B2B pricing strategies typically include (1) value-based pricing, (2) cost-plus or markup pricing, (3) competitor-based pricing, and (4) dynamic pricing.

Low price often drives B2C business where consumers are often willing to trade quality for price and often buy with more emotion. But this doesn't necessarily apply to B2B business where buyers make decisions based on far more than just price. B2B buying characteristics that vary from B2C include:

1. More complex decision-making process. Sophisticated buyers are motivated to help their companies be more competitive, successful, and profitable.
2. More rational and sophisticated buyers. Functionality, quality, and reliability are key factors where a business's reputation is at stake.
3. Longer-term buyers. Relationships, trust, reputation, customer experience, and services are essential.
4. More complex products, so relevant, timely information is key. Customers research solutions (yours and the competitors') heavily before engaging with your sales team.

McKinsey & Company have identified four proven B2B pricing strategies:

- **Margin Expanders:** Make incremental changes to existing price structure by differentiating pricing by product or by customer or raising or lowering prices based on competitive dynamics.
- **Revenue Drivers:** Make incremental changes to pricing structure to penetrate deeper into the existing customer base, including pricing new or different elements or changing how the offering is bought or paid to increase the spend per customer.
- **Pricing Disruptors:** A "radical approach" for companies in new categories or categories under significant threat. It attempts to

maximize profitability by redefining the pricing structure. This includes redefining how or what you price, sharing profits with customers, and applying innovative technology or tools to identify or capture more value.

- **Sales and Pricing Pioneers:** This aims to gain scale by drastically redefining pricing, including charging for results/performance, mixing free and paid elements, and "flexible" pricing, which gives the customer the power to decide prices.

In the SaaS space, pricing is a hot topic. Marc Andreesen, the perceptive California venture capitalist, said that "the No. 1 theme our companies have when they get really struggling is they are not charging enough for their product... The conventional wisdom in Silicon Valley is that the way to succeed is to price your product as low as possible under the theory that if it's low-priced everybody can buy it and that's how you get the volume. It's called 'too hungry to eat.'" He continued, "They don't charge enough for their product to be able to afford the sales and marketing required to actually get anybody to buy it. *And so they can't afford to hire the sales reps to go sell the product.*"

Raising your price, if done correctly, offers a number of benefits:

1. Attracts higher quality customers
2. Your customers value your offer
3. Your customers get better results
4. Your company can afford to offer improved or premium support

The result? Reduce or eliminate low-price customers who don't truly value your offering and add more long-term customers who "get" your value and are prepared to pay for it.

I've learned there's no cut-and-dried approach to defining effective pricing strategies. Not every strategy works for every B2B business. So you need to assess what works best for your market, your target customers, and your products or services.

Mitigating Customer Churn

Churn typically refers to users lost in a given time frame, but more important is *revenue* lost. It's usually expressed either as a dollar amount or a percentage. Revenue churn is generally due to customer cancellations or downgrading their SaaS subscriptions.

There may be many perceived reasons for customers to leave your company ("churn"). Most of them are wrong. It's typically *not* your product or its use, nor your competitor or your price. It's the perceived *value* the customer obtains from your company as a whole and your product. This is unique to each customer and changes throughout their ownership/use life cycle. Churn is the opposite of growth and signals that something about the value of your offering is not resonating with your customers.

There are three especially important factors with churn—results, trust, and relevance.

- Contrary to popular belief, customers don't purchase to solve a problem; they purchase to achieve a result. Their problem statement or specification is how they communicate a desired result. Since desired results often change, vendors need to understand the dynamics triggering the change.
- Trusted relationships are the centerpiece of customer loyalty. But trust doesn't come with the contract signing. It needs to be constantly earned throughout the sales cycle itself and beyond, during implementation and support.

- Vendor stickiness is driven by continued relevance of your whole offering to the customer's desired results. These may change over time. You need to be in tune and adapt before it's too late.

For SaaS businesses focused on smaller companies as customers, a 3–5 percent churn monthly is typical. For enterprise-level products, churn is typically less than 1 percent per month. However, early-stage B2B and SaaS companies can often have a churn of up to 15 percent for the first year as they discover their initial market and create an early revenue stream. Churn typically happens when a customer:

- Closes their account completely
- Cancels a subscription to a product or service
- Doesn't renew their contract
- Changes to another vendor

Focusing on the *value chain* rather than just one element is the secret to mitigating churn. However, this may require a shift in mindset from the various departments involved, starting with sales and marketing, but also including customer support and product management/development as well as senior executive leadership.

Four effective ways to mitigate churn are:

1. Assessing product fit to make it indispensable to your users—for example, by offering a dashboard of metrics providing key customer insights
2. Analyzing your customer experience and improving areas where needed
3. Negotiating multiuser contracts so that your product is adopted across the organization, thus increasing stickiness
4. Verticalization, described in the next section

Verticalization versus a Jack of All Trades

Horizontal B2B and SaaS businesses focus their product/service function-ality across many industries. By contrast, vertical B2B and SaaS businesses are focused on a highly targeted segmented audience within specific sec-tors and seek to dominate their niche(s). This can be an effective remedy for customer churn by differentiating along vertical lines. Although there is an initial cost and time to develop such a strategy and buy-in is required across your company, benefits of verticalization include:

- Developing a deeper understanding right across your entire orga-nization, of your customer and its needs, thereby enhancing the whole product fulfillment process and customer experience
- Better gross margins through volume economics where supply and domain expertise are concentrated in one industry
- Affiliate partnership networks develop and strengthen
- Stronger marketplace network effects where the value of each participant increases as the network grows, as does the stickiness of your offering

In summary, a vertical strategy enables you to:

1. Market more deeply within it and extend long tail coverage
2. Potentially own the supply chain
3. Develop a much more detailed and informed understanding of the buyer-seller transactional process and how best to market to it
4. Develop a deeper understanding of specific customer needs, contributing to an enhanced conversion funnel
5. Increase customer lifetime value by marketing to repeated, focused customer needs

6. Lower customer acquisition cost with a targeted, replicable offering

7. Create a highly defensible moat with partnerships, unique value delivery, a strong user community, and active referral network

Vertical Content Marketing

Implementing a verticalization strategy requires a shift to focus marketing budget on the selected vertical(s). Verticalized content marketing increases the relevance and credibility of your offering. Deciding whether to verticalize requires considering a number of factors, including vertical market size and uniqueness, your product-market fit, existing customer wins providing credibility, and your sales team culture and organization.

Your successfully verticalized content outreach communicates key signals to your potential customers. It says that you have customer proof since other similar companies have adopted your offering, that you value and understand the vertical, and that you are experienced in building and delivering your offering.

It does bring its own complexities however, since only so many marketing resources are available to adapt or generate vertical content. It's just as expensive to develop and maintain as horizontal content, yet only addresses part of your potential markets. Nonetheless, the more varied the markets you sell into are, the more vertical marketing can outperform horizontal content.

We have covered many topics in this chapter, and I hope you now more clearly understand that *"failing to prepare is preparing to fail."* Especially important is defining and understanding your entire customer journey and ideal customer profile and conducting thorough competitor analysis to identify gaps in the market. This will equip you to design a strong Value

Proposition, USPs, and ensure that your pitch will stand out and cut through the noise.

The question to ask yourself now is which sales channels are most effective? In Chapter 4, we will take a deep dive into what this looks like and carefully examine both channel and direct sales models as well as Enterprise versus SMB sales.

4

ONE-TO-ONE VERSUS ONE-TO-MANY (OR BOTH?)

I'll share with you a comprehensive understanding of the typical sales models you can pursue. Then I'll outline the pros and cons of each so you can decide which strategy is best suited for your organization.

"Gary, should we focus on Direct Sales or Channel Sales?" This is one of the more common questions I get from B2B and SaaS startups in my angel investing venture and Accelerator Platform offering. The answer varies greatly depending on the market you're entering, the competition, the product or service you're offering, and many other factors.

During my last twenty years in sales I've seen the good, the bad, and the ugly of both cases. And Lord knows, I've learned my lessons through the school of hard knocks in both direct sales and channel sales.

One of the toughest knocks happened when I first rolled out our channel sales program at my last company, WSM, and onboarded a high volume of resellers. Despite high levels of motivation, this approach never really reaped us any benefits because of their inability to subsequently resell our solutions. After months of presentations and pitches, heavy negotiations, agreements made, configuring partner support to their specific needs, and even training their reps, only a few customers came through the door to us. It was an utterly negative financial investment. Of course, I've also seen the complete opposite many times. The point is that no matter how systematic you are, you'll need to take a big leap of faith with little guarantee of success. So you have to carefully consider where to place your bets.

Conversely, I've also been kicked in the butt big time when going all-in with a prospective partner in channel ventures. At WSM, I negotiated for months with a significantly larger company than ours that also offered paid search management services and had 100x more resellers but in other digital marketing categories. After unveiling all our "secret sauce" by explaining how we managed campaigns at scale, enabled our partners to sell more, detailed our partner volume pricing, and much more, I learned a few months later that they had, despite assuring me otherwise and signing a nondisclosure agreement, gone all-in to build out their own PPC solution. As a result of months of diligent sales process and putting everything on the table, I had now enabled our new biggest competitor by trying to sell to them as a partner! I shall not reveal their name despite being heavily tempted to.

The same goes with direct selling where my stories are many. Several stand out. I discovered that one of my top-performing reps was selling all our customer data out of the back door to one of our direct competitors. As a result, we experienced high cancellations over the following months once commissions had been paid out to him. This negatively impacted the

THE ZERO TO 100 MILLION SALES BLUEPRINT

lifetime value since we weren't recuperating the high marketing and client acquisition costs.

Another blow to the stomach was at the peak of WSM's revenue trajectory, after we had been growing exponentially YoY for three years. Our growth rate brutally hit the breaks and even declined for some quarters. Everything became less effective. For example, the good leads were scattered across many reps resulting in highly fluctuating close rates. And our marketing as well as operational expenses skyrocketed, nearly leading us to bankruptcy.

Another painful experience was back at one of my old boiler room companies selling refilled ink cartridges to SMBs and overseeing nearly 100 sales reps in three different offices in Copenhagen. The recruitment and attrition of reps was a massive operation because the sales gig was so brutal that only one out of ten new hires "made it." In fact, the average tenure was less than two months on the phones before the constant harsh feedback and verbal abuse from prospects who, tired of being continuously cold-called, said things like *"Stop calling us and get a real job!"* or *"Do me a favor and go to the top of your building and jump off the roof, you f**king loser!"* just got too painful. Most reps quit within just a few weeks.

The result of this high attrition and the rather "creative" commission-only compensation structure we offered these young fresh-out-of-school graduates was an explosion of media attention after a journalist went undercover, took a job with us, and then wrote a dreadful article titled, "Sell Your Soul over the Phone" in a leading Danish publication, *Chili Magazine*. Of course it featured some of my recruitment pitches to prospective hopeful new hires to get rich fast, as well as an exposé of some of my high-pressure sales huddles and pep talks.

As I assume you're more familiar with direct sales, I'm going to start with channel sales.

For now, I'll spare you the pain of more negative experiences with both strategies. In later chapters I'll expand in greater detail, but the moral of the story here is that there are many pros and cons to consider with each approach, and it's very hard to give standardized recommendations for either. However, here are the key ones for each.

CHANNEL SALES: THE CONS AND PROS

Sometimes I like to turn things around when thinking how to begin with the end in mind by looking at the cons first.

The Cons

- **Less control** of your sales process since you are dependent on resellers. You have no ability to directly oversee the sales process, or manage or coach your third-party sales representatives. You can do your best to influence them by providing free sales training, sales and marketing collateral, and more, but in the end, you're relying on multiple external factors outside your control.
- **Less predictable** growth trajectory despite establishing targets and incentives for your resellers. They'll always have their own agenda and bottom line to consider before yours.
- **Brand risk** is at stake when going to market and having third-party sales representatives control the narrative of your brand and value proposition at a one-to-one level with prospects in the market. If a partner treats your customer or prospect poorly, expect your brand to take the hit. Your association with the partner negatively impacts your brand's reputation, and you'll be obliged to share responsibility for this negative treatment.

- **Reduced profit margins** because you'll almost always be expected to extend large discounts, incentives, or rebates to your resellers for them to be motivated to sell your solutions as a priority offering in their business. I've seen discount rates vary from 8–9 percent all the way up to 30–45 percent.
- **Potential channel conflict** and overlaps between partners and your direct sales team can make things quite messy, creating tensions between your in-house sales and your partner reps when competing for the same deal. Such partner channel conflict is difficult to prevent entirely, although you need to do your best to segment by markets and verticals. I've personally tried firsthand to compete with Google's and Microsoft's in-house teams. Although we always found an amicable solution, it's something to be aware of and carefully consider before rolling out a channel program that might create conflict with your direct sales initiatives.

And now...

The Pros

- **Effective scaling** of your revenue and customer base *if* you manage to successfully roll out a comprehensive partner enablement program, recruit the right resellers for your channel strategy, and nail just the right balance of financial incentives and stretch targets to motivate your resellers continuously and consistently.
- **Trust right out of the gate** can be expected and leveraged when you partner with a reseller who has a strong reputation and foothold in a local market. Through your partnership, you'll immediately be able to obtain good traction with prospects by being

associated with your partner's good reputation and trust in the marketplace.

- **Rapid testing** and experimentation is possible at a whole different level because of the sheer volume of resellers bringing your solutions to market. They can create a positive feedback loop and results that otherwise could take years to attain compared with your direct sales model.

- **Low cost of entry** to new markets, segments, and verticals since enabling resellers usually requires little up-front investment and much lower cost compared to launching a direct sales model with similar reach.

- **Low marketing/sales cost** for many channel sales ventures since if effectively constructed, one partner manager can often oversee 10+ resellers, and with the right mix of support vehicles (e.g., partner portals with collateral support or promotional offers for new client acquisition), you can expect a high ROI on partner marketing initiatives.

DIRECT SALES: THE CONS AND PROS

Now let's look at direct sales, again beginning with the cons.

The Cons

- **High cost** and low success rate is probably the most dreadful factor for most companies that try to build out their direct sales team. It's *very* costly to develop a sales team and often requires a large support network for them to be empowered to drive satisfactory results (i.e., lead generation, marketing and sales collateral, sales operations/admin support, sales management, systems and software, tools, bonus structures, etc.).

- **Scalability is hard** and painful with direct sales. Anyone who has managed a larger sales team can attest to this. It requires a lot of blood, sweat, and tears recruiting, training, onboarding, and developing reps, only to see an overall short sales rep life span, having few succeed (only one out of three reps usually meet quota). And then you have to struggle with retention efforts or renegotiation with your high-performing reps who suddenly become cocky and are quite aware of their market value and are open to explore new job opportunities from your competition if they have deeper pockets than you.

- **High barriers of entry** to new markets when compared to a channel sales strategy, since you're relying on setting up a new company (if in a different country), acquiring new offices, recruiting and managing personnel, and many redundant expenses from an operational standpoint.

The Pros

- **Higher margins** per deal because selling directly to your end customer requires no heavy discounts, rebates, or other incentives compared to selling through a channel sales distribution network of resellers and partners.

- **Better forecast accuracy** and predictability is expected since you'll have complete visibility over your pipeline, initiatives to meet quotas, and whenever needed in the sales process, be able to coach your reps to close more deals.

- **Full control** over your sales process with no dependency on external partners for revenue generation. If something isn't working or you're falling behind on targets, you can within reach, control most factors and your success "only" depends on your ability to execute.

Now that we better understand the pros and cons of these two go-to-market approaches, let's take a deeper dive into each for you to better gauge what's the right solution or mix for your venture.

CHANNEL SALES: SELLING THROUGH INTERMEDIARIES

The simple definition of a channel sales strategy is that you're relying on a distribution network of resellers, through partnership agreements, to sell your products or solutions under one of the following models:

- **White Label Partnership**, often called private label, where a reseller offers your solutions under their own brand to their customers. For example, this is the model we deployed at WSM where we offered White Label PPC Solutions to other marketing agencies that, either due to limited margins, lack of in-house speciality or capacity, chose to resell our PPC solutions over building out their own solution and team. This model can be quite attractive financially for resellers (and is very common in the digital marketing agency world) since a reseller chooses how much they want to mark up the price as a part of their own holistic solution. I once landed a large reseller that specialized in SEO solutions. To offer PPC as a value-add to their customers, they acquired our white label product at a 7 percent cost of media spend and sold it for 15–20 percent to their entire customer base. When you multiply that with $500,000 in monthly recurring revenue (MRR), that's a nice chunk of money for doing little to zero work, besides selling the solution of course, usually as an upsell initiative.

- Through the years, I've had the opportunity to play a leading role in establishing white label partnerships in a variety of verticals and business models, including:
  - » SEM and SEO Management Solutions and Software
  - » Social Media Management Solutions
  - » Mobile Application Development
  - » Email Marketing Software
  - » CRM Software for SMBs

- **Value-added resellers** is a co-branded marketing solution where a reseller often becomes a Certified Partner with a larger brand and is empowered to resell their products. Well-known examples of this include Google, Microsoft, Meta, HubSpot, and so forth, who all, besides having their in-house direct sales team, heavily rely on channel partnerships for growing their market share. In fact, after having previously worked with all of the above big brands for 10+ years, I know that channel sales in fact was their fastest growing sales model during the years I collaborated with them—that's how powerful channels can be if set up correctly.

  I've flirted with these partnership models at all levels of engagements—from my early days in channel through Radio NRJ where I established partnerships at a smaller scale with big media companies such as Havas Media, Carat, or OMD (fifteen to twenty-five sales per quarter) and at a larger scale as a Google Ads Premier Partner and Microsoft Ads Partner (200–300 sales per quarter).

- **Affiliate marketing** partnerships are typically scenarios where a company establishes referral agreements with third-party companies who in return get a commission for referring your solution to their prospect or customer. Quite commonly, this is a one-time referral fee, whereas the two other above-mentioned models usually yield perpetual recurring revenue-share agreements and the client relationship remains under the reseller's ownership. There are, of course, companies that offer recurring commission, but since the affiliate partner usually does not manage either the sales process or the ongoing account management, there's often little financial justification for a recurring commission model. Affiliate partnerships can, however, yield great returns if you acquire a large network of affiliates. It is often mutually beneficial when two companies that, for example, cater to different business segments, markets, or verticals, partner up with the objective of referring business to each other when a prospective client falls outside their scope of services and is better suited for the other party in the affiliate agreement. This allows both partners to add value to their prospects without making the investment to provide the service or develop the product.

I've set up quite a few of these partnership models, both as owner of my own businesses and as consultant for other companies. But since I've mainly operated in the B2B sector, I've never seen the volume of results as with the other partnership models, nor have I prioritized it much since there is often a limited growth impact due to one-time referral commission agreements. However, I know the opposite is true for many affiliate marketers who crack the code of generating traffic and source a great deal of revenue, especially with e-commerce and SaaS businesses that, in general, pay handsome commissions to their affiliates.

ROLES AND RESOURCES NEEDED TO 100X YOUR CHANNEL

During my last three years at WSM, I learned all the ins and outs of channel sales after onboarding 200+ resellers. Prior to that, I sat on the other side of the table in partnership agreements with Google and Microsoft as one of their leading resellers of PPC solutions.

As a result, it's safe to say that I'm a huge advocate of channel sales which, since I've experienced firsthand that if done right, has the ability to grow a business faster than most other sales models. The power of multiplication at scale and the compounded effect of continuously enabling resellers can skyrocket growth.

Although it's easier said than done, I strongly suggest at the very least, you consider the following roles, resources, setup, and processes.

Roles and Responsibilities

- **Head of Partnerships** is the equivalent to your Sales Director or VP of Sales in your direct sales division. You need a business-savvy sales professional who can develop your partner program and channel strategy—that is, planning, documenting, and rolling out partnership initiatives that, according to financial forecast, make the desired impact on your bottom line through strategic partnerships and alliances.

- **Strategic Partnership Manager (SPM)** is the hybrid between your Account Executives (AEs) and Account Managers (AMs) in direct sales. This person should be an eloquent, experienced sales and business professional, who holds a high degree of relationship-building skills and thereby can work closely with a dozen or so partners enabling them to meet your mutual growth targets and objectives.

- **Sales Engineer (SE)** is a hybrid between an engineer (i.e., strong technical understanding and use of your solution) and a salesperson. In my case selling digital marketing solutions, software, and custom applications, this was a needed support vehicle for our SPMs during the sales process to provide technical audits and answer questions regarding integrations and so forth. This is an important role if you're selling B2B and SaaS solutions and don't want to stall the deal closing process when the SPM faces technical challenges or questions that may hinder the probability of closing the deal.

- **Account Manager (AM)** as with direct sales, this is your day-to-day appointed contact who oversees the overall health of an assigned portfolio of mutual customers. They are responsible to address inquiries, stay on top of select accounts, and meet with partner reps on an ad hoc basis regarding specific accounts.

- **Marketing Development Representative (MDR)** is highly valuable with a channel sales program and especially if selling a more complex product and targeting a limited audience where inbound leads must be treated with utmost care to not miss out on otherwise potentially high-value opportunities. These more specialized salespeople with subject matter expertise can help bridge the gap between your partner marketing-qualified leads (MQLs) and your sales-qualified leads (SQLs).

- **Business Development Representative (BDR)** is also needed to effectively scale your channel sales programs. They are your conventional outreach-focused BDRs who aim to kick in doors and begin new partnerships, conversations that otherwise wouldn't come to fruition unless solicited via such outbound efforts.

Recommended Systems, Tools, and Processes

- **Partner Relationship Management (PRM) Portal.** In my last agency project we used Communities by Salesforce to layer a portal on top of our existing Customer Relationship Management (CRM) setup. This enabled us to give our resellers access to see all the notes, scheduled and previous tasks, activities, etc., of their customer base that we were managing on a white label partnership basis. This investment in providing complete visibility to what was going on behind the scenes from a logistical perspective was incredibly beneficial. Our resellers' AMs could, when probed with a question by one of their clients, directly access all the information on the client regarding what work had been done, why it had been done, the strategy, the expected outcome, and when again we were programmed to review the accounts.

- This transparency not only helped with the overall customer experience but enhanced the partnership potential by limiting unnecessary back-and-forth communication between our resellers' AMs and our AM or SPM. Additional worthwhile features and benefits to highlight with having a PRM include a robust content repository management system for sales and marketing collateral, analytics to demonstrate most popular docs/decks, etc., along with support ticketing systems, pipeline insights, performance overview, and special custom features such as "Request for Proposal" (one of the most popular partner enablement features I rolled out at my last channel sales company).

- Alternative PRMs on the market that I've used in various projects in addition to Salesforce's and can recommend are:
  » Allbound PRM

- » Channeltivity
- » PartnerTap
- **Quarterly and Annual Business Reviews** (QBR and ABR) are very important for the sake of partnership enablement and continued growth trajectory. Many channel companies don't put enough emphasis on this exercise as the partner portfolio grows and when things come up they can't keep the effort consistent. I truly believe that QBRs/ABRs are the cornerstone for success in any channel sales strategy and is a highly underrated growth tool for many businesses. The value of establishing quarterly targets with partners and measuring progress on key metrics, such as new client acquisitions, QoQ/YoY growth rate, churn rate, same-store growth, and product adoption rate, is mission critical for a mutually beneficial partnership.
- The primary KPIs I focused on during my QBRs with partners usually included:
  - » Total number of clients
  - » Total number of new clients acquired
  - » QoQ and YoY growth rate
  - » Customer churn rate
  - » Average spend per customer
  - » Average same-store growth rate (upselling)
  - » New product adoption rate (cross-selling)
  - » Partner budget utilization rate
  - » RFP-to-close ratio
  - » Amount of deals in pipeline
  - » Average sales cycle length
  - » New sales/marketing collateral and tools
  - » Co-branded marketing initiatives and new client acquisition events

- » Sales support initiatives (to co-pitch large deal opportunities)
- » Sales training needs
- » Overall partner feedback

Add to this the expected communication enhancement and feedback loops from this process, along with the elevated motivation levels a reseller often experiences when receiving this "love and attention" by the channel vendor and you can really begin to quantify the returns from these initiatives.

At WSM, one of my favorite parts of the venture was being flown out to San Francisco or New York by Google or to Seattle by Microsoft and getting wined and dined while talking shop. Rest assured that upon my return to our offices in Nicaragua or Miami I came back in full pitch mode and leveraged all the insights and support vehicles extended by their SPM at the highest levels.

A primary activity we covered during QBRs was collaborating on how together we could exceed the established targets or pick up on the slack if we were falling behind the curve. Co-marketing initiatives such as sales contests, joint case studies, video testimonials, or sales training were always part of the agenda.

When it comes to ABRs then, these are even more important in the big picture. You see, at the beginning of any partnership there are mutual goals and objectives put in place, usually supported by contractual agreements that detail out the financial rewards depending on the established targets. Although the QBRs serve as a good measuring stick to how things are trending, the ABR is the sum of it all and the time to assess the past year's business results versus goals and targets in contract addenda. The continued business objectives are revised and it's also the place and setting where priorities, opportunities, and goals for the upcoming years are discussed.

All of these initiatives, when working in conjunction with the right financial incentives, act as a catalyst for growth and I would even reason you shouldn't bother having a partner program and channel sales strategy unless you are capable of rolling things out with such partner support capacity.

Over my career I've participated in over 1,000 QBRs and ABRs collectively. I've witnessed the many ways these can take shape and their criteria for success. I won't go into detail, but suffice it to say that I'd expect you to treat them as you would a closing call with a high-value customer when the CFO and all the company stakeholders in the decision-making process are present. You need to make sure you come fully prepared with all pertinent metrics and data in place, have a crystal-clear agenda, and focus on mutual wins and opportunities along with areas of improvement. Like any other partnership, the desired outcome is always win-win-win!

- **Partner Onboarding Process** is the do or die in channel sales. God knows I've cringed many times throughout my journey when my team and I got this wrong, especially after spending months and sometimes years landing a new reseller. Like everything else in the world of business "first impressions are everything!" We always began with a kickoff call where the objectives were to introduce all the team members from each party assigned to this partnership, recap on objectives and goals, and then discuss next steps. Make sure to get this right, every time, without exception.

  What worked well for me was to underline to all assigned team members that although the partner had signed on the dotted line and committed financially, this was the ultimate test and last phase of the recruitment process. Now was the time where we'd either drop the ball or reinforce the value proposition we (I or other SPM) originally brought to the table and thereby activate the partnership effectively and generate profit. This is still a "dating process," and you must ensure to keep the excitement and energy level at its highest!

Furthermore, this is the time to adjust expectations and over-communicate on details. What are their communication and reporting preferences, culture, priorities, most important clients, and opportunities to prioritize. Although the goal should be process establishment, setting up systems, and process management, make sure that everyone sitting around the table who was not originally part of the negotiations and discussions is in *complete* alignment.

Last, a key initiative that I particularly focused on a lot up front was understanding the needs and gaps of the partner's team and resources. I was very keen to always invest up front initially with sales training and support for sales enablement initiatives like co-pitching. Not only did I create a foundation for long-term success with this approach, but by *overdelivering* I communicated the appreciation of this new partnership and created goodwill right out of the gate (that would save my ass down the road when I/or my team members dropped the ball on something).

- **Co-marketing Strategy** is where you double down if you plan to create a successful channel sales strategy. The objective here is to immediately and effectively create trust for your resellers through co-marketing tactics such as joint case studies, pitch decks, product explainers, or acquisition events. Here the aim is to collectively improve the effectiveness of tapping into the shared target audience and empower the reseller to convert prospects into joint customers. During my years working with several partners on both sides of the table, some of the more effective co-marketing strategies we rolled out were client acquisition events where we would have our BDRs and AEs spend a couple of weeks inviting prospects to an event, dinner, or similar social gathering, inviting a subject matter expert or thought leader of interest for our prospects, and further motivating them with special incentives if they went ahead and signed up for our solution on the night of an event.

One instructive success story was when we tried to upsell existing Google search advertising customers to increase their overall budget allocation with the objective of testing out a video marketing strategy with YouTube Ads. With the allotted co-marketing funds we could partly subsidize the video production process for the ad creative and thereby reduce the barrier to entry for them to test out the channel and then expand their overall budget with us.

DIRECT SALES MODEL: INBOUND, OUTBOUND, AND INSIDE SALES

Over the years I've built out direct sales teams for my companies multiple times. This is the most common sales model for entrepreneurs and business owners when launching their venture.

Direct selling entails you selling your products or services *directly* to your end customer. This can be done through outbound efforts such as knocking on doors (perhaps old school in this day and age), calling on prospects, driving your customers to your commercial physical location via advertising efforts, or locating your brick-and-mortar store in populated areas. Of course, nowadays a large and growing amount of direct sales happens online whether as e-commerce sales or via online demos and a follow-up process combining emails, calls, texts, and interactions across social media.

This model needs little explanation. Instead, I'll focus on why it's so damn hard and difficult for most entrepreneurs to build a successful direct sales department.

Challenge #1 is that hiring a large amount of reps for you to scale your business and train and motivate them to become effective, ensure they meet their quotas, and getting your sales department to become a well-oiled machine is really damn hard. You're dealing with Type A personalities who often have big egos, are competitive, yet in need of constant monitoring, management, and coaching. Consider that and then multiply by say twenty to thirty sales reps and you'll understand why many sales managers have one of the more stressful jobs known to mankind. They have to get other people to create results by motivating them daily, while dealing with high levels of attrition. Then, as soon as they meet their target for a month/quarter, resetting their goals (in many cases, even increasing them) and then start all over chasing down the impossible.

Challenge #2 is that most founders launch their business and sales efforts without having a plan! It blows my mind, since many entrepreneurs are highly qualified, smart, experienced, and educated subject matter experts who often have a detailed process and plan for their offerings and solutions. Consider, for example, a software engineer or an architect opening their new business venture. They are very process driven, have a suite of tools and applications to create their offerings, and would never take on a new client or a project without a series of meetings, asking probing questions, and creating a detailed plan of action.

However, when it comes to launching their business and sales initiatives, they have no plan in place in nine out of ten scenarios. They start by hiring one sales rep and give them full autonomy to contact who they want, create their own USP and messaging, manage contacts, interactions, and pipeline as they see fit. Subsequently they just expect new clients to consistently come month after month and with no struggles. Then, assuming that things work out miraculously in their favor with this approach, they're like, *"Great! That worked. Now let's scale that and hire one or more sales reps!"*

And this is when I *always* see the house of cards come down!

That's when I get contacted, once they realize this isn't working. Now we need to change this for better as of *yesterday* because at this point cash flow is usually stretched and frustration high.

What they could have done if they had begun with the end in mind and created a sales plan!

On the following page is an illustration that shows how sales are rolled out at most new companies, starting at the bottom, with just a pitch and a website. With little to zero planning or structure, they often have an inadequate foundation for scale. Later on this approach has to be reinvented and supported with a series of investments with external sales consultants, coaches, or advisors brought in to create the framework that was never put in place. Needless to say, you'll benefit tremendously if you flip things around and launch your sales plan with the end goal in mind—the opposite of this illustration.

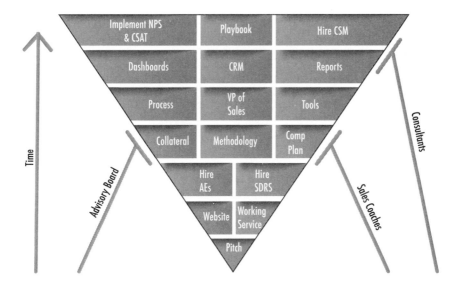

Most Sales Organizations Grow Without a Plan

CREATING A WINNING SALES PLAN FOR DIRECT SALES

Here's how I tackle a new sales process architecting project. First I assess the current sales plan and process in place (or lack thereof). Then I create a rainmaking sales plan that can be scaled, always with sustainability and profitability in mind!

Conducting Your Sales Audit (the Devil Is in the Details)

1. Evaluate your existing sales process.
2. Audit your sales tech stack and its ability to integrate and automate.
3. Examine your existing sales and marketing collateral.
4. Review leads and rate their quality.
5. Analyze all results and metrics by rep, lead source, seasonality, product, etc.

6. Examine current coaching framework.

7. Interview sales reps (top, middle, and bottom performers) as well as sales leadership.

8. Evaluate current compensation structure, bonuses, commission plans, and sales contests.

9. Listen to sales calls conducted: discovery, demo, and close calls.

10. Audit the CRM compliance levels and pipeline management procedures.

10 Steps to Creating Your New Sales Plan

1. **Market and customer research**
   a. Articulate your mission and vision
   b. Define your value propositions
   c. Company and solution overview

2. **Map out your customer journey**
   a. How do we set the right expectations, onboard and activate clients
   b. When and how to attempt to upsell and cross-sell
   c. How do we measure Customer Satisfaction Score (CSAT) and promote customer advocacy

3. **Develop or acquire a sales plan template and consider**
   a. Who is in charge of architecting this? In-house or external expertise needed?
   b. What will your compensation structure be like and how does it benchmark against market standards? You want to ensure that you attract, develop, and retain talent and have limited unnecessary attrition.
   c. What sales methodology do we aim to cultivate? Which books to read?

4. **Establish clear realistic goals**

   a. Sales forecasting and goal setting within 10 percent accuracy

   b. Establish KPIs and determine reporting structure

   c. Which metrics and activities will we use to measure progress?

5. **Resources needed**

   a. Develop a team structure and define responsibilities

   b. Identify sales tools and systems needed (see Chapter 13)

   c. Create a feedback loop and coaching plan

6. **Create a prospecting list**

   a. What determines MQLs and SQLs?

   b. Which lead qualification model to implement?

   c. How do you distribute leads to your reps, by criteria and processes?

7. **Formulate an action plan**

   a. Establish deadlines and milestones

   b. Who is responsible for what and are external resources needed?

   c. Which sales channels do you leverage and how?

8. **Create a budget aligned with targets and resources needed**

   a. How are you sourcing leads?

   b. Which marketing channels do you leverage?

   c. What needs to be included in your sales tech stack?

9. **Create your sales process outlining every single step**

   a. Write documentation for each sales task and activity

   b. Select the right tools and software to automate what's possible

   c. Determine lead qualification criteria

10. **Create all pertinent sales enablement materials, including:**

    a. Outreach sequences

    b. Pitch decks, scripts, pitch outlines, case studies, and white papers

    c. Rebuttal libraries, competitor score cards, and product explainers

Now you want to do internal audits of your sales plan and the defined process or hire external consultants to lead this. This should be done even if you're hitting targets continuously. It may just be luck, coincidence, or that you have a favorable position in the market. Auditing and optimizing your sales process every six to twelve months ensures that (a) you maximize your potential outcome and results to the best of your ability and (b) that you stay on top of the latest trend shifts in the markets, new technology accelerators, and that you *proactively* tackle the issues to make sure you never ever have a sales and revenue problem again.

ROLES AND RESPONSIBILITIES FOR DIRECT SALES EFFECTIVENESS

- **Sales Manager (SM)** is a critical role to hire initially when launching your company, especially if the founder isn't an experienced salesperson. Hire someone with experience right out of the gate so that you build the *right* framework for scaling from the beginning. They should be charged with doing proper market research (if this hasn't already been done or done correctly) and creating a sales plan encompassing all the above details. Now, before adding more team members to the equation, you have someone already in place who has designed the processes, proven that they work through execution, and established benchmarks for future hires.
- **Account Executive (AE)** is an equally important hire to get right from the start. Your AEs help you land your first customers and refine your pitch and messaging. And the first AEs establish the precedence for metrics that really move the needle for the next hire—for example, lead-to-closing ratio, average deal size, sales cycle length, contract renewals, etc.

- **Account Manager (AM)** You've already seen the value of impacting the average lifetime value per client and the corresponding metrics such as cross-selling and upselling ratios, customer churn, and referrals. And since the AM usually is at the helm of the client relationship, they're able to significantly influence it and support your time to profitability with their role. This is another position you want to get right immediately.

- **Business Development Representative (BDR)** does a lot of the tedious and heavy lifting work by conducting outreach, qualifying leads, conducting discovery calls, and so forth. Since it's considered an entry-level sales position, I personally like to hire folks with little experience for this role but with the right attitude and attributes. I motivate them to learn and perform as a BDR, by dangling the carrot of potentially growing into an AE through a career development plan with concise learning requirements, targets to consistently meet, and an assessment to pass to be promoted within a 1.5-2-year period. Many BDRs burn out before this time frame, so it's a good way, regardless, to motivate your BDRs to hustle at an extra level to meet their goals so they can be promoted.

Enterprise versus SMB Selling

Enterprise sales is *not* about selling products; it's about delivering *value* through results or outcomes, usually in the form of solutions, not products per se. Typically customers are large companies with complex decision processes involving multiple department stakeholders in long sales cycles (many months to over a year). Benefits of winning these deals include (a) brand credibility with Fortune 1000 customers (or their equivalent in countries outside the United States), (b) establishing significant initial and predictable ongoing maintenance and support revenue with only a few large deals, and (c) building deep, lasting "sticky" relationships with recurring maintenance revenue.

Enterprise sales is both an art and a science. But because of their length, enterprise sales cycles have more risk of things going wrong. Your competitors are waiting at the door to displace you. To successfully sell to these customers requires you to deeply understand the customer's industry, its organization structure, and key influencers, as well as a thorough knowledge of your product.

There are important key differences between Enterprise and SMB sales cycles. Failure to understand and recognize these can jeopardize your success. Of these, the most critical is your ability to identify and establish a relationship with *all* the relevant Enterprise stakeholders. The table on the following page summarizes the most important factors.

SMB SALES	VS	ENTERPRISE SALES
SMB Selling		**Enterprise Selling**
Small: <100 employees $50 million in revenue Mid-size: 100-999 employees $50 million - $1 billion in revenue		>1,000 employees. >$1 billion in revenue
Often single department involved with single stakeholder		Multiple departments involved with multiple stakeholders
More emotion in buying process; may be impulsive		Highly rational, analytical, deliberate buying process
Fast decision cycle (weeks or months)		Slow decision cycle (months to years)
Lower risk and more risk tolerant		Higher risk and risk averse
Often the CEO signs off		Multiple sign-offs with key stakeholders
Look for immediate or short-term impact on cash flow		Look for longer-term strategic benefits in multiple areas
Rapid ROI desired		ROI over longer term (3-5 years)
Rely on customer reviews & testimonials		Rely on internal analysis & third-party analyst reports
Easier to sell		Contracts and purchase orders required
"Hunter" sales strategy		"Hunter" and "Farming" sales strategies
Salespeople focus on immediate need of prospect and rapid close		Salespeople need to develop deep knowledge of their product and of the prospect's needs
Lower lifetime value (LTV) requires lower cost of customer acquisition (CAC)		Higher LTV justifies higher CAC

A SIDE - BY - SIDE COMPARISON

SMB salespeople need to be agile in responding to sales opportunities as often the customer is moving to quickly make a buying decision. They need to be adept at asking the right questions early to qualify the opportunity, uncover the key value drivers and position the business benefits of their solution. Successful SMB salespeople reference success stories for similar customers and use trial closes early and frequently to advance the cycle or disqualify the prospect.

Four critical success factors and key differentiators in Enterprise sales are (a) the ability to uncover core requirements versus desired but non-essential ones, (b) provide original insights to the customer, (c) show them a possible future with a long-term strategy, and (d) deliver value based on this.

Patience is required, combined with an organized plan of the relevant customer stakeholders' key criteria and timelines for decision. Usually a team selling approach is most effective, involving sales, sales leaders, pre-sales engineering, marketing, solution architects, development, customer success, and executive players from your side, each at the right time in the cycle. Finally but most importantly, you and your team need to truly understand the customer and learn to speak its language. Failure to do so effectively often dooms your process, enabling your competitors to outflank you.

Your Preferred Channel May Be a Fit Now or Later or Vice Versa

I know that I've poured a lot of information on you in this chapter. You may even be confused about which channel is right for you. Just know that very few get this right immediately, so the keywords here are *experimentation* and *patience*.

There are many factors set out in this chapter that come into play to decide which channel is right for you, or whether a combination of both is the winning recipe. During my last four companies, things always evolved for the better. In one case, we transitioned from direct to end up with a successful hybrid model after five years. In the next company, both channels were respectively highly successful; however, as the company evolved, one was better suited than the other at a later stage of the company's life cycle.

In summary, my recommendation is to carefully consider both options, run some small controlled experiments in select markets, then run the numbers carefully to assess the financial impact of each. Decide whether a direct model or channel distribution network optimizes sales and revenue. The most important thing is to ensure the right fit for your organization given the resources required for successful execution. Finally, take care you're not cannibalizing revenue if you're forcing growth through both channels at once.

So the million-dollar question is, do you have the skillsets and experience to make such judgment calls regarding what the best sales path is for your business? In Chapter 5, I challenge you to examine your strengths and weaknesses to better determine which resources you may want to bring on board for your company to be successful.

5

DELEGATE YOUR WEAKNESSES, DOUBLE DOWN ON YOUR STRENGTHS

An intensive chapter in which I'll empower you
for success by revealing your blind spot(s) and allowing
you to profitably focus on your passion.

At a personal level, I'm all-in when it comes to subjects like personal development, professional growth, self-awareness, and maximizing one's true potential. I believe that the key to happiness is living life fully and fueled with a strong sense of purpose and passion.

Hence, this is why my personal library on the subject includes almost everything and anything worthwhile reading on these topics published over the last century. That's also why for the last fifteen years I've been engaged with a personal coach who could support me personally and professionally.

I rigorously study personal development from thought leaders such as Tony Robbins, Jim Rohn, and Dr. Joe Dispenza. In fact, I'm so committed to this self-discovery journey that back in 2016, despite limited cash flow, I chose to invest $85,000 in a Platinum Partner membership with Tony Robbins's program. It was full of extremely valuable coaching and was worth every penny.

My point with saying this is that my accumulated learnings through personal experiences, coaching, and ongoing studies have convinced me that success and personal fulfillment *requires* one to go all-in on what matters for you, what excites you, and what you're trying to accomplish in life.

Double Down on Your Strengths

"Your work is going to fill a large part of your life, and the only way to be truly satisfied is to do what you believe is great work. And the only way to do great work is to love what you do. If you haven't found it yet, keep looking. Don't settle. As with all matters of the heart, you'll know when you find it."

—STEVE JOBS

"But, Gary, why the heck is this context relevant to me and for this book?" you may be asking yourself now *"I'm an entrepreneur who bought this book to learn how to sell and to grow my company."*

For me, as a serial entrepreneur, I've personally witnessed the impact of "welcoming mastery"' and doubling down on your strengths. No matter whether your core competence is sales, finance, or operations, or you're one hell of a software engineer or architect, you *can* fully embrace your natural-born talents and seek to become the very best in your domain.

Not only does this lead to greater personal satisfaction for most people, but it also empowers you to be more successful professionally either in your career or your own business.

A personal example. Back in 2016 with my previous company, we were growing rapidly, had surpassed nearly 200 employees (mainly bilingual staff in Nicaragua targeting US-based clients), exceeded eight figures in client management fees, landed exclusive contractual agreements with Google and Microsoft, and transcended $100 million in revenue/managed spend for our clients.

At this point, things were shifting from a company and operational standpoint. Instead of being a chaotic, high-intensity sales and founder-driven company, we were trending toward the need for a more corporate structure, detailed organizational chart, endless decision-making rules with an emphasis on processes, systems, reports, KPIs, and an infinite number of meetings.

Since I was "just" a sales guy with some degree of luck under his belt as CEO for this company, my partners and I decided that we needed some experienced help. So we selected a professional Board of Directors and added a full C-suite team to the equation: a CFO, COO, and CRO.

This help was especially required since we were also in pursuit of VC funding to further accelerate our growth, capture market share, and develop our own proprietary technology to support our existing offerings, with the objective of ultimately exiting the business with a large transaction after some years.

After recruiting a full executive team (not an easy task!) and within several months, I think everyone at the C-level was in agreement that I was not your conventional CEO. I clearly recall how our CFO and COO at one meeting began dropping hints about my education level (high school only) and suggested, in a quite politically correct and eloquent way, whether it might be beneficial for me to look into participating in a Harvard Business School executive education program.

As I never backed down from a challenge, and to some extent was in agreement with their recommendations about me complementing my skillsets as CEO, I participated in a Finance for Senior Executives program at Harvard.

For weeks on end, I was up all night, confused, searching on Google, stressed, and frustrated that I couldn't complete the assigned homework on analyzing complex financial reports, capital structures, capital markets, debt-to-equity ratios, financial restructuring models, and stock buy-back growth strategies.

To this date, I still get a headache when thinking back on those late nights at the ivy-covered Harvard campus in Boston.

Over the following quarters, much of my focus was on implementing and following these corporate financial principles and reporting requirements, while getting the whole C-level team up and running, as well as reporting on everything *comprehensively* during our monthly board of directors meetings with my partners.

I've rarely been less motivated and unfulfilled as those four consecutive quarters where I was bogged down with these responsibilities while the company nearly derailed toward bankruptcy because we failed to meet our growth targets (previously 60–70 percent YoY, consistently).

And I recall my frustrations and anger as clearly as yesterday. In the middle of an executive meeting with our C-level team, I raised hell demanding to know why we were consistently missing our sales targets by a large gap and churn rates were forever climbing high (a deadly cocktail for any B2B or SaaS-focused business). I walked out of that meeting only to march straight down to the second floor of our building where our sales team worked and called all sixty sales reps in for an impromptu sales huddle.

As I addressed everyone in that spontaneous session, I tried to motivate them, providing hope and aspiration about upcoming changes for our by-then highly discouraged sales team. They had also been part of a radical transformational journey with new processes, requirements, and sales methodologies, rolled out by our CRO and COO. But I realized it was likely too late for change at this level. A ship that big (200+ employees and 60 sales reps) takes a long time to shift course! Not as swift and agile as when we were twenty employees!

Instead, I "accepted" to step down as CEO and went all-in with my channel sales partner program MVP idea in order to help save the company by spearheading our then-nonexistent partnership program and reseller initiative.

The lesson learned here is that, as a leader and founder of a company (my baby!), there is no "picture-perfect textbook CEO." Never again *will* I let myself be influenced by others to believe I was lacking in areas and compromising my focus and value-add to the company by trying to take on those skillsets that weren't my strong suit in order to fit the mold of an ideal CEO.

All things considered, the primary reason we made the Inc. 5000 Fastest Growing Private Companies in America for four consecutive years was because our sales were *always* booming month after month and revenue kept flowing in skyrocketing our growth!

But during this difficult time, I was stressed 24/7, developed bad habits and addictions, had health issues, and went through a divorce. I'm sharing this personal and still painful story because I don't want you to make the same mistakes! Be true to who you are, *always*, and whether you're damn good at founding a company, coding programs, or your thing is creating mind-blowing designs, then embrace it fully. Double down on your talents and your strengths and aim to delegate your "weaknesses" to the *right* co-founders or team members.

Besides my personal learnings, a book that greatly impacted me on this journey and that I recommend is *Mastery* by Robert Greene. His main thesis is that *"mastery is not a function of genius or talent. It is a function of intense focus applied to a particular field of knowledge."*

THE RIGHT MARKETER(S) AT
THE RIGHT TIME FOR YOUR STARTUP

I'm blessed with having practiced, studied, and refined my sales and marketing skills to near perfection after nearly twenty-five years in the trenches. Interestingly, relatively few founders and CEOs come from a sales and marketing background.

Most founders are subject matter experts in their category, whether as an amazing chef, innovative developer, excellent software architect, or talented healthcare practitioner—and when going to market, they usually are hyperfocused on developing their offering, discovering product/market fit, and raising capital.

You guessed it. Near the bottom of their to-do list and priorities is setting up a demand-generation engine and sales machine.

And only upon landing their first customers, getting all the product kinks ironed out, and fixing bugs do they decide it's time to find a marketer for their company and get things going.

Often the challenge is that it's damn difficult to find the *right* marketer for your company. So new customer acquisition rates never reach established targets, and eventually the business runs out of cash and ceases to exist!

The priority for *any* founder right out of the gate should be to find either a suitable co-founder or key team member(s) who complement their own skillsets to ensure their venture becomes successful.

When opening my last company, WSM, the digital marketing agency headquartered in Nicaragua with funding from the Danish government, my former partner Alexander and I, after having been beaten up by online advertising in recent years with our broadcast/radio advertising model, decided our new focus should be selling digital marketing solutions with an emphasis on managed Pay Per Click (PPC) services.

As a result, upon landing in Nicaragua back in 2010, I found myself sitting in our house reading *Google AdWords for Dummies*.

Thankfully, very quickly, I realized this was not going to go well, so my partner and I agreed we needed to source a subject matter expert to join the company.

A few weeks later, I found a fellow Danish dude, Andrew, whom I knew sporadically from a few encounters at the gym back in Copenhagen. To his big surprise, I cold-called him out of the blue and pitched our plans for world domination in the PPC category and why I needed him on the next plane to Nicaragua to discuss a partnership constellation and our next steps together.

Andrew, to this day, is still a good friend and someone I consider to be one of the most gifted PPC specialists I know. Despite just having relocated to Malta, thankfully he saw there was some merit in our vision and shortly after, decided to join our project in Nicaragua back in 2011, just as we were about to open the business.

This was one of the best moves we ever could have made because my former partner Alexander and I, despite having successfully sold many radio advertising campaigns, were not your typical technical data-driven campaign optimization types that would thrive in a Google AdWords department.

So with Andrew's great contribution in building our offering and team structure, we were able to fill the gap in our skillsets, complementing my sales abilities. This resulted in exponential growth YoY. And one year we were even recognized as one of the fastest growing Google agency partners out of tens of thousands in its ecosystem.

But before you run out and begin cold-calling sales pros and marketers to join your project either as a co-founder or key hire, ask yourself the following questions:

1. Is sales and marketing going to play a major factor in the success of your company's launch?

2. How competitive is your domain and how "Blue versus Red Ocean" is your go-to-market strategy? The answer to this is going to determine how much emphasis you put in finding outstanding people with these skillsets.

3. Does your company have sales and marketing challenges that you as the founder are not capable of tackling?

4. What types of marketing and sales do you need the most help with? You can't expect to find a marketing unicorn who fully understands product marketing, communications, branding, and performance marketing. The same goes for recruiting a sales professional who has mastery of direct sales, channel sales, enterprise sales, and inside sales. Can your candidate design the entire sales framework or simply execute within an already established sales structure?

5. What's your timeline to find these sales and marketing pros? Can your anticipated burn rate permit adding these team members to the budget, or should you consider giving up company equity in order to get the right founding team in place?

So although this is predominantly a book on sales, hopefully you start to realize just how important the integration with marketing is and what resources are required to establish a true revenue machine for your company.

Creating the Perfect Founding Team

The most critical decision to make in a startup is not about the product or service; it's about the people—your founding team. This diagram illustrates some of the key characteristics and questions to consider:

Round Out Founding Team

Ensure you are the right person/team to solve the problem you are addressing

---

Founder Fit

Are you the right person to address that problem? Do you have...

- Adjacent experience?
- Experience in a certain domain?
- Family ties to a certain domain?
- Experience with the problem yourself (or someone close to you)?

> You do not need to have decades of years in the industry you are tackling. On the contrary, often outsiders disrupt.

Co-Founder Fit

It does not need to be your best friend (for some it may even be problematic to mix friendship and business relationships)

Take some time to get to know your potential co-founder and to have a certain level of trust

Ideally, you have known each other previously and you have complementary skill sets (CEO + CTO)

Based on personal chemistry and professional compatibility, you have a shared vision of what you want to build and why

Founding Team Fit

Ideal founding team investors are looking for...

- Complementary founding team whose skills are diverse
- With essential skills to the core of their business and industry in which they are competing
- Horizontally smart, able to get things done, and ultimately getting along (strong cultural fit)
- Usually consisting of 2-4 people
- Whose equities are split evenly

Founder Alignment: Personality, Values, and Vision

Since I launched my first company, The DVD Specialisten, back when I was nineteen years old and still in high school in Denmark, I have started and exited six companies and always with co-founders and partners. And let me assure you, in case this is your first time partnering with someone, going into business together with a partner is a rocky process and almost equivalent to a marriage, especially when things become challenging—and they will! Or conversely, when you become successful and profitable, and things really take off, is when you'll often get surprised and learn things about your co-founder and partner that you never saw coming!

From my experience, with the limited amount of time we have available as busy entrepreneurs/business owners, it's mission critical *where* you spend your time, focus, and energy. The difference between channeling your energy toward constant internal conflicts, misalignment, power plays, and so forth versus spending your *entire* focus truly devoted to external efforts—that is, marketing campaigns, outreach, new client acquisitions, client nurturing—is often the make or break point for many companies with several founders.

As a result, before entering any new partnership, either as angel investor or co-founder/partner, I've learned to always implement a process of proper assessment and vetting of my potential business partners.

The outcome of this exercise has been very helpful for my levels of excitement, job fulfillment, and positive synergies in the companies I'm involved in.

And yes, as an outcome of this process, I've actually turned down many high-potential projects I was otherwise ready to get involved in! You see, for me, attaining success is not everything—by far! As Tony Robbins is famously quoted as saying:

> *"Success without fulfillment is*
> *the ultimate failure."*

You want to make sure that you select the *right* partners for your company so that your success doesn't come with the price tag of misalignment, unproductive conflict, and potentially a bad breakup. Establishing partnerships and starting a business with someone is even more stressful than being in a relationship or marriage. When you get married, there's "just" you two to agree on things, plus possibly a few kids to wrangle as well (I'm not saying it's easy of course).

However, with your business, you'll have to juggle and agree on how to handle hundreds or even thousands of high-demand clients, sneaky control-obsessed investors, and employees who seek inspiration and better compensation, professional development, and motivation. Add to that a variety of other external stakeholders such as key partners or vendors, and you have a lot to juggle. So safe to say that unless you do your due diligence properly when selecting your co-founder, it's quite probable that you'll end up either unfulfilled or in an ugly "business divorce."

To combat this, as one of the initial phases in my angel investment or partnership establishment process (see the diagram on the following page), I conduct a series of interviews where both myself and my prospective co-founders go through a rigorous process answering a set of 50+ questions to ensure that we are in alignment, discuss potential risk factors for our partnership, identify areas of disagreement, and essentially determine whether there is, besides the shared business vision, a healthy basis for a productive forward-moving partnership.

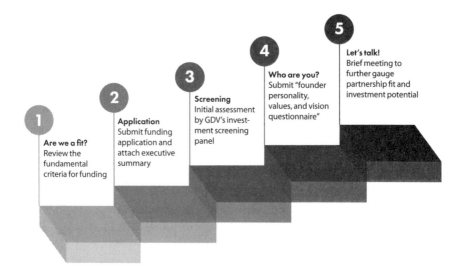

1. **Are we a fit?** Review the fundamental criteria for funding

2. **Application** Submit funding application and attach executive summary

3. **Screening** Initial assessment by GDV's investment screening panel

4. **Who are you?** Submit "founder personality, values, and vision questionnaire"

5. **Let's talk!** Brief meeting to further gauge partnership fit and investment potential

I call this my "Founder Matchmaking Process" which you can access from the book website www.0to100million.com along with other resources.

Questions on Founder Personality, Values, and Vision

Below is a selection of questions to ask your potential future business partner(s) *before* diving into negotiations about share allocation, equity, investment size, and going to market together.

- **How Do You Operate?**
  - » What are your strengths and superpowers?
  - » What are your weaknesses?
  - » What words would your coworkers use to describe you? What would they want me to know about what it's like to work with you?
  - » How do you deal with conflict? Describe a time you dealt with it well and a time you didn't.

» What's the worst interpersonal conflict you've dealt with? How did you handle it?

» How do you cope with stress?

» How do you arrive at your convictions? What are some mental models you use to be creative, solve problems, or make decisions?

» Describe your work style. What techniques/tools and so forth do you use for personal productivity?

» How many hours/week are you dedicating to work? For how long? What sounds good? What sounds like a nightmare and unacceptable? Do you have different expectations for different phases of the company's life span (i.e., planning to work 24/7 in the beginning, but once we reach XYZ goal, it drops to…)?

- **Roles and Responsibilities**

  » What would you want your role to be before we reach product/market fit?

  » How do you see your role changing as the company starts to scale?

  » If your role becomes unavailable entirely (e.g., if the board hires a professional CEO or an experienced executive after a while), what would you want your new role to be?

  » Areas of expertise and responsibility. Please rank yourself in these areas on a scale of 1 to 5.

  ____ Sales

  ____ Marketing

  ____ Product Strategy

  ____ Design

  ____ Engineering

  ____ Operations

_____ Recruiting

_____ Finance

_____ Leadership

_____ Company Building

_____ Legal

- **Corporate Structure and Funding**
  - » Where should our startup be based? How do you feel about remote or distributed teams overseas?
  - » Is there anything I should know that may materially affect your time or legal status as a founder (e.g., Visa, Green Card, criminal record)?
  - » How should equity be set? What's your philosophy on the employee equity pool?
  - » What should our approach to employee compensation be, including cash and equity?
  - » How much money should we raise (i.e., "zero; let's be as boot-strapped as possible" to "as much as we can")?
  - » In the range of "bootstrapped small business" to "go big or go home," where do you want this startup to go?
  - » What matters most in a founder/partner? If you were doing reference checks on a VC or potential board member, what traits would you be looking for?
  - » What does an ideal company exit look like for you (i.e., "work on company for one to two years and sell for seven figures" to "work for seven to ten-plus years, reach nine figures in revenue and then IPO")?
  - » What do you think about the time frame and pace of success? Are you planning to take the longer path? How long is too long?
  - » What number would you sell at? How would that change if you

got extra liquidity from your existing positions?

» Can one co-founder fire another co-founder? Can someone else fire a founder?

- **Personal Motivation and Drivers**

  » Why do you want to start this company—in general and in particular right now?

  » What does success look like for you? What motivates you personally?

  » What impact do you want us to have? Is your startup objective "getting rich" or "changing the world" or a hybrid? If so, what's the mix?

  » Is control or success more important (i.e., are you willing to step aside if the company is more likely to have a financially successful outcome, or is it important for the founders to stay in control of the company's destiny?)?

  » Who are your heroes? Or who do you admire the most in your organization/family/friends and why?

  » What are you most proud of in your work career or life to date?

  » When have you taken a chance when others did not? Or when have you been willing to take an unpopular stance to support your beliefs? What was the outcome?

  » Name a few of the products, services, or companies you love the most and describe what you like about them.

  » Is it possible to build a wildly successful company without burning out or damaging other parts of your life (family, health, etc.)? How do you plan to balance things and prevent burnout?

- **Commitment and Finances**

  » Will this company be your primary activity? Do you have any other time commitments?

- » What is your expected time commitment right now? How do you see that changing in the next six months, two years, longer term, and so forth?
- » What is your personal runway? Current financial burn rate? Would you invest more of your own money (ideally retaining higher equity in return)?
- » What is the minimum monthly salary you need to "survive"? What is it to be comfortable? Finally, what is it to feel like you've "made it"?
- » What should the policy of co-founders advising/consulting with other companies be?

- **Team and Culture**
  - » Are there any immediate mission critical roles for the company that aren't currently fulfilled that might be a challenge (or expensive) to recruit for?
  - » Complete the sentence: It would make you proud to hear people describe this company's culture as _____.
  - » What's your philosophy on how to attract and retain amazing people? Tactically, how would we make this happen at our company?
  - » What processes or techniques would you use to get the most out of your team? For example, how would you help them become better managers or achieve their goals?

- **Co-Founder/Partner Relationship**
  - » How would we resolve personal conflicts between ourselves?
  - » What happens in the scenario where we aren't growing?
  - » In every partnership, there are times when a partner might breed resentment if certain dissatisfactions don't change over time. How would you deal with a situation like this?

- » If needed for a special skillset, what would you think about bringing on an additional co-founder/partner?
- » In case this becomes part of our partnership's evolution, how would you go about handling a startup divorce?
- » Now we know each other's weaknesses, passions, needs, and constraints, how are we going to make each other successful? What would it take to feel truly partnered in this adventure?

DANGLE THE CARROT: EMPLOYEE STOCK OPTION PLANS

Depending on your success with finding the right co-founders to partner with or the level of expertise/experience you're aiming to hire for, you might want to consider leveraging the power of creating an employee stock option plan to give your headhunting for core team members some extra ammunition.

In my most recent companies, as a default I always allocate a minimum 10 percent of total shares toward an employee stock option plan that I use when building out my core team.

Stock options can be an *incredibly* powerful tool if:

- Your idea has merit
- You're good at pitching the vision of your company
- Perhaps as in my case, you have a good track record with building businesses and selling them
- You're a subject matter expert in your domain

A widely held guideline is to *"Hire slow, fire fast,"'* but for me, the most important element in the success equation is to *hire the very best people possible*. Stretch your budget as much as you can to get A players on board. I'd personally rather hire one A player than a team of three to four B players.

Jim Collins (one of my all-time favorite authors) in his bestseller *Good to Great* analyzes the principles of 1,400 successful companies over forty years. He identified eleven companies with similar characteristics that went from *good to great* and one of the key common factors was that they all focused on the concept of:

> **First who, then what—get the right people on the bus.**

In other words, these eleven companies put a tremendous effort in hiring the *right* team members knowing that the *what*, *when*, and *how* can be figured out later and, better yet, together as a team.

For this reason, if you want to reach out and snatch away a talented employee from another successful company that likely has deeper pockets than you, it *really* helps to attract talent by offering stock options. To do so, you need to elaborate on the benefits of such and how they become minority owners instead of "'just" an employee. And you need to consider how that can translate into a larger payout within a reasonable time frame if the company gets built up to its anticipated valuation and is sold.

On the following page is an example of a stock option plan I rolled out for one of my companies which shows the share allocation together with the estimated dividend payout along with the big carrot—their payout after five years if the company reaches projected EBITDA levels and is sold on a standard industry benchmark multiplier. In this case I used 8x EBITDA, but it varies depending on market, solution, customer volume, whether the technology developed is proprietary, and other factors).

Equity & Dividend Payments

Shareholders	%	2022	2023	2024	2025	2026	2027	Exit (8.0x)
CEO	3.0%	-$5,336	-$10,367	$11,146	$30,429	$55,582	$81,046	$853,630
COO	3.0%	-$5,336	-$10,367	$11,146	$30,429	$55,582	$81,046	$853,630
CFO	3.0%	-$5,336	-$10,367	$11,146	$30,429	$55,582	$81,046	$853,630
CSO	2.0%	-$3,557	-$6,911	$7,431	$20,286	$37,055	$54,030	$569,087
CTO	2.0%	-$3,557	-$6,911	$7,431	$20,286	$37,055	$54,030	$569,087
PPC Director	1.0%	-$1,779	-$3,456	$3,715	$10,143	$18,527	$27,015	$284,543
SEO Director	1.0%	-$1,779	-$3,456	$3,715	$10,143	$18,527	$27,015	$284,543
Gary Garth	85%	-$151,177	-$293,721	$315,801	$862,151	$1,574,830	$2,296,291	$24,186,187
<<Enter Employee Here>>	0.0%	$0	$0	$0	$0	$0	$0	$0
<<Enter Employee Here>>	0.0%	$0	$0	$0	$0	$0	$0	$0
<<Enter Employee Here>>	0.0%	$0	$0	$0	$0	$0	$0	$0
<<Enter Employee Here>>	0.0%	$0	$0	$0	$0	$0	$0	$0
<<Enter Employee Here>>	0.0%	$0	$0	$0	$0	$0	$0	$0

Regardless, in this case, when aiming to hire a very savvy and experienced COO from a leading SaaS company whose current pay was a tad higher than what I was offering, I instead leveraged the 3 percent stock option and emphasized how we together, as partners, could build up this great company and that without any of their money invested (all mine in this event), they could still cash out nearly $1 million after a target of five to seven years. That's a nice little savings account to build up when combined with good compensation and ongoing dividends. Without this, I doubt I could have landed that COO.

Besides the above-mentioned use case, below I highlight the following benefits for you when creating an employee stock option plan for your company:

- **Interest Alignment:** As author and management consultant Peter Drucker is credited as saying, "*What gets measured gets managed.*"

Hence why issuing stock options to your core team members and executives can be a phenomenal mechanism to get everyone on the same page with regard to overarching objectives and goal alignment.

- **Attrition Mitigation:** Attrition of team members can be dreadful to a company's growth momentum, especially when they are core team members who are leading your teams and conveying the company's vision on your behalf. If they leave the company in the middle of its journey for whatever reason, it not only consumes your time and energy to find a suitable successor but can also possibly cultivate doubt among other internal and external stakeholders regarding your company's ability to execute on your overall mission and potential. Most employee stock option plans vest over four years with a one-year cliff. This means that the employee is "forced" to stay for a longer period of time to get the value of stock options realized. This can sometimes be the tipping point factor for them to not leave your company before the finish line is crossed and thereby function as an attrition mitigation tool.

- **Budget and Cash Flow Reduction:** The EV/EBITDA ratio (Enterprise Value to its Earnings Before Interest, Taxes, Depreciation, and Amortization) is a popular valuation method used by investors to determine the fair market value of a company. And in the case of getting your core team members aligned working toward a future large exit strategy, having a unified focus on reducing cost for the benefit of improving your EBITDA can be very impactful—also for your interim bottom line and the size of your/their dividend payments.

- **Cultivates and Rewards Performance:** A common condition exercised by companies when offering stock options is to combine the vesting period with another condition—meeting their established annual KPIs. So whether it's for your Chief Revenue Officer or Chief Financial Officer that you've issued shares in your company, if you establish achievable yet stretch targets as KPIs for them, their motivation to vest their shares by meeting their established KPIs can in many cases provide you with a healthy ROI since they are driving incremental performance and profits.

- **Risk Compensation:** If you, like me most recently, are pitching a core team member to join your company and they're already working at an established company that pays them handsomely (in my case more than I could afford), they're taking a rather big risk joining your startup even if you match their current salary. After all, while there are no guarantees in life or business, they'd be giving up their stable income at an already established company and taking on a risk by joining your as-yet-unproven company that's up against the world statistically speaking. Issuing stock options and dangling the carrot of a future large exit payment in some cases can, for someone who is more risk averse, be a deciding factor for them to join your company.

In this chapter, we identified why it's important as a founder or sales leader to put your ego aside, assess your weaknesses, focus on your strengths, identify the resources required to realize the vision of your company, and create alignment to develop the perfect founding team.

Now, in Chapter 6, we turn to look at a mission critical element for success—setting the foundation for a data-driven sales environment that will empower you to make decisions based on facts over opinions and emotions.

6

IN GOD WE TRUST; EVERYONE ELSE BRINGS DATA

I'll make sure you've got your eyes on the prize at all times and leave the emotions and opinions out of the equation for what really matters—measuring results.

O ver the past two decades while selling advertising to SMBs in various formats (from broadcast media to search and display ads) in Europe, the United States, and Latin America, I've repeatedly been surprised how, without exaggeration, nine out of ten business owners during my sales calls didn't know the answers to questions such as these:

- *"For every ten leads your business gets, whether phone calls or contact form submissions, how many of these inquiries turn into a paying customer—two out of ten, five out of ten, or seven out of ten?"* The difference can be the distinguishing factor between profitability and insolvency.

- Another classic is, *"What is your most effective advertising method to acquire new customers? And what is your cost per acquisition via that advertising channel?"* The answers I usually receive to this question, or more accurately the lack thereof, aligns perfectly with the old saying accredited to the very successful American merchant John Wanamaker, *"I know half the money I spend on advertising is wasted, but I can never find out which half."* The problem is that he said this back in the early 1900s and now, a century later, it is possible to track every penny spent on advertising. So no excuses for not knowing!

- Similarly, I get a deer-in-the-headlights look from prospects when I ask the question, *"What percentage of your customers are you able to upsell and to cross-sell other products?"*

- Last, a critical factor when starting up your cash-constrained, bootstrapped startup, and a "must answer question" in my experience is: *"What is your average sales cycle length? How long does it take, on average, for your prospects to go from initial contact to becoming a customer with a sale?"* This metric significantly impacts your time-to-profitability ratio and burn rate.

By now, you probably have a better understanding of what resources, partners, or hires you need to consider in order to create a high-velocity demand-generation sales and marketing machine. Perhaps you also better understand how your go-to-market strategy should look like—either via direct or channel sales or both.

But *before* you start pouring your money into advertising, reaching out to prospective clients, or begin hiring for your sales team, let's devote deserved attention to the creation of your data-driven sales metrics measuring process to cover all steps of the customer journey.

Congratulations if you've already answered these, making you a "one out of ten" entrepreneur and putting you ahead of the competition. And if not, this exercise can help you answer the above-mentioned questions. But more importantly, it will help you reach profitability sooner than later because you'll be able to let data *empower your decision-making process* and allocate your limited budget toward the efforts and resources that give you the biggest bang for your buck.

Truly understanding all customer acquisition metrics for your business benefits you in either of the following scenarios:

(a) Helps you realize that you're up against the wall with your current setup. Your business model is not viable and/or perhaps you don't have the financial resources to sustain your burn rate or sufficient funds to acquire the tools, staff, and resources to realize your targets.

(b) Elevates your existing business plan and financial modeling in place with a robust data-driven, realistic sales and revenue forecast. Based on this, adjustments to required resources allow you to fully understand your "time-to-profitability rate" and whether you can get there with your current setup or need to bring in help.

Before we dive into the specifics of defining your key sales metrics that steer you toward building a truly sustainable and scalable business, let's consider the formula for reaching profitability (the overarching objective for *any* business). It takes into account three key cost areas as well as monthly recurring revenue (MRR), the predictable total revenue generated by your business from all the recurring revenue streams in a particular month.

$$\text{Time to Profitability} = \frac{\text{Customer Acquisition Cost} + \text{Customer Onboarding Cost} + \text{Customer Retention Cost}}{\textbf{MRR}}$$

NUMBERS DON'T LIE

One of the most common challenges I witness from inexperienced sales managers is that they have never taken the time to truly break down their entire sales process from a metrics standpoint. Instead they often dive directly into establishing sales KPIs (usually handed down from their leadership) by just passing the baton to their sales team.

So first, let's take a moment to separate *sales metrics* from *sales KPIs* because that's usually where the mistakes begin.

Sales metrics are what truly move the needle because they're the data points that measure the performance of all your activities during the sales cycle. These are what you want to carefully monitor and coach for improvement gains.

Sales KPIs are equally important to establish, especially at an organizational level. Typically they are defined as an improvement in achieving a target—for example, xx percent growth in the number of clients acquired next quarter or xx percent incremental revenue gains from cross- and upselling initiatives.

Benefits of establishing KPIs for most organizations include:

- Helping you monitor the overall health of your company and whether you're falling behind on targets vital for the survival of your business

- When falling behind on targets, KPIs, if measured carefully, provide the ability, with time, to make appropriate adjustments or resource allocations to get back on track with performance
- By the ongoing collection of, and reporting on, KPIs, you'll be able to set proper benchmarks for performance. Based on this, you can analyze your patterns and monitor improvements in sales over time and connect them to strategic initiatives you have rolled out
- Supporting the execution of your overall strategic business objectives by quantifying these into measurable outcomes

But sales metrics and corporate KPIs must go together. Although establishing KPIs is usually done by most senior executives and business owners, fingers are often pointed in many directions at the end of a sales quarter when targets are missed, if the *sales metrics* haven't been detailed or reported on. They can clearly show what, when, and who needs improvement for your sales team and organization to meet its targets next time around.

Sales Metrics That Matter

The establishment of sales metrics varies *greatly* depending on your organization and product offering, but from my experience with most companies I consult with, primarily in the B2B and SaaS markets, the following sales metrics are key to implement and monitor early to fast-track your time to profitability. There are many ways to present these metrics. I've chosen to begin at the top with annual recurring revenue and then trickle things down from there. However, that doesn't mean that one metric is necessarily more important than another.

1. **Annual Recurring Revenue (ARR)** is usually one of the key metrics for most businesses in B2B and SaaS, or companies with

a subscription-based business model where an agreement stipulates a contract length. It provides a macrolevel overview of revenue.

$$ARR = Total\ contract\ value\ (including\ upsales, cross\text{-}sales, etc.)\ /$$
$$Years\ of\ contract\ length$$

2. **Average Revenue Per Account (ARPA):** I first learned this expression when selling paid search campaigns and establishing a partnership with Google and Microsoft. The constant focus and question was, "Gary, what's your average revenue per advertiser (or account)?" I now understand why this was such a priority. This number reveals your company's ability to focus on its highest impact verticals or market segments, while also revealing whether you have established an appropriate budget allocation with the client and your ability to upsell or cross-sell them. Usually, ARPA is expressed on a monthly basis (although can be annual).

$$ARPA = Total\ revenue\ /\ Number\ of\ clients$$

3. **Monthly Recurring Revenue (MRR)** is equally important as ARR. It just zooms in by showing the company growth month over month. From my experiences, since customer churn plays a key factor in such a growth model, it's important to keep a constant micro overview of this metric instead of just macro such as ARR. In the SMB space, it's most common to establish a twelve-month contract length with an evergreen model for renewal/continuation, whereas a contract with several years length is more common for Enterprise solutions and high-ticket software sales.

$$MRR = ARPA \times Total\ number\ of\ active\ customers$$

4. **Average Deal Size** reveals the average dollar amount per deal that your reps closed. It's an important metric to monitor since if understood early in the sales cycle, it can enable sales leaders to prioritize their support efforts toward the highest impact opportunities that drive the most growth for your company. Similarly, it can also help identify if a weaker sales rep is "underselling" your solution—that is, always going for the light package, easiest sale, and perhaps needs coaching or a boost of confidence to raise the bar and aim to increase his/her average deal size.

   Average Deal Size = Total sales revenue / Total number of new sales

5. **Average Profit Margin** is an estimation of how much profit can be expected from your total sales revenue, and although a good profitability indicator for a company, it should be used cautiously. This is true especially if your company sells multiple products since the weighted average may be influenced significantly by a product/solution with a higher-than-usual margin yet is not the primary product sold.

   Average Profit Margin = Net Income (Revenue – Expenses) /
   Net Sales × 100

6. **Customer Lifetime Value (LTV)** is another key metric to monitor since it gives you a clear indication of how valuable your customer is financially. This is also an important data point for your business since it helps you work on the measures that can impact your LTV and thereby the company's profitability. Examples include extending the time frame your customers stay with you or your ability to expand the revenue per customer during their journey with you. And every smart marketer wants to understand this metric in order to amplify their new customer acquisition

strategies to the fullest and maximize the growth potential as much as cash flow allows it.

$$LTV = ARPA \times Average\ lifetime\ customer\ value$$

How to Measure Customer Lifetime Value

Average Order Value | Average Number of Transactions per Customer | Customer Retention Rate

Customer Lifetime Value

Example: Digital marketing agency with monthly plans

A digital marketing agency with many services and pricing tiers has an ARPA of $720/month. Clients in average stay with the agency for 22 months.

LTV = $720 (ARPA) x 22 (months) = $15,840

7. **Customer Acquisition Cost (CAC)** is the sum of all costs and resources required for you to land a new customer. It's the Holy Grail metric for most smart marketers who are looking to maximize their company's revenue. If you understand all related metrics such as LTV and profit margins, as long as your CAC is financially favorable, and you have capacity for growth, my mantra has always

been to put the pedal to the metal on your sales and marketing activities and leverage the growth potential fully. Fluctuations in advertising cost or new competition entering the market are all factors that can significantly impact your CAC, which is why you want to understand and maximize it fully to fuel your growth trajectory.

$$CAC = Total\ cost\ of\ sales\ and\ marketing\ /$$
$$The\ number\ of\ customers\ acquired$$

8. **Same-Store Growth (SSG)** is a term that originates from the retail industry and reveals the effectiveness of a company's ability to increase its revenue per customer. However, while I worked with Google and Microsoft as a channel partner, this metric was one of the top focus areas in every single QBR. So safe to say, it's no longer just for retailers. Your ability to influence this metric can, in my experience, drastically impact your overall profitability since you've already sunk the investment in your CAC so your SSG is just pure icing on the cake.

$$SSG = [Total\ sales\ current\ year\ /\ Total\ sales\ previous\ year - 1] \times 100$$

9. **Customer Churn Rate** is the rate at which you lose customers either as they breach contract, drop off your subscription model, or decide not to renew their contract with you. This is probably the king of all metrics in my book. And I learned the hard way that unless you control this metric steadily for your business, no amount of new sales can make up for a high influx in cancellations, eventually causing your growth rate to stagnate. Furthermore, as mentioned before, this metric is one of the main drivers for increased profitability. Monitor it like you would your bank statement!

$$Churn\ rate = Number\ of\ customers\ lost\ /$$
$$Starting\ number\ of\ customers \times 100$$

It costs **6-7x** more to gain a new customer than it does to keep your present customers

A **5%** increase in customer retention can result in a **25 - 95%** increase in company profitability!

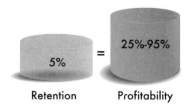

5% Retention = 25%-95% Profitability

10. **Customer Retention Rate (CRR)** provides intel regarding your ability to retain your customers over a given period of time. Like customer churn, it's an important metric since its outcome can lead to valuable coaching initiatives to quantify the efficacy of both your marketing strategy and customer service levels. What good is landing a large deal with an expected high LTV if your customer retention rates all of a sudden plummet with revenue, then flowing out the back door?

   CRR = Number of customer beginning of year
   – New customers gained / Initial customer volume × 100

11. **Lead Conversion Rate (LCR)** is the percentage of qualified leads that turn into paying customers. If you've ever been in sales, you know this is a metric that you're measured on a continuous basis. And as a sales manager or business owner, there's tremendous growth optimization potential in this metric. Not only can it reveal how to better optimize marketing efforts, but it also reveals areas of improvement by which reps need more coaching and

with further inspection *where* they're lacking during the sales process. Conversely, just like a basketball coach would when you wish to win an important game, you usually want to give the ball to your top-scoring player when it's crunch time!

LCR = New customers gained / Number of qualified leads × 100

12. **Average Lead Response Time** is the time it takes from you receiving an inbound lead (usually via email or contact form submission) to one of your reps contacting the prospect (and I'm not just talking about an automated reply message here). Since most buyers usually fill out three to four different company contact forms besides yours, and studies show how a one-minute lead response time can drive a 391 percent increase in conversion rates, you want to keep your eyes on the prize here and continuously optimize this process.

Back in the days when I ran big sales teams and software such as Chili Piper didn't exist, I went to the extreme of installing a large flashing light on my sales floor that would be triggered every time a new inbound lead came in. Then my sales ops team would jump all over it to assign it to the best suited available rep, while the reps would get emotionally psyched and mentally prepped hoping it would be assigned to them. Safe to say that my LCRs always have performed above market standards because of this focus.

Anything else just doesn't make sense to me! It's mind blowing to read studies that show how US B2B companies have an average lead response time of forty-two hours! Why the f**k would you pay hundreds of dollars per lead (applies for most industries) only to be sloppy and nondiligent regarding how you treat them? The difference in outcome when multiplied by hundreds of leads monthly can equate to millions of dollars in incremental revenue for your business.

Lead response time = Time lead received/created
– Time lead was contacted

13. **Demo-to-Close Ratio** is the ratio of solution demos conducted by your reps to their ability to convert that to a paying customer. I find it more the rule than exception that most B2B and SaaS companies conduct what I consider ineffective solution demos. It's incredibly important to coach your reps how to conduct demos and to create processes to help them. You've already spent a ton of money generating the lead, had the discipline to get them on the phone, and during your discovery call determined they actually qualify for your solution, and then you drop the ball at the "finish line" when it's time to *wow* them and convert to a customer.

   The best way I can explain the demo process in my previous companies is that we made it almost like a broadway show. I leveraged all the intel from the discovery call and subsequent research to customize a demo process that catered to their specific needs. Then I made sure to show success stories in their category (not generic ones), focus on features that benefit their use case, and have all my tabs and windows prepared in sequence so that I'm like a boxer getting as many punches in as possible to score points before I eventually go for the knockout. (More on this in Chapter 10.)

   Demo closing ratio = Demos conducted / Total sales × 100

14. **Proposal or Deal Win Rate** measures the ratio of deals landed versus the amount of proposals sent out. By closely measuring the effectiveness of your team's ability to convert proposals into customers, you can again drastically tilt the scale in your favor

from a coaching and sales process standpoint. And by leveraging proposal software technologies such as Proposify, PandaDoc, or Conga, you can obtain user analytics that reveal how your prospect engaged with your proposal—that is, how much time did they spend in each section of your proposal, did they skip some sections all together, which case studies got the most attention, and whether they submit repetitive comments or questions to certain topics in your proposals. All of this intelligence is another valuable "Smarketing" topic initiative where your sales and marketing teams can collaborate on how to move the needle in your favor when it comes to proposal win rates.

Win rate = Number of deals won / Number of quoted opportunities × 100

15. **Deal Lost Rate** is just as important to dissect as your win rate. More importantly, you want to study this metric for coaching and feedback purposes by examining the underlying reasons for loss—for example, was it to a competitor, and if so, to whom? Are there any patterns you can discover? Was it because of budget issues so you need to better qualify leads? Or was the deal simply lost because of lack of competence by your rep to convey the right message and earn the prospect's trust in your solution?

All these lessons are valuable opportunities to either coach reps or adjust your process. This feedback is often more valuable than your successes. Like Michael Jordan once famously said, *"I've missed more than 9,000 shots in my career. I've lost almost 300 games. Twenty-six times, I've been trusted to take the game winning shot and missed. I've failed over and over and over again in my life. And that is why I succeed!"*

Lost rate = Number of deals lost / Number of quoted opportunities × 100

16. **Deal Slip Rate** is a key metric for budget forecast accuracy and can be the difference between a smooth operation thriving profitably and a messy, chaotic, stressful business environment constantly living in "react mode." For example, if a large prospect has committed verbally to get started in Q1, but for XYZ reason the deal gets pushed to the next quarters, this is deal slippage from a forecasting standpoint.

    In my last company, when selling white label digital marketing solutions to other marketing agencies, the ability for us to provide the service was contingent on hiring, training, and certifying staff to be able to manage advertising accounts effectively. Creating a hiring forecast aligned with our sales forecast three to six months down the road was mission critical for success and profitability. A high deal-slip ratio meant we would hire too many people versus the demand/work taking place so our profit margins would therefore decline. Thankfully, this was never the case on my sales watch—rather, the opposite. In fact, we couldn't hire and train quickly enough. Regardless, that's why deal slippage is critical for forecast accuracy.

    Deal slip rate = The number of deals that didn't close /
    The number of deals expected to close × 100

17. **Sales Cycle Length** is the time, on average, it takes your reps to win a deal— from initially getting the lead assigned, qualified, demoed, proposal sent, deal negotiated, and finally getting a signature on the dotted line. This is another valuable data point for sales leaders to coach and influence deal success probability by aiming to spot delays in the sales process that eventually can put the deal at risk. Additionally, when coupled with a predictable

high-velocity lead-generation process, understanding your average sales cycle length is a powerful combination to secure forecast accuracy and become profitable.

Sales cycle length = Total number of days to close deals / Total number of deals

18. **Pipeline Coverage** provides an estimate of your reps' potential deals in their pipeline versus their sales quota. This is very valuable intel to monitor on an ongoing basis if you want to coach your reps effectively. It's equally important to ensure that the majority meet their quota to beat the industry benchmarks of only one out of three reps doing so. For example, if your rep has $100,000 in short-term pipeline coverage and their quota for the month is $40,000, they have 2.5x pipeline coverage. And once you know their average deal closing ratios, your average sales cycle length, deal size, etc., you can predict to some extent if they can hit their quota by the end of the month by understanding their pipeline coverage. And should the probability be low, then you can push the right buttons and ask for extra effort or time to be put into work. You can even issue additional incentives to spark their motivation levels since in many cases your rep might already have given up on your current month/quarter and be sandbagging to increase the likelihood of meeting quota during the next cycle.

Pipeline coverage = Potential sales in pipeline / Sales quota

19. **Quota Attainment Rate** is the percentage of sales that your reps close compared to their established goals for that time. When aiming for areas of improvement, this is another key metric to monitor and carefully examine. It helps you create better hiring

profiles, training schedules, identify common traits and activities performed by overperforming versus underperforming reps, and indicate how well your sales organization is performing as a whole. Last, when talking about forecasting accuracy and understanding how this impacts your bottom line, focusing on improving your quota attainment ratios is invaluable for your sales growth and effectiveness.

Quota attainment = Sales won / Sales quota × 100

20. **Lead Scoring** is a sales and marketing metric that indicates how valuable a lead is or where they are in the sales funnel (the closer the lead is to converting, the more valuable it becomes). When assigning leads to reps and setting quotas, one cannot get around lead scoring. It's like a golf handicap, not for the sake of scoring the reps' ability to close deals but rather to establish a realistic view of how many leads and at what value are expected to convert into deals based on the lead score. It's not fair to establish the same budget for two reps if one gets all the high-value, perfectly suited leads in high demand of your solution, when the other gets assigned leads that don't necessarily have a high commercial intent. These are the prospects who aren't actively in need of purchasing a solution like yours and perhaps are not even a good fit for your company. Lead scoring is not only valuable for sales and marketing alignment, but it also empowers sales efficiency, levels the playing field, and supports your budget forecasting predictability.

Lead Scoring = Not a simple formula. "Leads are evaluated subjectively, usually on a score from 1 to 100, and requires an analysis of firmographic data, demographic data, the online behavior, existing technology in place, and so forth.

20 Key Sales Metrics

Annual Recurring Revenue (ARR) · Average Revenue Per Account (ARPA) · Monthly Recurring Revenue (MRR) · Average Deal Size · Average Profit Margin

Customer Lifetime Value (LTV) · Customer Acquisition Cost (CAC) · Same-Store Growth (SSG) · Customer Churn Rate · Customer Retention Rate (CRR)

Lead Conversion Rate (LCR) · Average Lead Response Time · Demo-to-Close Ratio · Proposal or Deal Win Rate · Deal Lost Rate

Deal Slip Rate · Sales Cycle Length · Pipeline Coverage · Quota Attainment Rate · Lead Scoring

Five More Sales Metrics That Matter

You thought we were done! Think again. There are five more sales metrics that I recommend you carefully monitor:

1. **Outreach Sales Metrics,** for example, related to your email campaign rates. Say for every 100 emails you send out, you want to assess the email open rates, reply rates, reply to call schedule rate, email opt-out, and email sent to deal win rate. This intelligence drive improved performance if adjusted accordingly by A/B split testing headlines, messaging, calls to action (CTAs), and much more.

2. **Sales Hiring Metrics** are those I often experience sales leaders ignore, but they are equally important for your sales

organization's growth potential. How can you expect your sales team to meet established growth KPIs and targets if they don't have sufficient sales staff trained and ready to effectively manage incoming lead volume, and considering your overall sales metrics like sales cycle length, LCR, demo-to-close ratio, etc.? The same goes for measuring your sales rep turnover rate—that is, the average time it takes a new rep to break even or the average time it takes your HR team to hire a new rep. After all, without the appropriate resources in place and a highly motivated, well-functioning, and consistent sales roster, you can certainly kiss goodbye to anything even close to budget forecast accuracy.

3. **Lead Generation Sales Metrics** support the important collaboration between sales and marketing to collectively push toward target achievements. Measuring and optimizing the efficacy of MQLs turning into SQLs, or the volume of new leads added to the pipeline, are important for your demand generation engine to be oiled and tuned on an ongoing basis. The same goes for the percentage of leads dropped and the reasons for such, as well as the lead assignment process optimization efforts.

4. **Sales Process and Tool Adoption Metrics** are perhaps difficult to quantify in detail, but from my experience this is where a good Sales Ops team can justify its existence and ROI within your company. What good does it serve the company to spend tens of thousands of dollars on some new swaggy sales enablement tool if only 25 percent of your sales team adopts the tool in their day-to-day workflows. The same goes with analyzing, optimizing, and then documenting sales processes with the objective of improving sales metrics. If your reps don't adopt the processes you have created, the desired outcome will be nonexistent, and

the heavy time and budget allocation that your sales leadership, sales ops team, or perhaps external consultants have invested will go entirely to waste.

5. **Sales Productivity and Activity Metrics** are good measuring sticks to gauge where and on what activities your reps are spending their time—very, very valuable when it comes to coaching and process creation. It goes without saying that you want as many repetitive and tedious sales admin tasks automated and optimized so that your highly paid sales reps can focus on what they're best at—talking with prospects, charming them, winning them over, demonstrating value, and earning their trust. All these are activities that require direct contact either over the phone, in person, online, or via any other medium. If you optimize sales activity metrics with the objective of having Sales Admin, Sales Ops, and related automation tools strip away as many non-value-added sales activities as possible for your reps, this effort directly translates into your sales reps' happiness, their performance, and your bottom line.

Hopefully, you now clearly see a common denominator for most of the above-mentioned sales metrics, and that's how they showcase the performance of activities within a select time or task within your customer journey. Armed with this data, the right sales manager or business owner can identify areas of improvement, evaluate individual sales rep's strengths, weaknesses, and activities, and then create tailored training initiatives or implement processes to improve the given metrics and the overall business outcome.

It goes without saying that measuring all these metrics for your company requires some legwork and investment. You can't just hire staff to manually spreadsheet yourself out of this task. It requires some investment and select sales tech stack components such as a well-configured CRM and dashboard/sales analytics tools (more on this in Chapter 13) which are indispensable if you want to get this right. But the fruits of your investments will not be worthwhile and you will not be able to scale your company profitability without this approach.

The chart below provides you with a macro view of the sales metrics and how they intertwine with each other on your path toward profitability.

Key Metrics to Understand Time to Profitability in B2B and SaaS

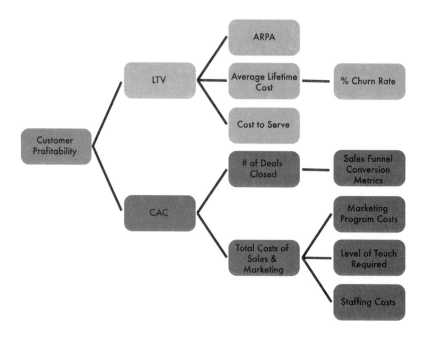

"SMARKETING" IS REINVIGORATED
BY METRICS AND DATA

One of the more common pitfalls companies fall victim to (including yours truly) is letting their sales and marketing teams become completely siloed and operate with different strategies and priorities. There's a number of reasons for this, often pointing right to the top leadership who fail to grasp the extremely negative impact it can have on revenue performance and staff morale. The concept of "Smarketing" expresses the process of integrating sales and marketing objectives into a unified strategy.

One of the most effective ways to foster marketing and sales alignment is by establishing and agreeing on sales metrics right out of the gate and then collectively working on improving all these indirect revenue and profit-generating metrics.

An effective way is to *begin with the end in mind* and use some of your previously defined sales metrics *to calculate backward*. Then, based on industry standards, determine how much (a) marketing resources are required and (b) where to amp up your coaching efforts in order to hit your established targets by using the following 10-step lead calculator, which I use in both my Accelerator Platform and marketing agency.

In this hypothetical example on the following page, I start with looking at the overall monthly sales quota ($15,000). Then using a set of metrics calculations as shown, we can drill down all the way to determine how many leads are required to come respectively from marketing (105 MQLs) and the sales reps' own prospecting efforts (9 SQLs) in order to hit the target.

10-Step Lead Calculation Method

Step 1.	Define the MRR target you have established per rep	= $15,000 MRR target
Step 2.	Define your monthly revenue per customer	= $1,500 MRR/deal
Step 3.	Determine how many deals need to be won monthly	= 10 deals/month
Step 4.	Determine your average LCR (# of SQLs to win 1 deal)	= 33.33% win ratio
Step 5.	Calculate # SQLs needed to reach MRR target	= 30 SQLs [all channels]
Step 6.	Determine SQL ratio between Inbound and Outbound	= 70% / 30% lead split
Step 7.	Calculate # of SQLs needed from Inbound	= 21 SQLs [Inbound]
Step 8.	Define the conversion rate of inbound MQLs to SQLs	= 20% conversion rate
Step 9.	Calculate # MQLs marketing needs to drive to get # SQLs	= 105 MQLs [Inbound]
Step 10.	Define # SQLs sales rep must generate via Outbound	= 9 SQLs [Outbound]

If you aren't taking this suggested approach, you'll likely bang your head against the wall. As often happens, your marketing director manages the relationship with your marketing agency (who have their own priority metrics, by the way), while your sales manager is running hard pursuing new sales targets, resulting in everyone's failure to achieve targets at best, and a lot of unproductive finger-pointing or worse, as illustrated below.

The conversation, in a B2B or SaaS company for example, quickly becomes something along the lines of this (perhaps a bit rudimentary and exaggerated but I'm trying to make a point about *why* detailing sales metrics is key for your success):

Business Owner: *"We must grow revenue by 25 percent this quarter and get fifty new clients on board."*

Sales Manager: *"I need leads. A lot of them if I gotta meet that 25 percent sales growth KPI!"*

Marketing Manager: *"I need 25 percent more budget to generate enough leads for sales."*

And then the end of quarter comes around:

Business Owner: *"Not only did we miss our target by a mile, we also spent 25 percent more on marketing than originally budgeted. We're bleeding red this quarter."*

Sales Manager: *"I missed the targets because the leads marketing assigned us were poor and most suspects didn't even want to speak with us or have enough budget."*

Marketing Manager: *"Sales didn't follow up on the leads properly and were so desperate to close deals quickly that they discounted heavily. So that's why we didn't hit target."*

This conversation would never have taken place if the twenty-five suggested sales metrics were in place. Why?

A business owner with metrics such as CAC, LCR, ARPA, SSG, and more in place would be far better suited to understand exactly what it would take in order to grow their revenue and book of business by this rate and also whether the increase in marketing budget allocation should translate into profitability and by when (average sales cycle, LTV, margins, etc.).

And since sales and marketing would share the same metrics and have insights to the same data, a more collaborative conversation would likely take place by asking questions such as:

- *How can marketing help sales by providing a series of blog posts, white papers, case studies, or other resources that can help influence our win rates?*
- *How can sales provide better feedback to marketing on leads per channel in order for marketing to better understand some of the intangibles*

of paid advertising lead generation and better optimize the ad spend per channel?

- *How can we align initiatives and establish cross-departmental KPIs in order to collaborate better and meet our overall company growth targets?*

- *How can sales provide better feedback to marketing on what our prospects and customers are asking for so that we can improve our direct response campaign messaging?*

- *How can marketing support sales better to reengage leads by implementing lead-nurturing initiatives that can reignite interest from otherwise cold prospects?*

With all of these considerations, I hope it's now obvious to you why your company as a first priority—right after doing your research and building your sales plan, before hiring—should establish all pertinent metrics per your expected customer journey. Otherwise, you'll find yourself saying the following phrase in meetings a hundred-plus times a year (and obviously not the way to go!):

"If we have data, let's look at data. If all we have are opinions, let's go with mine."

PS Here are a few additional tactics I've used over the years to create better alignment between sales and marketing. I recommend the following:

- Run cross-departmental contests with joint company outings, trips, etc., to better build relationships and understanding of each other's team members.

- Run a biweekly or monthly sales and marketing meeting where departments work together.

- Implement career trajectory paths that allow sales to move into marketing roles in your company and vice versa (when suited

THE ZERO TO 100 MILLION SALES BLUEPRINT

to the candidate of course). You'll be surprised how much that can influence collaboration.

- Place your sales and marketing offices right next to each other. Or better yet, put both teams in a big open office space with desks next to each other.
- Agree on terminology and assign each department responsible for educating the other on otherwise "mystical" concepts to limit misunderstandings.

As a little incentive for you to take action on this concept, here are some stats from recent studies showing that companies with strong sales and marketing alignment are:

- *Sixty-seven percent more efficient at closing deals*
- *Achieving 20 percent annual revenue growth*
- *Seeing 208 percent growth in marketing revenue*

Tell the Story through Numbers and Visualization

Most CRMs such as Salesforce, HubSpot. Microsoft, Monday.com, Zoho, PipeDrive, and a long list of hundreds of smaller ones in the marketplace do, to some degree, offer reporting capabilities for you to monitor and improve your sales metrics. However, very often, this requires ongoing adjustments and expensive consulting gigs with high-paid CRM implementation companies. I've personally spent hundreds of thousands of dollars on this. And as every business is fluid, new products get rolled out, and adjustments are made to your processes and go-to-market strategies, they'll need ongoing corrections, for a fee, either as an internal or external cost.

I believe that's one of the main reasons many companies fail to either incorporate sales metrics and, if they do adopt them, fail to religiously aim to optimize them. The same goes for those claiming they lack resources and instead attempt to manually import all this data into spreadsheets, create pivot tables, and design manual dashboards for the sake of reporting. Adoption of these dashboards will be limited to the few data-driven individuals on your team, and the impact of getting collective visibility and focus on metrics will be absent.

Thankfully, there's a few alternative methods to quickly and cost-effectively create dashboards that are interactive, visually appealing, tell a story that is actionable, and can drive performance.

A few of my favorite dashboard technologies I've used for sales metrics adoption over the years are:

- Google Data Studio
- Tableau
- TapClicks
- Power BI
- DataPine
- Klipfolio
- Grow
- Domo

On the following two pages are a few sample sales metrics and KPI dashboards (from Klipfolio) that paint the picture of how you can present the data and make it visible within your company. In fact, I always have several monitors highly visible in my departments 24/7/365 just to showcase metrics.

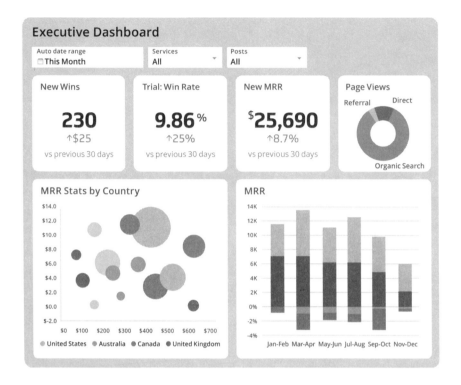

In this chapter, I presented you with a comprehensive list of twenty-five sales metrics that truly matter and elaborated why you should closely align these across your teams, including marketing, sales ops, HR, and finance.

In the next chapter, I'll unveil a number of important best practices when it comes to hiring, onboarding, and developing a team of sales champions irrespective of your budgetary constraints.

7

GREAT SALESPEOPLE
ARE MADE, NOT BORN

*Will empower you to build a highly successful sales team
despite limited resources and funds. It centers on the notion
that you shouldn't try to find the golden goose—
that "one in a million" born salesperson—but rather create
a system to continually produce sales superstars.*

"*He's a natural-born salesperson!*"
Many times over I've heard people describe me as such, as well
as other top performers in other sales organizations I've been blessed to be
part of. The fact of the matter is that in most cases, that statement couldn't
be further from the truth!

In my case, up until my early twenties, I was the complete opposite of
what you would characterize as a natural-born, talented salesperson. I was
shy, introverted, lacked interpersonal skills, and couldn't hold a conversation if my life depended on it!

So how did I become a top performer on every sales floor I stepped on later in my adult life? Like most other sales champions I've come across, hired, and developed over the past twenty years, I had three key ingredients that I built on.

1. **Hunger for more in life.** As a young kid, living with my single mother in the suburbs of Copenhagen, we were certainly not poor, but safe to say, we didn't have money for anything other than the absolute basics. From my early teens, I was a basketball enthusiast (at 6' 5" I had to be), quickly dazzled by the culture associated with NBA superstars. Like many kids, I aspired to be like one, live the flashy lifestyle, get all the girls, and more! When you play basketball, and you're a kid, your kicks are *extremely* important status symbols. Michael Jordan was at his peak during my young basketball journey, and I remember the agony I felt of not being able to buy the new AJs like my teammates and instead having to wear some cheap, worn-down Converse kicks instead. It may sound shallow, superficial, and in hindsight, completely stupid (aren't we all when we're kids?), but that hunger to acquire material things was a huge driver setting me up for success in sales. I found a path to earn a lot of money that I couldn't otherwise. That drive empowered me to survive my first sales gigs, where I absolutely sucked. I probably would have given up if I wasn't blessed with the hunger to earn money and acquire the things, experiences, and lifestyle I aspired to.

2. **Desire to prove myself.** Everyone, depending on their social conditions and upbringing, has a different set of values and emotional drivers that shape every decision they make in life (see Chapter 3 on psychographics). In my case, I'm certainly driven by two major emotional needs:

THE ZERO TO 100 MILLION SALES BLUEPRINT

a. The need to feel significant

b. The assurance of certainty

The first of these has been a major catalyst for my sales career trajectory in which I had to prove myself over and over again both as a sales pro and entrepreneur. You see, growing up as a "poor" kid—tall, skinny, socially awkward, and not blessed with any special God-given talents—I was eager to change this perception and my self-limiting beliefs by proving myself, growing in confidence, and creating a new identity.

I struggled in high school and didn't have the grades or resources to go to an ivy league college. But I quickly realized after my initial sales gig, where I witnessed other young kids doing phenomenally well financially and socially, that my path to significance was via entrepreneurship and fueling my success in business by becoming the best salesperson in the world!

Now, some twenty-five years later, after my first sales job, reflecting on my emotional needs back then and assessing my journey, it's evident that without this strong appetite to "prove myself," I probably wouldn't have made it in sales or business!

3. **Analytical with desire to learn.** Because of my hunger and desire to prove myself, I was able to develop a learning skillset in areas that interested me. Whether it was how to sell and make money or, in my teens, play the point guard position in basketball (despite being slotted into the center role) so having to learn ball-handling skills and prove folks otherwise, I acquired one of the most valuable attributes in becoming a successful salesperson—the ability to learn! For many years, I've made it a priority to read or listen to a new audiobook every two weeks (about twenty-six books a year)—all books on business, sales, psychology,

personal development, or autobiographies from proven entrepreneurs. This thirst for knowledge, fueled by my values and emotional needs, has been central to my success. It has enabled me to consume so much information that, although not born with special talents, I've been able to develop myself to become a sales and business expert by studying others with prior success in related fields, applying their theories and recommendations, and experimenting on my own.

HIRE FOR ATTITUDE AND ATTRIBUTES, THEN TRAIN FOR SKILLS

So as you've now done the exercises of mapping out your customer journey, and defining all the key sales metrics, perhaps you've begun to realize that going on a head-hunting recruitment mission to find *a proven, experienced, and already high-performing* sales rep is going to require you to dig deep in your pockets and cash out a salary that perhaps is higher than your startup budget or current finances allows.

In fact, I'd go so far as saying that despite how well funded your project is, I'd *never* recommend you go out and just hire top sales performers from other organizations and teams. My vote would *always* be to create and develop your own sales talent (of course with a few experienced key sales team members to support laying the foundation).

There are so many layers to consider regarding what leads to the high performance of your current experienced sales hires, and what they bring to the table in their current or last job where they are/were a top performer, that don't necessarily apply to *your* sales methodology, customer segment, and market approach.

Here are a few examples of what I mean:

- If your candidate previously had immense success selling an SaaS product to SMBs, that doesn't necessarily translate into equal success at your company if you're offering an Enterprise-focused solution with a more complex and longer sales cycle. He/she would have to begin a whole new learning curve, and success in this new role would also depend on factors such as their coachability and adaptivity. Wouldn't you agree?

- Or what if the characteristics that drove high performance at their last job were fueled by the candidate's unique ability to build rapport, their charisma, and ability to earn trust with prospects? Yet, at your company, sales outcomes usually derive from problem-solving and customizing solutions by understanding their business processes in great detail using superb probing abilities. I don't think this former sales superstar would even be in the top 20 percent at your company, right?

- Another scenario I've encountered many times is when a number one sales performer at a B2C-focused sales team transitions to B2B sales. They're usually used to handling incoming inquiries and often have a strong product in their hands to sell. This doesn't mean they're bad at sales. Conversely, their sales performance skyrocketed because they had amazing probing abilities, listening skills, and were able to connect both the potential pain and pleasure to the product they were pitching their prospect.

However, when transitioned to B2B sales and dealing with buyers who are less emotional, more rational, operate with budget limitations, require ROI calculations about the impact of a purchase, etc., then the former B2C sales superstar finds themself struggling in their new B2B role. Often they may not even cut it after the initial induction period due to sheer frustration and disappointment in the change in status from the hero to a below-average performer.

Don't get me wrong. Later in this chapter, I'll share some tips on how to successfully headhunt top sales performers from other companies in your domain. I'll also show how to mitigate the potential of them not succeeding in their new role at your company after you have paid them big bucks to transition their career trajectory to your organization.

I've developed a rule of thumb when building and scaling a sales team that I call the one-to-five ratio. For every sales superstar hire I bring on with prior success in a similar role, I aim to hire five sales newbies that I develop from the ground up. I found that provides the right balance by not letting external hires with proven track records in other companies (and who have certain expectations about how things are done, processes, good and bad habits, culture, etc.) influence your sales methodology and culture too much.

Conversely, this provides you with some experience on the floor that can help validate your best sales practices, approach, and generally bring some real-world experiences and value to the table. Then your "fresh into the school of sales" new recruits have some support from these more senior salespeople, but at the same time you maintain better control in shaping the behaviors you want in your sales organization, the culture, sales methodology, and which technologies to use.

This has proven over the years to be a perfect model for scaling sales teams with the right balance of effectiveness versus budget optimization since your approach of producing sales superstars internally will be *significantly* more cost-friendly for the payroll section in your company budget!

The DNA Blueprint of Your Future Sales Champion

Now, the million-dollar questions: What do you look for in candidates when aiming to hire your future sales superstars? What characteristics should you scout for in a candidate who lacks sales experience? And how do you create a framework for this to work at scale and in collaboration with your talent acquisition team?

During the last ten years alone, I've hired more than 1,000 people whom I personally met and either interviewed initially or took part in a final interview (usually fourth or fifth in a series of interviews and assessments). You see, for me, and as I stated in Chapter 4, hiring the *right people* for your startup is probably one of the biggest factors to determine your success! Many, many other entrepreneurs, authors, and business experts share this notion, but rarely have I heard sales leaders put the same emphasis on this when hiring a sales team; in fact, from my experience, it's often quite unstructured and with little strategy behind the efforts. After all, it's "just" sales, right? Nothing is as complex as product development or engineering. WRONG!

World-class sales hiring is probably the single most important factor in determining the success of your company! Let that sink in for a second. Again, with no consistent high volume of sales in your company, there's no growth. With no growth, there are no new hires to be made, products to be developed, new markets to be conquered, new roles to be created, funds for marketing campaigns to be designed, promotions, salary increases, opportunities to make an impact, etc.

So with this notion and when hiring 1,000+ people over the years, despite everything else going on in the business (sales to be made, processes to be created, constant fires to be put out), I still prioritized and made time to sit in on thousands of interviews. During this process and very informative experience, I began detecting patterns for sales excellence and so developed a set of twenty characteristics that I think define sales superstar talent.

In summary, if you can find inexperienced sales candidates who possess the majority of the below-mentioned characteristics, under the assumption that you have a good onboarding process and coaching framework in place (more on that in the next chapter), then you'll be almost guaranteed to build a high-performance sales team that can deliver outstanding results with predictability and consistency.

1. **Goal-Oriented:** This is probably one of the characteristics I primarily look for in a potential rising star. You see, in sales, you're constantly pursuing goals: the goal of landing XYZ client, the goal of reaching your monthly/quarterly quota, and even the constant partial milestone goals of scheduling a meeting, sending out the agreement, and getting the payment. So if an applicant is highly goal-oriented, this is a huge plus in my book. Even if it's personal goals such as "Gary, I'm taking this sales role because I know I can make a lot of money, and that's how I can realize my dream of buying a house." Another good example is an applicant who is goal-oriented with regard to their career trajectory. For example, my absolute top sales performer at my last company consistently outperformed the other best reps by 2–3x in revenue. When I interviewed him and explained our performance-based sales career ladder and showed a trajectory of him potentially moving from a Junior Rep to Sales Director, his response was, "Gary, I want to know what it takes to get your seat." Now, that's a goal statement I love!

2. **Passionate:** Prospects can easily detect if a sales rep is enthusiastic about their job and the solutions they're selling. This may be difficult to attain if you're selling some product or service that makes

THE ZERO TO 100 MILLION SALES BLUEPRINT

less of an impact on the world, but there are always ways to spin this as a founder. For example, at my last company, despite us "just" selling digital marketing products for tech companies like Google and Microsoft, we instead put the focus on events where we helped change a small business around for the better by generating leads and sales they otherwise wouldn't have attained without our help. Another angle was highlighting how we were indirectly changing economics for the middle class in a third world country by offering salary levels previously unheard of from other companies. Our entrance in the country forced all other bilingual-focused companies to up their salaries to compete with us.

3. **Prior Success:** Now, this is not necessarily restricted to sales. It can also be in sports, academics, business, or any other competitive area of their life. If a candidate has a proven track record and became number one In their field or recreational passion, they have already demonstrated to you they can be committed, disciplined, hardworking, goal-oriented, and responsible. Nobody can reach that level of success, whether as a top athlete or academic, without demonstrating those qualities. Now the question is for you to identify whether you believe they can transfer those very same qualities to their upcoming role in sales. The right sales leader knows how to push those buttons and reignite those behaviors, and with such, you have a very strong foundation to develop a sales superstar.

4. **Curious:** This is an incredibly important characteristic for the process of creating a high-performing sales rep. They have to be constantly curious about the market, their competition, how they can sell better, their prospects, what their goals are, their challenges, how to keep up to par with product updates, and much more. In

today's connected world with ease of access to information online, anyone anywhere can find answers to most problems—if they're just curious enough to seek the information. Few people bother to put forth the effort, and that's why curiosity can go a long way in sales. A good way to identify this characteristic is simply to assess how many questions the applicant asks you before, during, and after the interview has taken place.

5. **Coachable:** For me, this is almost a deal breaker when hiring a candidate. How can you develop a potential sales superstar if they cannot embrace feedback, reflect on areas of self-improvement, and then apply it? A top performer is almost always committed to their own professional development and constantly looking for ways to improve. They are able to park their ego on the back seat and listen to feedback from their customers, peers, or managers. From my experience, regardless of the levels of talent, if an applicant isn't receptive to your input during a fictional role-play scenario or assessment during the interview process, I'd rather let the candidate go in favor of a hire who may require extra coaching effort but conversely listen and apply your feedback.

6. **Disciplined:** Sales is a tough environment. It requires a strong, determined, and disciplined mindset to daily go through countless rejections, setbacks, and disappointments and then continue with the activities required to pursue one or more partial victories during the day. Imagine going through two or three setbacks in a row during the morning and then needing to elevate your mindset and attitude for your next meeting. That kind of bounceback mentality requires disciplined behavior! I prefer to hire people who are fit, exercise a lot, are in good shape, and eat healthy since getting in shape requires a certain degree of disciplined behavior.

You don't grow muscle without determination to consistently hit the gym.

7. **Energetic:** Perhaps it's just my Type A personality, but I don't find that someone with low energy can get the job done. I want people who have things to do, goals to meet, and are constantly eager to advance. That requires high energy, and when translated to sales, it's usually a strong factor in determining success. A little trick I do is to pick up applicants at the HR office or downstairs and accompany them to the interview room. If they walk slowly, they're already points behind before even starting our interview. If your company has bold and lofty goals, you must surround yourself with a team equally energized to get shit done!

8. **Enthusiastic:** A key for success with sales. There's plenty of competition in any business, and if you don't convey a strong sense of enthusiasm for your product and the opportunity to do business with your prospect, then forget it—you've already lost the deal. So how do you detect enthusiasm during an interview and screening process? First and foremost, keep track of whether it's consistent in interview one, two, three, and four. Second, remember that communication is not just our words. In fact, the words we speak account for as little as 7 percent of our communication. The rest is our tone of voice, body language, and posture. So look for their overall ability to project enthusiasm through emotions and how they communicate with you. Someone slouching during the interview or talking super slow and quiet gets only five minutes of my time in an interview. They're not going to make it in sales.

9. **Problem Solver:** Real sales is all about solving problems and creating desired results. Taking the time to truly understand the client's needs, challenges, industry, opportunities, etc., in order to

help the client with a customized solution is what a true problem-solving salesperson does every day. Boiling down an often highly complex and long sales process can be as simple as first asking relevant, challenging questions and with that intel identify possible problem areas for improvement. Then, based on that intelligence, suggest solutions to help the customer achieve their targets and goals. I usually conduct role-plays during interviews and give a hypothetical use case in which I ask an interviewee to "sell me" in order to gauge how good they are at this process. And if they fail, I provide feedback through questions to see how coachable they are on their second and third attempts.

10. **Good Collaborator:** This is almost a do-or-die for developing a sales champion. The more you sell, the more you'll have to collaborate with other internal team members in your company whether they be marketing, admin, operations, finance, or fulfillment. The same goes for external collaboration, whether it's your partners or team at the client's company. Good collaboration skills are a necessity. Trust me, you don't want a lone-wolf sales superstar who is ego-driven and doesn't get along with your other team members. It never ends well, and the worst you can do is accept such behavior since it deteriorates the morale of your other staff.

11. **Committed:** To their targets, to their clients, to driving results, to learning, to always walking into a meeting on time and being prepared—you name it. Commitment goes a long way in the game of sales. Thankfully, this is somewhat easy to detect during an interview process. Just look at their past jobs, projects, and accomplishments. Have they shopped around and stayed less than a year in each job? Do they bring up how they attended this course or that workshop but have good excuses for why they don't have the

certificate, the result, or recommendation at hand. Those are all signs of someone who lacks commitment and is a "dabbler."

12. **Challenger:** Being a "devil's advocate" is a strong quality in a salesperson. A top performer doesn't just accept the status quo. You want folks around that if something isn't right and can be improved, they speak up. They're constantly pushing for the better. For themselves, their peers, company, and clients. You want to embrace this behavior in your future sales reps because you'll never succeed at scaling your company to something great if you're just surrounded by a team of "yes sayers."

13. **Responsible:** A no-brainer attribute needed for a high achiever in any category. But especially in such a performance-driven environment as sales, with constant ups and downs, a true sales superstar is someone who can take full responsibility for the outcome, whether success or failure. The right candidate owns their result and does not pass blame on the "bad leads" they were assigned or that they had personal problems that impacted performance, or that XYZ prospect didn't come through as promised. They'll do whatever it takes and put forth extra work as needed when behind on targets. Even more important, they'll aim to be ahead of the curve at all times so they have room for the predictable unexpected events that always occur in the game of sales.

14. **Good Listener:** Non-negotiable for me in an applicant. Long gone are the days when a strong pitch, charisma, and being extroverted were attributes that defined a good sales rep. Today's top performers take a consultative approach to selling. They ask a lot of good, intelligent questions that get the buyer thinking. And, of course, they listen carefully to understand their prospects' true goals and challenges to ensure they can help solve their problems. This can

sometimes be identified by providing insights and asking questions in a way where a candidate with good listening abilities will be able to pick up on your approach and reply to your questions referencing what you said earlier during the interview.

15. **Good Storyteller:** "This reminds me of one of my customers who signed with us a few years ago. Rich is his name. He was in a similar situation as yours and..." One of my best sales reps at my former company loved to start off his position statement like this after asking a whole series of questions. You see, storytelling goes thousands of years back in history and is how many lessons were passed down. So we are naturally drawn to stories because they appeal to our emotions, and that often leads to actions, such as buying. Not all purchases can be defined as rational decision processes but rather are based on our need to seek pleasure and avoid pain. Some of the best salespeople I've encountered master the two skills of superbly asking intelligent questions and then tying that up with solutions that are presented partially via storytelling. If you come across this combo, hurry up and make a job offer to that candidate.

16. **Intelligence:** Many argue this is perhaps an attribute that doesn't necessarily equate to success in sales. And although it's true that intelligence isn't sufficient, it has proven to me in many events to be an important factor in becoming a leading sales professional, especially in the domains I navigate (digital marketing, tech, B2B, and SaaS). Sellers today, within a short time span, are expected to quickly dissect and understand different business models, identify hidden areas of opportunity, and then effectively communicate complex solutions to prospects in a simple fashion, all requiring a high degree of intelligence. The same applies to the ability to learn

and understand the changes in these fast-paced industries where constant evolution happens. I try to identify intelligence in applicants, not in a conventional way by issuing IQ tests but instead by conducting assessments on issued reading material or giving fictional scenarios during a role-play. This allows me to gauge their ability to grasp the situation, ask the right questions, and attempt to provide solutions based on knowledge they acquired during that process.

17. **Hard Worker:** The best phrase I know for this is one I heard tech billionaire Mark Cuban say when describing his early entrepreneurial days: *"Work like there's someone working twenty-four hours a day to take it all away from you!"* This kind of relentless, resilient, and persistent attitude toward the application of hard work to reach success is a requisite in a top performer. I have come across many, many hires where I was utterly impressed with their job interview performance and score on assessments conducted during the interview process, but the ones who lacked the ability to work hard (admittedly very difficult to gauge during the interview process) were *always* outperformed by their peers who consistently outworked them despite having fewer talents. Hence during reference checks with their former employers, I now always ask about an applicant's ability to grind hard.

18. **Purposeful Positioner:** My first sales manager told me that I should have a purpose with every conversation and interaction I engage in. A true sales professional is able to shift mindsets, crush roadblocks, and get a prospect to understand their vision by always positioning their solutions with a strong purpose and explaining why they *need* it. This skillset does require work, training, and experience to some degree, but I have found that by

asking applicants about something they're passionate about, I can gauge whether or not they can become a strong positioner of our solutions by the level of how they pitch me and whether they can convince me.

19. **Product Knowledgeable:** In today's internet-driven world, this is key. Most buyers have conducted at least basic research before reaching out and speaking with a seller. They're not seeking knowledge they can find on a simple Google search. If your reps are able to fully understand their product and how its benefits and features can help their prospective clients, they'll be able to deliver their pitch with more authority and credibility, therefore enhancing the buying experience. Your reps don't have to develop the knowledge at the level of a product engineer, but the better they can understand all the ins and outs, the more effective they'll be as a salesperson. A way to identify your next sales rep's ability to absorb and understand product know-how can be to issue a white paper, product explainer, or links to a few blogs prior to your next interview and then question them and see if they understand the context and can explain what benefits could be particularly relevant for your prospective customers.

20. **Confidence:** An absolute requisite for any top-level sales performer. If they don't believe in themselves, the company they work for, or the solution they're offering, then how the heck can you expect a prospect to believe in them? Any buyer usually knows that some risk is associated with acquiring a new solution, but if the seller isn't conveying optimism and confidence that mutual success be attained through this transaction, you can't expect any buyer to move forward with a deal. I'd go as far as stating that all successful salespeople are confident.

The DNA Blueprint of Your Future Sales Champion

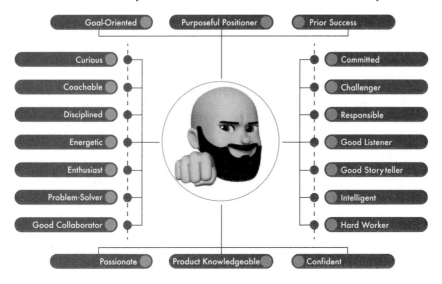

Hiring and Onboarding Sets the Precedence for Excellence

Before I spend a lot of time, energy, and resources finding the candidates to join my sales team, I prepare for them to hit the ground running by establishing a robust and consistent hiring and onboarding plan.

Too many companies just "wing it" when it comes to onboarding new sales reps. Sales employee attrition is notoriously high compared to other professions. Not only is it a hard craft to master and sustain, but without experience and no onboarding plan, you're almost doomed to fail. Not surprisingly, data from HubSpot shows that the average sales turnover is 35 percent (nearly three times higher than other industries at 13 percent).

According to CSO Insights, there's a 16.2 percent higher chance that your reps hit their quota if there's an effective onboarding process in place. That seems like a fairly good statistic to invest in if you want to improve your company's bottom line.

Now, as with everything else in sales, the devil is in the details, so before you get your HR and Training department or an isolated sales executive with no finger on the pulse creating your sales onboarding plan, make sure you give this exercise the adequate attention to maximize efficiency and profitability.

What has worked best for me is to make onboarding a company-wide project by making hiring efficiency metrics visible and treating this process as you would a sales process. By company-wide, I mean having your reps spend a week with your product fulfillment team so they get to understand the "other side of the table" regarding the post-sale process. Or getting Sales Ops folks heavily involved with creating CRM and sales tech stack manuals, processes, and training so that every rep fully understands the tools and support vehicles at their disposal from day one.

The same goes for Talent Development with regard to establishing goals and motivating reps to tackle all the adversity to be expected in their new role. Equally important is to have your AEs sit with your SDR/BDR teams so that there's full understanding of how they position the value of an appointment with them, typical pitfalls they encounter daily, and as a result, create better cross-departmental synergies.

This way, everyone's on the same page, and you can collectively aim to improve your sales hiring and onboarding process. On that note, here are a few recommended metrics for you to consider monitoring and making visible to all stakeholders within your company's sales and revenue departments:

- Percentage of sales management time spent recruiting (screening résumés, head-hunting, networking, interviews, etc.)
- Average time to hire for new sales reps (i.e., from the day you publish the opening to the day the job is fulfilled (not the actual start date)

- Percentage of job offers issued that are accepted and rejected
- Average sales rep turnover/attrition rate (equally as impactful on your bottom line as customer churn)
- Average tenure of sales reps within your company
- Percentage of sales reps that succeed with advancing their sales career development plans and being promoted (more on this at the end of this chapter)
- Average cost to replace a sales rep—for example, job directory cost, advertisements, talent acquisition team, prorated overhead cost, and time for new rep to meet breakeven
- Percentage of sales hires that hit quota after onboarding process and average time for them to break even or become fully productive

This may seem like a lot of work, but my point is, why take all the time to hire, onboard, manage, coach, and then *not* look to optimize the process, especially so considering the positive bottom-line impact in increasing the likelihood for new hires to hit their quotas?

Additional data that supports why you should invest heavily in your sales processing, hiring, and onboarding tells us:

- The average ramp-up time for a new sales hire (i.e., before they become productive and profitable) is between six and nine months. What kind of financial impact to your bottom line could be made if you shortened this by say, 30–50 percent?
- On average, it costs between 1.5 and 2 times a sales rep's salary to replace them with a new candidate.
- The average sales rep tenure is a mere eighteen months. Given the above, just imagine the financial gains you could attain if you extended your sales rep tenure to, say, thirty-six months?

- According to Gartner research, only one-third of sales reps end up meeting an organization's expectations and hitting their sales targets.
- Your reps have options. A quick search on Zipcruiter showed 2,546,395+ sales jobs in the United States alone. In today's post-COVID and now highly accustomed remote job workforce, your reps can apply for a new sales position worldwide without worrying about relocation.

Your 30-60-90 Day New Rep Onboarding Plan

So the million-dollar question is, *what does an effective new sales rep onboarding plan look like?* How can you reduce your sales rep turnover significantly and boost profits by 2–3x the amount of your reps that meet their quota?

It all begins with a paradigm shift within your organization and especially at the top of the food chain. If you religiously monitor, support, and enforce improvement on your sales hiring metrics, rest assured that it never takes place.

A way to look at new sales onboarding is by creating a comprehensive 30-60-90 day plan where you include all the following elements and extend additional coaching on an individual basis as needed. But remember, no two reps are the same, so there will always be a need for personalization according to needs.

- **Before they start**
  - » Communicate clear expectations for the role, not just the usually "fluffy" job description expectations but in detail what sales activities will be required to meet quotas, i.e., average amount of calls per day, emails sent, time spent on LinkedIn for social

selling (also in spare time), and how many interactions with prospects are expected across all channels.

» Align their personal goals with your objectives. Make sure to uncover these (financial, motivational, career advancement, etc.) and share with all pertinent stakeholders so that you can remind the new candidate of the carrot dangling in front of them as the tough gets tougher on the job, and they need a reminder of why they're there.

» Provide them with a comprehensive company overview (from your pitch deck) and elaborate on all important elements of your company such as vision, values, employee benefits, training, career trajectory initiatives, and so forth.

» If possible, after the employment contract is signed, I like to invite them in for a full day monitoring the sales department *before* their first day so they can understand how a regular day at your workspace looks and can prepare themselves for what's soon to come. If you have a larger company, provide a full tour of your facilities.

» Reading material. Don't overload them with study material before they start, but many appreciate any content that can help them hit the ground running (especially since your selection of hires should be eager to learn and be competitive).

» Ensure that all paperwork and preparation is fully executed (information collected, contract signed, company emails created, welcome emails sent, employee handbook circulated, etc.).

- **Day 0–30**
  » Conduct a product training session "on steroids." Too many companies fail in this area, figuring their reps don't need much product training. The fact of the matter is that today's

top-performing reps are solutions advisors and consult prospects on how to solve their problems. Most industries demand they become subject matter experts and know the ins and out of their solution offers.

» Develop a "Sales Department Wiki" or collateral bank that is constantly updated. Make sure the initial induction process covers all relevant information such as company and product knowledge, your industry, key partners, possible compliance, and regulatory information.

» Emphasize that they become familiar with key customer case studies and testimonials such that they can recite them during a call in a storytelling format as if they had sold that particular customer themselves. Encourage them to become storytellers in all their customer interactions.

» Processes, processes, processes. Success leaves clues, so make sure they can go from 0 to 100 as fast as possible by learning your ideal sales processes and following them.

» Sales methodology training, lead qualification criteria, psychological triggers of your pitch, and value proposition should be covered in great detail. This is where your sales leader should take initiative to own the approach and create confidence that things are done the best way.

» Per your research done from Chapter 3, provide them with an understanding of your target market, ICP, and the competition. Make sure to include an overview of your mystery shopping process. Provide any competitor scorecards for them to become *highly* familiar with.

» Provide a user-friendly, easy-to-understand manual that includes shortcuts and time-saving feature explanations on all your sales technology; most importantly, key tools such as CRM, dialer, email software and sales enablement/outreach tech, lead enrichment tools, etc.

» Conduct daily role-plays on how to prospect, pitch, do demos, probe customers, etc. Align it with your buyer personas so that it's customized as in a real-life sales scenario.

» Provide a comprehensive overview of your entire customer journey. This may seem redundant, but the less you silo your sales team from other company functions by teaching them the entire journey, the more likely they are to perform at a higher level, understand and respect their colleagues, and be engaged across the company.

» Issue scripts or call outlines and conduct daily role-plays. Compare and play recordings of previous successful "ideal" calls made by your experienced reps across the entire sales cycle. That way, not only do your new reps get to model their "deal pitch" but also understand how the prospect or customer is handled during the next steps of your sales cycle.

» Set up meetings with key stakeholders across departments, as you find it necessary, not only with your sales leadership. I always include three departments in that process:.(1) Product Fulfillment/Engineering (how does the "magic" happen?), (2) Customer Service/Customer Success (What do our customers love? What do they hate?), and (3) Marketing (to understand the market, USPs, ICP, competitors, etc. in depth and to shine extra light on any questions your reps have in these areas so they fully understand how and why a new lead eventually lands in their lap).

» Digital footprint. Walk them through and provide templates for how this should look. Prospects check out their LinkedIn and other social media profiles to know who they're dealing with. If they have an unprofessional appearance, they lose opportunities and suffer financially. Fix this right out of the gate by setting expectations and providing support. I recommend getting marketing involved here for professional headshots, banners, etc.

- **Day 30–60**
  - » Pair them with an experienced sales rep to shadow and be mentored by. An effective way to increase the mentor's engagement is to provide a bonus incentive for them paid out 50 percent when the new rep graduates from the initial 90-day sales onboarding process and 50 percent once the new rep meets your productivity metrics (i.e., becomes profitable). Another method to incentivize mentors to do the best job possible is making success with this process a requisite for job advancement.
  - » Once they begin actual selling, set realistic goals that require a high degree of effort but are achievable to attain early wins.
  - » Provide training and explanation of your established written email sequences and snippet library. Explain what tests you've done to demonstrate why these work. And although they can be optimized like everything else in your processes, you don't want new reps to come in and start over with their own email messaging experimentation. Let them pick up where you left off. But that requires education and reasoning to obtain buy-in.
  - » Provide a list of recommended reading material—for example, industry blogs to keep up to par with trends, videos by subject matter experts, podcasts, along with two or three "must-read" books that support your sales methodology.

» Listen to their calls and conduct weekly, if not daily, feedback sessions where you also include their mentor so they can reinforce your coaching principles and insights.

» Begin reviewing their sales activity data/metrics and share with them. Provide feedback so that you create a feedback loop, understand potential areas they need more training on, as well as communicating what sales activity levels you're expecting and for which they're being monitored (calls, emails, demos, proposals, follow-ups, CRM compliance, etc.).

» Walk them through your rebuttal library and conduct role-plays so they are prepared as best as possible for their sales calls and the inevitable high volume of excuses and objections prospects throw in their face every day.

- **Day 60–90**

  » Reinforce the month one product and market training. It's now been thirty to sixty days since the first classroom session and now they're entering the "real life" of sales. Why? People forget 70 percent of the information they learn during their training within one week—70! And up to 87 percent within a month.

  » Have weekly collaborative sessions with marketing where they guide where to find useful case studies and collateral within your Sales wiki/collateral bank so that they know exactly where to find relevant case studies to share, valuable statistics and data, ROI calculations, product explainers, and everything else that help them more effectively guide your prospects down the path to purchase.

  » Have your experienced reps provide solution demos on a weekly basis so new reps learn how to master this critical skillset. As mentioned before, it comes down to a science to integrate storytelling, evidence, and entertainment all highly customized to the individual use case of the prospect.

» Conduct ad hoc call reviews (by sales coach/manager).

» Do ongoing role-plays to practice negotiating tactics, objection prevention, and handling.

» Take exams and necessary certifications to make sure they fully comprehend product training.

» Establish monthly performance reviews to support weekly feedback sessions.

» Have Sales Ops conduct CRM, tech stack usage, and process compliance feedback as needed. This is very important! You want to establish the correct habits that foster performance immediately and reinforce them.

» Establish adjusted personalized goals for the next three to six months per their performance, ambitions, and your career path progression plans. Make sure to push their comfort levels and establish lofty stretch goals now that they have been acclimatized to sales and your organization. Most reps prefer to "underpromise so that they can overdeliver," especially in a stressful sales environment. But peak performance won't ever come in their comfort zone.

Picking the Right Sales Hire Candidate(s)

Now that we have boiled down characteristics that define your future sales champions, you have plans for onboarding them in place, training, and incentives, it's time to pick the winners to join your sales team. How can that be done more effectively in addition to a robust candidate sourcing and interviewing process?

I like to test people and see if they can walk the walk instead of just talk the talk which comes naturally to most sales applicants. Here are a few proven and recommended ways to do such:

- **Sales Role-Playing Exercises**
  - » This exercise is ideally conducted before your assessment center activity. Usually this consists of a few whiteboard sessions conducted by your sales manager after the second or third interview. They're better suited to assess sales skills and coachability instead of your HR/Talent team which should be more focused on overall screening and interviewing to find the best suited candidate based on characteristics, prior experience, motivation, compensation level, etc.
  - » In these "spontaneous" scenarios, unlike the assessment center where the candidates have time to prepare, the sales manager provides some basic information and conducts a role-play scenario with the candidate. The goal is to see how they articulate themselves, gauge how quick they are on their feet, and how they improvise. Equally important is to understand how receptive they are to coaching feedback and how adaptive they are to instruction about what they could possibly do better if they just did XYZ accordingly.
  - » It's also an opportunity to better understand how familiar they are with your industry, the market, your company, and its solutions.
  - » In addition, this allows you to judge how much research they've done prior to the interview.
- **Required Reading**
  - » This can be done by assigning a White Paper or short book as their preparation, typically for the second and third interviews.

» I personally *love* this exercise since the right candidate won't mind investing time to study this prior to the interview. In other words, they're already performing to go above and beyond to land the job. The candidate with the wrong mindset or who is not sufficiently motivated may be reluctant to do a reading assignment and may even complain about why they were asked for this before even being hired. Next!

» With this exercise done and prior to your assessment center, you can now better gauge their ability to learn, communicate complex concepts back to you, and see how they can transfer acquired knowledge as ammunition in role-play.

- **Sales Candidate Assessment Centers**

    This exercise should be one of the last steps in your hiring process. In other words, after a two- or three-step interview process with the talent acquisition team, HR, and Sales Manager but before the final interview with your CEO.

    The assessment center is where you can test the final short-listed batch of sales applicants. This is a way for you to test them on:

    » How they collaborate with others in a project setting

    » Whether the characteristics you identified as valuable during the interview process stand the ground once tested in a more realistic on-the-job environment

    » Their comprehension, learning and writing capabilities by issuing a sample of your actual training to gauge how they capture information, their note-taking, and how receptive they are to the concepts you'll be teaching them

    » Conduct fictitious selling scenarios where they are given a situation and then asked to conduct discovery and demo calls over the phone with one of your sales managers role-playing to be the prospect

» A selection of questions and emails from fictional selling scenarios to assess their grammar, written articulation, eloquence, and the overall structure in written communication

- **CEO/Owner Interview**
  » I personally always do these interviews—without exception. I want to (a) make sure the Talent Acquisition department continues to raise the standards and aim for A-players only, (b) have the opportunity to weed out candidates at the finish line in case I detect something we missed throughout the hiring process, and (c) have an opportunity to communicate *my* clear expectations to the candidate before being hired.

  » A good filter to be certain the candidate is worth betting on (recall the costs explained earlier regarding sales rep turnover) is for your bottom-line responsible person, the CEO, to prioritize being part of the hiring process and gauging the candidate. From my personal experience, I emphasize having the candidate ask me questions since, at this stage, these can reveal *a lot* that may not be easy to identify if you're the one asking questions.

  » I'd argue that eight out of ten candidates at this stage should be hired—otherwise the prior steps need to be optimized and your talent acquisition team needs to up the game. You don't want to waste your time with this, but you should be the final step in the process. Showcase to all candidates that they are important to the organization by getting face time with you, hearing the vision from the horse's mouth, and also ensuring that all stakeholders agree on a hire to avoid pointing fingers if it doesn't work out.

To recap, my recommended sales hiring processes are as follows:

1. Talent Acquisition Screening and Interviewing (including fundamental skillset assessments, etc.) one to two interviews usually
2. Book/White Paper reading assignment
3. Sales Manager interview including reading assignment, assessment, and role-play
4. Assessment center with top sales candidates participating
5. Final interview with CEO

DRIVE ENGAGEMENT BY PATHING SALES CAREER DEVELOPMENT

"If you want 1 year of prosperity, grow grain.

If you want 10 years of prosperity, grow trees.

If you want 100 years of prosperity, grow people."

—CHINESE PROVERB

Many business owners and senior executives I work with who aim to hire for attitude and attributes over experience and skills, thereby building a salesforce more cost-effectively, face a real challenge when trying to hire Millennial or Gen Z candidates. Most are discouraged in doing so and share statements to me such as:

"Gary, the problem with these young Millennials is that they come in here with a sense of entitlement and act as if they own the effing place!"

or…

"Gary, I'm going to shoot my brains out if I bring on one more of these high-demand Gen Z sales reps who believe they can run the entire place after just a few victories on the phone and a little taste of success."

The truth of the matter is that I, too, more times than I can recall over recent years, have been annoyed and frustrated when hiring this new breed of sales folks, who often bring an abundance of entitlement and presumptuous behavior to the table.

One thing I've learned after spending the last twelve years living abroad, partly in the United States but mainly in Latin America, is that one should not, and usually cannot, no matter how hard they want to, try to change the culture in another country when launching their business there (more on this in Chapter 14).

Instead, you must embrace their culture, holidays, way of life, priorities, etc., and adjust your approach accordingly. Look to pivot your go-to-market strategy so that it aligns with their customs and culture. As an example, when we first launched operations in Nicaragua, it came to me as a big surprise how many holidays there were in Latin America in contrast to the United States. In particular with one holiday, called Semana Santa, I learned the hard way when forcing the team to come to work then so we could fully service our US-based clientele. That was a big mistake because the holiday was sacred and my staff were very upset. Instead, I needed to adjust my approach and find another solution.

And the very same goes for hiring, training, developing, and motivating Millennials and Gen Zers for your salesforce!

We are living in a new era—a social media-driven world, with access to most information at our fingertips, shortcuts preached for anything and everything, and where *convenience* is the new magic phrase. Add to this the amplification of instant gratification, gaming with rewards, instant social media dopamine triggers, and the fact that there's more wealth created than ever before. No wonder these young people expect and want to see immediate progress!

My recommendation, and this worked for me when scaling my last company to its peak of ~300 young employees between twenty and thirty-five years old, was to leverage this notion of them receiving swift rewards when exceeding expectations and performance.

It took a few attempts, but what worked well for me in my "Recruitment and Onboarding Packages" for applicants and new hires was to lay it all out and cultivate a spirit of *"We expect you to step up to the plate, study, work hard, deliver, grow, and then advance career-wise. If you grow, we grow! As simple as that."* The packages included career path trajectories, employee testimonials, success stories, income calculators based on our commission structure, and more.

This worked *really* well, as all of a sudden I had folks competing, putting in extra effort by working late, coming in early, and helping their peers to demonstrate good attitude and leadership skills, instead of just being entitled and crossing their arms, as executives at other companies experience. Why? Because our approach was 100 percent transparent and they could relate to it from gaming and sports where the rules are laid out *before* the game begins. They knew if they performed at a certain pace for a given period of time, without high fluctuations in performance, maintained output at the top of their class, and developed their skillset, a promotion was theirs to lose.

Here are two examples of such an approach at my last company.

- **From Sales Development Representative (SDR) to Account Executive (AE):** SDRs probably have the most brutal job in the company with a turnover rate 2–3x higher than other roles. When hiring a new SDR, what made a good impact was laying out performance metrics and training requirements from day 1.

For example, after the onboarding process, if an SDR met their monthly quota (24 appointments with ≥33.33 percent LCR) and took the Google AdWords Search certifications, they could apply to become a Junior AE (a closer). At this point they had to continue setting appointments for themselves mainly but would also source leads from inbound as well as from other SDRs. In this role they would need to meet their revenue targets for six months straight ($8,000 in new monthly recurring revenue), study for the remainder of the Google and Microsoft Ads certifications, and conduct a series of account audit protocols with yours truly.

This way, we ensure that if they met their quota, passed the certifications, and learned the processes, we now had a new lethal AE on our hands and we'd scale up our demand-generation efforts and grow our book of business. On average, AEs made 4–5x more income than an SDR, so motivation and effort were at an all-time high after we rolled out this program.

- **From Junior Account Manager to Team Account Supervisor:** In our corresponding department where clients were serviced and managed, our holy metrics were customer churn, upselling, and cross-selling. This was an equally stressful position for the Junior AMs, especially when dealing with cash-constrained SMBs who took a leap of faith with the AE and our proposed paid search campaign solutions, despite having a limited budget and in many cases (e.g., service businesses) themselves having a subpar sales process. As a result, many leads we generated on their behalf via Google AdWords campaigns fell through the cracks because of their inability to handle them adequately (a very, very common scenario for most companies). The AMs also had their backs up against the wall when assigned a new customer. What could extend the LTV and mitigate customer churn was proper expectation setting, extensive reporting, and proactive communication.

This is why we also decided to increase motivation levels and create a transparent career path progression plan presented during the hiring process. So after the product training and certification process (usually about three months), once they were assigned clients and grew their portfolio to $10,000+ in recurring monthly management fees, if they could sustain customer churn rates ≤5 percent month over month for more than six months while growing their existing book of business by 20 percent with upsells and cross-sells, they could apply to become an Account Supervisor Trainee and co-manage a team of six to eight AMs. If done successfully for six-plus months, they could be promoted to Account Supervisor. Next steps were Senior AM, Director, and various VP roles.

See the sample career path trajectory mapping on the following page. This example is not from my previous company, but we added a similar image to our "Your New Career Progression Is Waiting" booklet. You might think that it's too much, too exaggerated. But hey, if I can dream big as a seventeen-year-old taking my first sales job and get to this level with no education, just pure grit, goals, and big dreams, who am I to tell my employees otherwise?

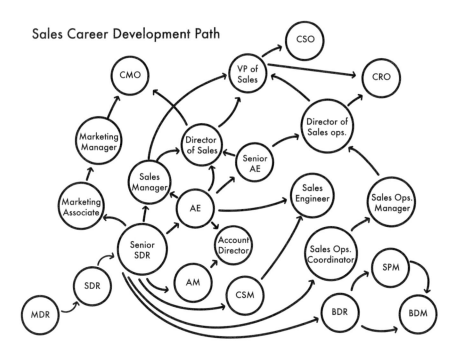

Sales Career Development Path

I do recall these initiatives receiving a lot of criticism from our then-Board of Directors and senior executive. Conversely, I'm very proud of being attributed as the mentor and catalyst for many former employees who now work all over the world, some with high-paid jobs in Silicon Valley, others now entrepreneurs running big agencies. And more than I can count advanced from their initial entry-level $800/month salary position to now working for large brands as supervisors, managers, directors, and CEOs earning upward of 20x from when I brought them in and "sold them" on the vision that this was the place to be if they wanted a stepping-stone to make something out of their career.

Hence why the message from the very first interaction with a prospective hire throughout the hiring and onboarding process should be that they're the master of their own destiny in your company. They set the limits for growth. You may start today as a Sales Development Representative (SDR), but that doesn't mean you cannot become our VP of Sales five years from now. Our mantra was that we do everything in our power to support you to accelerate your career progression trajectory—from training, to mentoring, to paid courses or whichever criteria we identify needed to be developed for you to grow your abilities and skills to get promoted. All you have to do is bring your best to the table every day, grind, and understand that there are no handouts in life. You need to work hard, prioritize, stay committed, and *earn it*!

Now, you don't have to follow my elaborate approach in this task, but if you want to gain traction with this younger workforce, especially in sales, then lay out a concise progression path and support with training and enthusiasm and cheer them on the way to help you make money, especially if you want to optimize your sales hiring and productivity metrics and increase your bottom line. This exercise is a requisite to implement and is further backed by data from Deloitte showing that employee loyalty is decreasing rapidly, to an extent that 44 percent of salespeople plan to leave their job within two years, and SiriusDecisions data shows that 89 percent of salespeople leave their current role for higher pay.

But I promise that you can significantly change those statistics in your favor by implementing the above-mentioned recommendations for hiring, onboarding, and maintaining an ongoing focus on career development.

> *By beginning with the end in mind,*
> *you now can see why hiring for attitude and attributes over*
> *skills can best position your successful growth.*

In the following chapter, we are going to discuss a subject that many companies get wrong—selecting the right sales leadership that fits with your type of company and culture. I outline my sales management success formula, how to create your sales playbook, and the key characteristics of a successful sales manager.

8

SUCCESS LEAVES CLUES

*I'll give you the ingredients needed to take
your company from launch to a highly scalable stage
by identifying patterns that work and amplifying them,
while eradicating less effective methods.*

ongratulations! You've now hired your first sales reps, onboarded them effectively, and enabled one or more to consistently hit your established targets. Relevant sales metrics are being monitored. While you aim to optimize performance further, it's evident that significant continued growth requires you to replicate the success of your first rep(s) and begin building out your sales team to scale the operation. Now is the time when the men get separated from the boys from a sales leadership standpoint. Or the women from the girls!

I've done it too many times over to make the same mistakes again now. After I finally "cracked the code" on sales, got traction, and looked to scale from say five to twenty reps, or from ten to fifty, only to experience that the incremental revenue growth didn't correlate with the corresponding accumulated expenses—more CRM licenses, increased lead generation costs, extra layers of sales admin and operations. All this while my top-performing reps complained about receiving poorer leads all of a sudden. This is a very common scenario for many startups in growth mode and almost inevitable unless you have a structured coaching process in place and make it a strict discipline to scale your successful models with processes and systems.

One of the more challenging experiences I have had with this scenario was back in 2012 when we nearly ran out of cash. My two partners stepped out of the business. We agreed that I'd stay in the business as the only full-time executive and try to turn things around. There weren't even funds for a salary, so my partners agreed that if I turned around the losses from $40,000–$50,000/monthly to $10,000 profit (very modest target, yes), then I'd be honored with a $5,000 monthly salary. If I took that to $50,000, we'd increase it to $10,000.

That was a turning point for me. Although appointed CEO, my focus was getting on the phones, taking leads, closing deals, and showing the few reps we still had employed who believed in the vision that we were a company with a future.

We had various creditors calling daily asking for money for unpaid bills, and this required my attention of course. But simultaneously, I prioritized speaking with prospects and closing deals. I therefore decided to create a fake persona—David Duran (how I came up with that name I just don't recall). But David would be the enthusiastic, high-energy, and attentive salesperson all leads would be greeted by when calling in and asking about our services. Conversely, when our operator messaged me about a creditor or the bank calling to speak with senior management, then I'd put my CEO hat back on and a calm, conservative, and solutions-oriented Gary would speak with them about a payment installment solution or similar.

Now, I'm not advocating that you need to create dual personalities to scale your sales team. But I had to do this to quickly shake off the stress and worry triggered by speaking with debt collectors, only to pick up the phone two minutes later to speak with a lead that cost us hundreds of dollars to generate (cash we didn't have). Getting a closed deal was imperative for me.

Being up against the wall like this turned out to be a blessing in disguise. Very quickly I was closing deals at a 60–70 percent conversion rate (one month I closed twenty-one deals from twenty-one leads). This enabled me to set the precedent for success within a now-growing sales department with reps who again had a North Star they could aim toward.

My schedule was brutal. I was up at 4:30 a.m. or 5:00 a.m. every day, hit the gym for an hour, took a quick shower, kissed my daughter goodbye, and arrived at the office by 7:00 a.m. before the first reps showed up. Then I prepared my notes for our daily 7:30 a.m. sales huddle. This behavior, with me directly acting as sales leader, instilled healthy habits among our eight to ten sales reps.

Being there as the first person on the floor, prepped and ready for everyone to show up, kicking off the huddle consistently on time at 7:30 a.m. so that late sales folks would be grilled and ashamed if they showed up late, and getting everyone tuned and ready to perform by training the team every morning—these are ways I led by example.

I always did role-plays, listened together to a recording from a sale made the day before, provided feedback, and had a sales contest with a cash SPIFF payout announced for the top performers of the day. The combination of daily grit, coaching reps, and fueling them with constant motivation and belief were the key elements that took us to profitability within five months (giving me my first salary in six months). Within the next couple of months we climbed to $50,000+ in monthly profits.

Now it was time to scale, so I asked my HR department to find a potential sales supervisor whom I'd mentor and groom to help me take the next step.

As it turned out, finding an experienced digital marketing sales supervisor was nearly impossible in Nicaragua. So instead, I hired a young inexperienced kid, and for the next couple of months I followed my previous agenda, and after 5:00 p.m., I sat with him every day to listen to his calls, coach, do mystery shopping together, calling our competitors, documenting everything, and developing lengthy word-by-word scripts for our reps to follow.

My first script outline was sixteen pages long and included everything from relevant quotes like, *"Half the money I spend on advertising is wasted; the trouble is, I don't know which half"* (when a prospect I was auditing an account for didn't have revenue tracking installed on his advertising campaigns). In addition, I added screenshots and instructions on how to pause the screen-sharing session to then look for opportunities within the prospect's ad account while asking probing questions related to their performance and operations.

All these small lethal details combined enabled me to close deals at ~70 percent month over month when the previous standard was 25–30 percent for our top performers.

SCALE SUCCESSES ONLY—DON'T REPLICATE MEDIOCRITY

- *Forty-eight percent of salespeople never follow up with a prospect.*
- *Twenty-five percent of salespeople give up after the second attempt to contact a prospect, 12 percent after the third attempt, and less than 10 percent of sales reps make more than three contact attempts.*
- *Only 2 percent of sales are made on the first contact, 3 percent on the second contact, 5 percent on the third, and 10 percent on the fourth. Eighty percent of sales are made on the fifth to twelfth contact!*

Let those stats sink in for a second. Now consider how similar numbers would impact your bottom line or even the existence of your company, if you were to pay top dollars for leads only to lose out on 80 percent of the projected sales due to inadequate sales rep behavior and lack of processes.

That's why when I cracked the sales management code back in 2012 and aimed to scale our sales team, I followed my own "Five Elements of Sales Management Success" formula. I believe this played a big part by first mentoring to become our top sales performer and then scaling the sales team from ten reps to nearly fifty reps within eighteen months by 2014.

My Sales Management Success Formula

The following elements of the formula are drawn from my previous company experience as follows:

Daily Morning and Evening Sales Huddles

- **Showcase victories by reps and highlight customer successes.** With a focus on the positive, these motivational activities were almost always part of every huddle. Sales is a tough nut to crack for anyone. Playing recordings of successful calls well handled by a colleague or reading a recent client testimonial are small elements that can go a long way. That's why having both huddles each day is key in my book. Get people ready and fired up in the morning, then send them home by ending the day with a recap and some words of encouragement if needed. Make sure folks leave the office holding their heads high and ready for the next day's battle.
- **Call feedback and collective coaching** was a quick and effective way to get everyone engaged during our huddles. I'd request my sales ops to listen to some calls and pull a recording or two from

my reps each day. I'd then play the calls and pause to probe the team for feedback. This was highly effective because the team came together and shared their experiences. Even the slightly nonchalant top performers would participate eagerly to demonstrate their know-how and provide recommendations of how a prospect's question could have been answered differently or how they would have handled a given scenario. It got to the point where my sales ops had to turn down requests from reps eager to get their calls pulled for feedback, so we created a rotation system.

- **Sharing best practices** was a key element in raising standards and cultivating excellence. I don't believe our sales organization would have developed such high lead conversion rates and grown as fast as we did if it wasn't for this exercise. Too many sales organizations are siloed and best practices aren't distributed frequently and effectively. But by having daily huddles and continuously prioritizing twenty to thirty minutes of coaching in our daily sales meetings produced results. I'd always have a quick whiteboard session or pull up a screenshot of search results, account demos, etc., to run through scenarios with the team and ensure that the sales processes developed were actually understood. Soon enough my team, and especially the top performers, were striving for promotions and would take turns at the whiteboard explaining to the team how to conduct various processes.

Incentive-Based Mentorship Programs

- **Individual coaching amplified via a mentorship model** is a great way to supercharge your coaching efforts while nurturing your sales reps with leadership potential. I've mentioned mentoring programs as an effective method to onboard and train new reps, but in this specific use case, as frequently as possible, I'd make sure to include both the mentor and mentee when providing coaching to the mentee. This way, the mentor would learn how to provide feedback, fully understand the concepts, and then be able to reinforce the coaching later when supporting the mentee. I found that, especially when the mentor focused on process and was ambitious for career growth, they would take an extra active role, and this resulted in an effective farming system to develop new reps as well as sales management protégés.

- **Replicating behaviors and strategies that work** is often the end result of efficiently rolling out mentoring programs. However, the key to success is ensuring that the mentor is following your established sales methodology, best practices, and processes. Now I had several reps, and you most certainly have too, who despite not following your processes verbatim and by doing certain things their own way, get very good results from personalizing select processes and doubling down on their own strengths.

  For example, I had several reps who were masters in asking the right questions that led to many sales but couldn't close deals effectively, yet because of their strong ability to ask burning questions, many deals would come through anyway. Or in another example, a rep was so eloquent in pitch presentation and incredible at building rapport with the prospect that despite below-standard probing and their low volume of sales calls, they would crush their targets. But both scenarios are less than ideal for mentorship models. Ideally you want to pair up new reps with experienced reps who follow processes to a tee so that the new ones adopt all your best practices, thereby increasing the new sales rep success ratio within your organization.

- **Fostering organizational development and promoting from within** is, as discussed in Chapter 7, a hyper-effective way to develop talent and mitigate sales rep attrition which otherwise can be devastating for growth for many sales teams. Add specific KPIs that define success to the mentor program so it's not just a "fluffy big brother" support element but rather goal-oriented and with mutual benefits, considering that an experienced rep has to sacrifice some of their highly valuable call and client activities to support their mentee. If constructed in a fashion where everyone wins and you compensate accordingly for the successes, you dramatically increase the odds of scaling successfully. If, like I did, you include mentoring programs in your sales career development plans for experienced reps eager to advance up your career ladder, you can supercharge your organizational development.

Leading by Example

- **First in and last out of the office** is a non-negotiable element of a sales leader in my book. You need a general who, like William Wallace in the movie *Braveheart*, doesn't command his troops to go to war with force and from behind but rather mobilizes them forward every time by being there and riding into battle head-on. Immediately after my sales huddle kicked things off, instead of going to my desk to answer emails or look at reports, I always tried to make it a priority to pick up the phone and make some calls to encourage the same behavior and get my sales troops to attack the phones as well. The same goes for the end of day. As the boss, many feel rightfully entitled to leave early or focus on other activities. However, few things are as powerful for sales department morality and loyalty as having a sales leader who sticks around to help close a late-evening deal or provide support with an important proposal that has to get out.

- **Crushing targets and going above and beyond** to hit department targets should be evident for any sales leader, but too often many hide behind their past results and glory, relying on their team to do all the selling. You always want your sales leaders to stay active with their own selling. For me, it fuels a level of confidence that money can't buy. Your reps genuinely respect you for it and more eagerly "go to war" with you daily to help get the results for your company. I know of many sales leaders who instead apply fear-based management tactics and rely only on carrot-and-stick motivation strategies to get their reps to perform. That never works in the long run and is often a result of the sales leader's fears of failing, not coming through, or being beaten performance-wise by his reps. All such egocentric behaviors mean you have the wrong sales leader at the helm of your sales department. You want a leader who *loves* the hustle, day in and day out, alone and with their reps, ready to do whatever means necessary to meet and exceed targets.

- **Developing a winning culture** is cultivated best when starting at the top and trickling down throughout your sales organization. Winning means never quitting, always doing your best, and constantly pushing the limits. Just because you hit targets and you're a success doesn't mean winning. You want a sales leader and culture developed from asking questions like "How could we have done better this month?" or "Did we really maximize the potential of this opportunity?" This behavior can only be fostered if it comes genuinely from your sales leadership. If instilled properly, this can boost your growth beyond expectations since continuously raising the bar with such questions make you outcompete most competitors and set new standards for your industry.

Documenting and Developing Processes for Success

- **Sales methodologies and lead scoring** are needed to create standardized processes, implement systems, and establish expectations that can be scaled across a larger or growing sales department. You may have initial success without this in place, but I guarantee things evolve into anarchy and complete chaos if you don't grab the bull by the horns and establish standards and guidelines. I implement my own combination of "The Challenger Sale," "Spin Selling," and "Consultative Selling" as methodologies. For lead qualification criteria, I initially used BANT and, later on, MEDDIC. But I continuously experiment and am flexible. However, my reps knew what to do, what was expected, and what language to speak when it came to what to do, how to do it, and what the benchmarks were. This only comes into place if you make a deliberate effort to develop and document your processes into standardized guidelines.

- **Script development, pitch eloquence, and rebuttal library** are unmerciful ongoing required elements that go hand in hand with success in scaling any sales department. Developing and maintaining these is one of the quickest and most effective ways you can make an impact on your reps' ability to meet their quotas. Of course it's not a one-trick pony, and if your sales activities and metrics aren't up to par with standards, a perfect script or demo outline won't do the trick. But *success does leave clues*, in any profession or trade, if you replicate the approach, process, and delivery of your sales scripts and messaging down to the smallest details and effectively roll out across your team, you'll very quickly see previously underperforming reps turn up the heat and begin hitting quotas.

The key here is not to just incorporate what you think sounds best, most impressive, or is most effective but rather to use statistical validation of the data and language to incorporate into your pitch. Very often we are dazzled by lengthy phrases that sound great, so we include them in our pitch and messaging in a speech-like fashion, but the reality is that sometimes less is more and another choice of words is more effective. Personally I like to use Conversational Intelligence software and tools such as Gong.io to identify pitch patterns that move the needle and then incorporate them into call scripts and rebuttals to roll out across the department in a unified fashion.

- **Metrics-driven coaching with daily reports for visibility on performance** is needed if you want a structured and systematic approach to growing your sales team. Numbers don't lie. If you make it a habit to go less with your gut feeling as a sales manager and always study the metrics before conducting your one-on-one weekly sales coaching or feedback sessions, then you'll get better adoption and effort to improve by your team. They'll see the correlation in the data to areas you're motivating them to improve, whether it's their prospecting efficiency, demo-to-close success rates, or ability to upsell deals or create a sense of urgency to shorten their sales cycles if significantly longer than your department benchmarks. Using data to demonstrate the opportunity for improvement, to compare with benchmarks, and to establish targets for what success looks like makes your coaching and constructive criticism quantifiable and much more likely to be embraced by your sales reps.

Focus on highest-impact activities

- Spending most of your time coaching middle and top performers is something I took on or adapted to sales after reading Winning. In his bestselling book, Jack Welch highlights the importance of nurturing a superior performance work environment that helped him maintain very high standards while he was at the reins of GE. I believe that Welch's 20-70-10 rule is highly applicable to sales leadership and is a surefire way for you to boost performance within your sales team.

  Too many sales leaders, including yours truly previously, fall victim to spending most of their limited and valuable coaching resources trying to get underperformers (the 10 percent) to perform. The downside is in ignoring or undermining the impact of focusing on top performers (the 20 percent) to have them advance their performance, be motivated, and grow into more senior sales positions, while also creating a structured coaching system to get your middle performers (the 70 percent) developed toward the 20 percent top-performing levels. From my experience, this change in coaching effort can 10x your growth and revenue almost overnight while helping the underperformers if you document and coach them on the successful methods of your top 20 percent along the way.

- Prioritizing helping to advance larger deals goes hand in hand with my previous point regarding where to spend most of your time. It's a nonintrusive way to effectively support your high-performing reps, establish your credibility and respect as a sales leader, and make a significant impact to your company's bottom line. As your team grows larger, this can only be accomplished by having an automated pipeline review management process in place. With this, you can proactively intervene and support reps when they need help without them being consciously aware of the need to seek help in closing the deal. If you master this process, the positive ripple effects within your sales organization can be tremendous since you'll fuel new levels of excitement and motivation by constantly pushing deals across the finish line, fueling the sensation of success for your reps.

Identifying sales collateral that can make a high impact on your sales process should, as mentioned in Chapter 6, be a collaborative effort with your marketing team. However, make no mistake, your sales leader should take the lead with this initiative. He/she has the pole position when it comes to identifying opportunities for collateral creation that can really move the needle and its adoption among your teams. These might include product explainers or pitch inclusions to frequently asked questions or client success stories with ROI stats. Your marketing team is a tremendous resource for successful execution by creating a strong collateral library. This is most effective if your sales leader is deeply in tune with your sales process and working in the trenches with your sales reps. That way, valuable content and support vehicles for quota attainment can be created.

> *Winning means never quitting, always doing your best,*
> *and constantly pushing the limits.*

Inspired by Maslow's hierarchy of needs that shapes human behavior, we can think of a Sales Manager's need structure in a similar fashion:

A Sales Manager's Hierarchy of Needs

- Caffeine
- Tools, training, and incentives in place for scale
- Tech stack aligned with sales process
- Organized framework and processes
- Enriched lead list and database management
- Realistic targets and resources for execution
- An engaged team and culture buy-in

CREATING YOUR SALES PLAYBOOK

At this point in developing your company's revenue engine—you've identified your sales methodologies, lead qualification criteria, developed scripts, email sequences, and much more—it's time to document everything and put it into writing by creating your Sales Playbook.

In simple terms, your Sales Playbook is your one-stop resource for all the critical information that enables your sales reps to follow your established best practices and maximize your performance as you aim to scale your sales organization.

Just like you want a standardized new sales rep onboarding process, you've now matured your sales process and department to such a degree that for you to add sales managers and directors to the equation, you need a streamlined overview of your go-to-market approach. This is obviously not an easy task since you need to consider almost everything and anything that goes into your sales process. Without it, much will be left to guesswork for your team, and that can be a breeding ground for bad habits that you want to avoid at all costs. Now that you've finally addressed most of your critical sales management requirements, your continued growth is "simply" a matter of replicating success and adding team members at the same level of efficiency as when you were just a small team.

The scope of your ideal Sales Playbook may arguably vary and I've seen quite a few versions over the years. My first playbooks were boiled down to a handful of steps and suggested processes that left much room for interpretation and imagination when it came to best practices. Slowly but surely, by a series of trial and error and with many lost opportunities later, I've now developed what I consider to be a comprehensive Sales Playbook Framework which I've rolled out in quite a few companies by now, either as an owner or consultant.

There are many ways to go about crafting your Sales Playbook. I've made many attempts at creating playbooks for companies large and small across a variety of verticals, and as a universal recommendation, I encourage you to develop it as a joint initiative with several stakeholders in the company, including your reps, sales ops team, and marketing. The more people you get involved and the more they participate in sharing best practices, the more likely you are to attain full buy-in for what becomes your sales department's operations manual.

Here's an outline of the topics I usually recommend including in your company's Sales Playbook:

1. Company overview
2. Organization chart and responsibilities
3. Solution overview
4. Sales process and customer journey overview
5. Key performance indicators and sales metrics
6. Lead qualification criteria and disqualification process
7. Buyer persona overview
8. Elevator pitch, USPs, and value proposition
9. Research to conduct prior to each sales call
10. Call scripts for each stage of the process, e.g. discovery call, demo call, presentation call, and close call
11. Suggested questions for every step in the sales process
12. Common objections and rebuttal library
13. Email sequences, templates, and snippets
14. Solution demo samples
15. Deal agreement samples and negotiation tactics
16. Competition overview
17. Overview of marketing resources and sales enablement materials
18. Training schedule and sales career development paths
19. Tech stack manuals
20. Compensation plan and commission structure

The Characteristics of a Superstar Sales Manager

"Never promote your best salesperson to be your sales manager." I'm sure you've heard or read that a few times over your career. And truth be told, when dealing with the entire process of designing, building, and scaling a sales team, together with everything else that goes along with it, I've found that

hiring or developing sales managers has been one of the most challenging tasks of all.

I've made all the mistakes possible in this arena. I've promoted my best sales rep to be my sales manager, only to not equip him with appropriate support and coaching. I just assumed that he'd develop his managerial skillset as easily as he did his sales talents that made him my selected candidate in the first place. The outcome led to mutual frustration, poor performance, a setback in sales team morale, and unfortunately, me letting go of an otherwise highly talented sales rep who was a pure rainmaker.

Conversely, on several occasions I've looked outside my organizations to bring on sales leadership and must painfully admit that here also, with a few exceptions, things quickly went south and soured almost every time. And at nearly every occasion, the scenario played out the same way. I identified a sales manager candidate from the same industry, usually working at a larger competing company, who could benefit from transitioning by taking a step up the career ladder and perhaps grow from Sales Manager to Sales Director or from Director to VP. Often I was impressed with the candidate's know-how and maybe even a little wowed by the many suggestions or ideas they brought to the table of new things we could implement during the interview process. Then, sadly, every time after just three to six months of tenure in the new role, the outcome was the same. The fit was just not there. It was only a matter of time before we parted ways.

This scenario is equally painful as the first one of promoting my best sales rep. Often I'd have to dig very deep in my pockets to incentivize the career transition of an otherwise highly successful sales leader in my current organization.

So what did I do wrong? In the first scenario I mistakenly assessed the best sales rep based on their *sales* skills and expected that we'd develop the *managerial* skills sooner or later—wrong. Even after having done it a couple of times without success—each time ramping up the support elements, leadership training, and promotion criteria—it went sideways quickly. I finally began to run experiments. This time I looked for sales *leadership* characteristics to develop *within* my top 20 percent performers instead of purely *sales* performance. And there is a big difference, as I learned.

In the second scenario, which occurred many times over my last twenty years building companies, the negative result happened so often that frankly now, I'm not an advocate of hiring externally for such positions. In fact, I'll do it *only* as a very last resort. From my experience, at least in my scenarios, there was always a big gap in culture and methodologies, despite my rigorous hiring process. Worse still, there was always a big difference in how they were used to running things and what we needed within our sales organization.

If they transitioned from a larger competing company, they often had entirely different expectations when it came to what sales execution meant and the support required from marketing, sales ops, admin, etc. They were used to following processes to a tee but didn't have the intuitiveness to create things, run experiments, and roll up their sleeves to architect, develop, and then scale things. They were used to getting directives on what was expected, how to do it, and then just execute accordingly. And these principles and behaviors were often so ingrained that it was almost impossible to alter the course of how they did things.

These experiences underlie why to this day I hold the very strong opinion that *a founder should rarely give up control of their sales strategy and development*; that is of course contingent on whether, like myself, they have acquired the skills to do so in the first place.

Obviously, this isn't the case for most founders, and not always can you rely on finding a golden match co-founder (as described in Chapter 5, that's not an easy task). So what's the right approach to take when it's time to build out your sales team and develop your first sales leader(s)?

What Managers Think Reps Want

Confidence · Organization · Processes · Rewards · Time Management · Communication

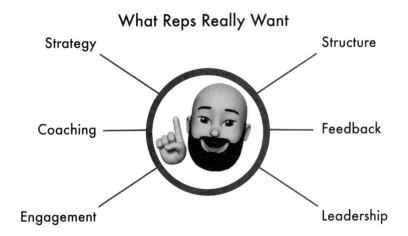

What Reps Really Want

Strategy · Structure · Coaching · Feedback · Engagement · Leadership

The Ten Sales Manager Traits to Look for
When Promoting from Within

I've just established how difficult it is to find or develop a superstar sales manager. And many would argue that certain other characteristics I've identified are necessary for the makings of a great sales leader. However, with the goal of making it realistic to find someone suited from within to promote and develop, I've prioritized the following ten characteristics. Why? So you don't get stuck trying to chase down the golden goose and instead "just" search for some good eggs that you can hatch.

1. **Great Coaching Abilities:** This is the number one trait I look for, having clearly established that the buck doesn't stop after new rep onboarding. Sales coaching is, if there's any such thing, the only element I'd categorize as the "secret sauce" when it comes to sales management efficacy. And I break it down into three aspects:

   a. **Integrated and Ongoing:** Coaching should be a part of your sales manager's weekly check-ins with reps. Don't just talk about quotas, metrics, or lead quality/quantity. Feedback is what makes the difference! This includes regularly listening in on calls, doing call reviews at all stages of the cycle, and win-loss analyses.

   b. **Skills and Product-focused:** Although product training is important, sales skills often trump product knowledge. Make sure your manager is spending enough time teaching reps the psychology of selling (as I discussed in Chapter 2) and not just dump marketing collateral in their laps. We all know that emotions affect purchasing decisions, so make sure to teach your reps the triggers and how to move the needle forward with appropriate persuasion techniques and establishing authority with prospects.

   c. **Customized Training:** Whether you hire a training firm or use in-house specialists (the latter being my strong preference), your sales training program should always be specific to your product, market, *and* company values. Furthermore, I recommend you lay out and document the *entire* training curriculum for your sales team—that is, from onboarding as BDR to AE—so you don't limit the growth trajectory of high-potential, talented, and ambitious new hires.

2. **Emotionally Intelligent:** Hiring or promoting a sales rep to sales leadership without them having a good portion of emotional intelligence (EQ) is a surefire way to unwittingly boost your sales rep attrition. You must hire a candidate who can manage a diverse team of sales individuals with different personalities, needs, desires, and emotions. The right sales leader earns loyalty and commitment from his/her team by showing empathy and reacting appropriately based on their reps' individual needs. Your manager must also be able to leverage this connection to develop improved strategies, predict better outcomes, and increase the effectiveness of the overall team. After all, it's people, usually with high levels of emotion and motivation, that make up the core ingredient of any sales team. *People come before your processes and systems.*

3. **Confident and Courageous:** This is another non-negotiable trait of your future sales leader. They, with utmost certainty, will be navigating stormy seas at a daily level and have to always communicate confidence and strong leadership abilities. And this even when behind on quota for the third consecutive month with senior management breathing down their necks, inflation hitting the market more than ever, or when the competition is killing you. They must convey complete certainty that we overcome this—fear not, we shall pass the stormy weather, and things get better. And despite being up against the wall, a great sales leader knows how to request the change and growth needed from their team members so that solutions are solved collectively. Not an easy task, but without these abilities, rest assured some sales leader from

another organization in growth mode will be able to persuade your reps to jump ship, promising a better environment with more stability and opportunities for career advancement.

4. **Master of Motivation:** Both at a departmental level and also individually, understanding how to trigger the best development of the hand you've been dealt is key for a sales manager. Very often, almost hourly throughout the day, with the ability to juggle and prioritize a million different things, top sales leaders aim to bring out the best in every team member. How? By supporting and motivating them through focusing on their people's *strengths over weaknesses*. Even at the heart of distress during challenging times, your sales leader must convey confidence and always be calm, cool, and collected so their team doesn't lose faith and motivation.

5. **Powerful Recruiter:** This is likely one of the more frequently overlooked skills when looking for a sales leader that can drive growth for your company. We introduced in Chapter 4 the concept of "First Who, Then What" by Jim Collins and in Chapter 7 the common challenges of hiring, developing, and retaining sales talent to mitigate the otherwise financially disastrous impact to your bottom line of low sales rep engagement and continued high turnover. Although you have the support of your talent recruitment team and leadership to source talent, I've always looked for a sales leader who single-handedly can attract the very best available sales talent.

6. **Great Communicator:** I never ignore this quality in a sales leader who is supposed to double or triple your growth by rallying the troops and making them go above and beyond expectations. I'm not just talking about their communication abilities with clients or closing deals. More importantly, there will be countless

complicated and challenging messages to communicate to your team as you embark on your sales department growth trajectory. Changes to comp plans, raised targets, price changes, unexpected external challenges such as market conditions that impact performance, new competition entering the market, or a change in leadership within your company all need to be effectively communicated. The right leader knows how to present the core facts to their reps while focusing on the opportunities in each situation that come your way. This is a talent that few possess. Needless to say, it can change things for the better when done right since the sales leader empowers the team to be fully accountable for its successes *and* failures by communicating properly and setting the right expectations. However, the inability to communicate successfully can have a profoundly negative impact on your reps' morale and performance. So do not, at any cost, overlook this criterion.

7. **Analytical and Data-driven:** In today's marketplace, this is another key requisite to developing a sales team. Sure, emotional intelligence and motivation go a long way to help reps, but a sales leader who can support their decision making with strong data as evidence will far more likely be able to get buy-in from their team. By being analytical in their thought process, they can usually ask the right questions, despite not necessarily having all the answers, and thereby get support and engagement from their team. That's the definition of true leadership for me—asking the right questions and getting everyone involved. You don't want the know-it-all superstar who always pretends to have answers for every scenario. And this also goes for your candidate's knowledge of sales tech and ability to extract data for decision making. Last,

by being better at analyzing gaps and opportunities for improvement, sales leaders are better equipped to facilitate change by making things easier and launching coaching and process development initiatives where needed to close the gaps.

8. **Experienced in Sales:** Critical but maybe not as good as your top performer. It can't be their first rodeo, and they must have been at least a top 20 percent performer. I've tried before to hire external candidates with strong operational, leadership, and communication skills, but if your sales leaders lack sales abilities, they'll have a hard time with (a) gaining respect from their team members and (b) their coaching approach, which may often lack some intangibles that are hard to detect but result in less favorable outcomes.

9. **Excellent Time Manager:** This is arguably right up there with coaching abilities. Pipeline reviews, motivational pep talks, sales huddles, hiring, cross-collaboration with other departments, sales admin work, and a hundred more tasks will overwhelm the inexperienced candidate who lacks the ability to continually prioritize and organize their agenda for maximum efficiency. Quite often there simply aren't enough hours in the day to get everything done. This is almost a deal breaker attribute if you're looking for a sales leader who can make the desired impact without crumbling under pressure or in no time being overworked and overloaded.

10. **High Integrity:** This means doing the right thing always, including when people aren't looking. And in a competitive stressful environment like sales, it can be tempting at times to take a shortcut or loosen your standards. Integrity is something that goes a long way in leadership and in getting team members to follow you

in both the good and the challenging times. After all, if you stay consistent with what you preach and your corresponding actions, you will eventually gain the deserved respect from your team. And this often substitutes greatly for any other attributes your sales leader may be lacking.

Below is an overview of ten attributes that your ideal Sales Manager should embody. Instead of looking to bring in an external candidate with proven experience, aim to identify internal candidates with such attributes, then promote from within, and develop him/her into your superstar Sales Manager.

Key Sales Manager Attributes

1. Great Coaching Abilities
2. Emotionally Intelligent
3. Confident and Courageous
4. Master of Motivation
5. Powerful Recruiter
6. Great Communicator
7. Analytical and Data-Driven
8. Experienced in Sales
9. Excellent Time Manager
10. High Integrity

With this overview, I hope I've equipped you with learnings and guidance on what to look for in your next superstar Sales Manager so that you can avoid the costly mistake of selecting the wrong candidate.

Now let's take a look in Chapter 9 at what it takes for you to create a lead generation engine that can supercharge the growth of your team, including how to build personalized sequences that invoke strong interest with prospects, how to deploy multiple channels in combination, and how to leverage sales collateral that triggers high reply rates and interest.

9

THE RIGHT MESSAGE, TO THE RIGHT PEOPLE, AT THE RIGHT TIME

*An invaluable playbook on how to
cut through today's noise and get your message
across to your prospective new clients.
And from a new client acquisition standpoint,
it makes sure you spend your limited and highly
valuable time catching the right people.*

I had a lightbulb moment back in 2019 when, at my last company, I successfully rolled out a channel sales program in the form of a white label offering. Up until that point, I had sold digital advertising solutions across a wide range of industries in B2B, B2C, SMB, and Enterprise. But I had never sold solutions to our previous competitors—other marketing agencies.

In less than two years, I managed to onboard 120+ resellers of all shapes and sizes. Some were conventional marketing agencies, others creative agencies, quite a few SEO agencies, and of course, many paid search agencies like ourselves.

But now they were no longer competitors of ours. Instead, they had become strategic partners. So potentially were the hundreds of other agencies in my pipeline with whom I had a close dialogue exploring ways for us to establish a mutually beneficial partnership model. At a reduced cost, we could fulfill their clients' campaigns on Google and Bing, and they would mark up the cost of our white label service 2–3x. Their clients would get subject matter experts to support PPC management via their existing agency, and Google and Bing would see growth in otherwise non-existing or stagnated PPC portfolios. The true definition of a win-win-win-win scenario!

This also meant that the barriers and secrecy I otherwise previously experienced when attending quarterly partner summits at Google or Microsoft and connecting with other agencies were completely removed. Now we had a common objective, and we were there not to indirectly compete but rather to help each other.

As we rolled out the program, I anticipated that the majority of our approximately 120 marketing agency partners would look to us mainly for support with account management. But after speaking with hundreds of marketing agencies, rolling out partner satisfaction surveys, and probing how we could help our marketing agency partners with growth, many instead asked for our assistance with lead generation and new client acquisition. I was baffled.

I knew after having worked with 5,000+ direct advertisers over the last decade that most B2C and B2B companies had challenges with lead and demand generation (at least at a profitable rate). But to learn that even the vast majority of *marketing agencies*, the ones supposed to help other companies with their lead generation efforts, also identified lead generation and getting new customers as their number one growth constraint was a real eye-opener!

The more I investigated this, I learned that other tech and platform companies—for example, WordStream or CallRail, which also had an agency-focused business model—reported similar results. Below is a snapshot of a WordStream report supporting my finding that 63 percent of marketing agencies find their biggest challenge is acquiring new clients.

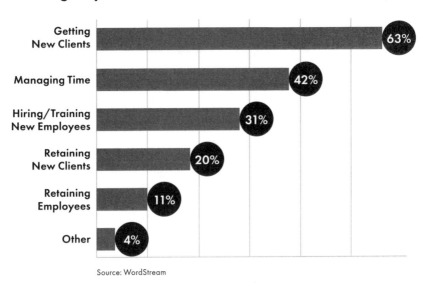

What Are the Biggest Business Challenges Your Agency Will Face this Year?

Source: WordStream

This is further supported by HubSpot data showing that 61 percent of marketers rank lead generation as their number one challenge.

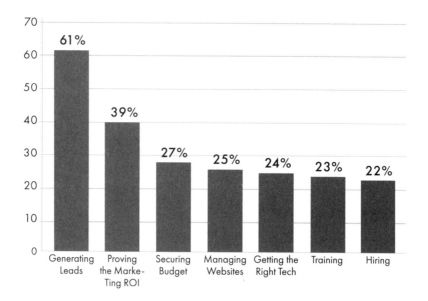

Biggest Lead Generation Challenge
Company's top marketing challenges

Equally surprising was my discovery of how few of our agency partners relied on "practicing what they preached" when it came to generating leads and acquiring new customers. In my partner surveys, I was shocked to learn that less than 2 percent of our agencies cost-effectively used PPC advertising or SEO to generate leads for their own sales reps. The vast majority lacked a structured effort and were therefore relying on outbound methods, such as cold calls and emails, to acquire new business.

My findings were again supported by partner surveys conducted by other channel sales companies, such as the snapshot on the following page of WordStream's 2020 "The State of the Internet Marketing Agency Report," where combined online marketing efforts across all channels account for only 20 percent of lead generation sources.

What Is Your Agency's Main Source of Acquiring New Clients?

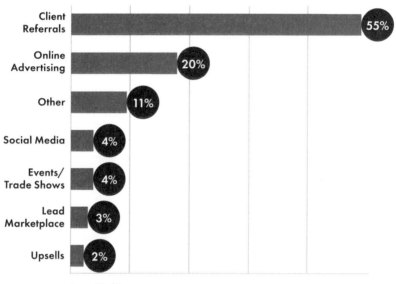

Source: WordStream

I now realized I was on to something and why we had been fortunate to grow our book of business exponentially over the previous years. I had cracked the code on outreach campaign efforts after a lot of trial and error. And even though that helped us reach the status as one of the fastest growing companies in the United States four years in a row, it was also what supercharged the growth of our agency partner model—sophisticated outreach campaigns at super-low cost. *Contacting the right people, with the right message, at the right time*—this was a huge differentiating factor to other players who, unlike us, would sit and wait around for client referrals or have moderate outreach campaign efforts that they never managed to scale due to inefficiencies.

In the next sections, I'll break down step by step how you can create a similar hyper-profitable outreach campaign strategy that can support your inbound marketing efforts and rocket-fuel your growth.

DON'T PITCH THE BITCH

A scene from the movie *Boiler Room* (2000) clearly stands out in my memory of sales movies, and I watched it dozens of times back in my early twenties when starting my sales career. Nicky Katt, playing Greg Weinstein, instructs his new sales protégé, Giovanni Ribisi, played by Seth Davis, saying:

"We don't sell stock to women. It's just not worth it. Don't pitch the bitch."

And although the context here is highly discriminating and sexist, it does take on the same level of importance when conducting a highly effective B2B demand-generation campaign. You want to make sure you're only pitching relevant people by crafting a hyper-customized message tailored specifically to that persona. Despite it being an automated email sent to hundreds of somewhat similar prospects, it's so effective and targeted that you're never ever "pitching the bitch."

And building a strong lead list is, in my opinion, one of the most important tasks for you to take on as a founder or sales leader in order to ensure success with your sales and company. It all starts with leads, and without the right ones, you'll never gain any traction with your sales process.

DEMAND GENERATION VERSUS
LEAD GENERATION

Before we dive into ways to solicit interest for your business, let's clarify two popular concepts: demand generation and lead generation. I hear these terms thrown around loosely by sales and marketing folks. Even business

THE ZERO TO 100 MILLION SALES BLUEPRINT

owners and startup founders often get confused when they explain to me how they intend to ramp up their new client acquisition strategy.

You see, demand generation and lead generation are two completely different beasts each requiring different strategies and efforts depending on the size of your company, position in the market, and marketing budget. The following diagram illustrates this difference.

Demand Generation vs. Lead Generation

Demand Generation

Top of the funnel marketing activities to increase brand awareness and create interest in your business.

Lead Generation

Bottom of the funnel marketing activities to drive leads from prospects with a high commercial intent.

A limited marketing budget may call for a lead generation campaign where you aim to capture prospects at the bottom of the funnel when they're specifically searching for your services or products. These are usually high-buying-intent search queries where the buyer knows specifically what they are looking for but are searching for vendor alternatives, customer reviews, promotions, bundles, etc., before they end up selecting a company to make their purchase.

A very common setup for such a lead generation approach could be a paid search campaign with Google Ads or Microsoft Ads using carefully selected keywords targeting only search queries that indicate a strong commercial intent by the searcher/prospective buyer. This approach can secure a very strong ROAS and ROI, but the flip side is often limited lead volume and growth opportunities. Also, you're targeting the absolute bottom of the funnel, which is often crowded, shark-infested, Red Ocean waters where you'll compete on price against a series of competitors.

Data from "Search Advertising Benchmarks," a 2022 report by WordStream, shows that competitive sectors like Legal Services, Business Services, or Dentistry, for example, run advertisers' cost-per-lead prices of $80+. From my experience, this is usually on the very low end resulting in a high volume of disqualified leads with low conversion rates. This means that with lead conversion rates of 5–10 percent, it costs a business between $800 and $1,600 per new customer they acquire with this lead generation method.

Conversely, if your company has an adequate marketing budget, a demand generation campaign may be better suited, especially if you're aiming to grow your customer base and market share through new client acquisitions.

Now, I'm a big advocate of running paid search campaigns, but I would never ever put all my eggs in one basket and depend for my business growth on fluctuating advertising costs combined with the uncertainty of rising prices. Nor would I compete solely on budget against larger companies/advertisers with deeper pockets.

Now you're probably wondering: what the heck is the solution, Gary? The answer—a combination of top-of-the-funnel campaigns such as paid social media, programmatic, display, and YouTube advertising, along with paid search, content creation, and a strong account-based marketing strategy, can do wonders to fuel your new customer acquisition efforts.

The Larger Upper-Funnel Opportunity

First we need to understand that the marketing strategy most companies rely on targets running ad campaigns highlighting their core features, benefits, credibility statements, and pricing. However, this effectively communicates to only 3 percent of the market. That's the audience actively searching for a solution like yours and ready to purchase sooner than later.

In Jeremy Miller's book *Sticky Branding*, he expands on this model and breaks down your audiences into segments according to which buying stage they're in. Steve Richard of B2B sales training firm Vorsight also elaborates on the concept that only 3 percent of your market is actively buying, 56 percent are not ready, and 40 percent are poised to begin. And there are many other marketing books such as *Sell Like Crazy* by Sabri Suby with stats that showcase similar data of only ~3 percent of your target market being actively in the process of purchasing.

From my experience, percentages for the marketing funnel fluctuate greatly depending on your geo, industry, price point of solutions offered, and level of competition. The following classic marketing funnel demonstrates where your sales and marketing efforts should take place if you aim to create a truly scalable, predictable, and profitable client acquisition strategy by effectively targeting the entire upper funnel of your prospective customers.

In summary, you need to decipher cost-effective ways to effectively engage the 97 percent of your target market who are currently either unaware of having a need for your solutions, not interested, have an intent, or considering it but not yet committed to allotting a budget to purchase from you. The following graphic illustrates the marketing funnel.

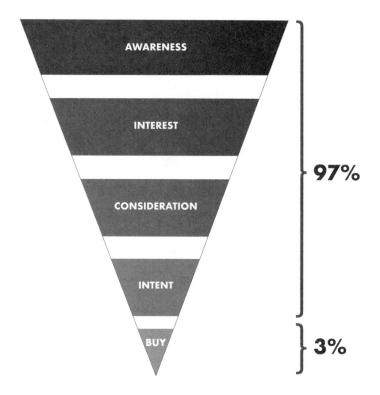

The V12 Engine in
Your Demand Generation Machine

So what's the first step in creating a sophisticated and highly cost-effective outreach campaign?

Remember those exercises we conducted in great detail during Chapter 3? Failing to prepare is preparing to fail. Now is the time again to apply all this intelligence when building out your "Lead Inventory Depository." In other words, combine all the insights learned while collecting your firmographic, demographic, and psychographic data, buyer personas, competitor intelligence, USPs, and value proposition. Putting this together in a structured fashion will supercharge your new client acquisition efforts.

At a high level, the idea is for you to lay the groundwork to begin a multichannel outreach strategy that is powered with the right content marketing tactics. And by groundwork, I mean begin building a highly segmented lead list of target prospects that (a) meet your ICP criteria and (b) can benefit greatly from your solutions, even though they aren't fully aware of it yet—that is, the 97 percent of your target audience.

To show you concrete examples, I'll give you two use cases of how I designed such processes and outreach models with my former marketing agency for (a) our direct sales business selling digital marketing services to direct advertisers such as dentists, lawyers, and home builders and (b) our subsequent reseller channel sales business model selling white label PPC services to other marketing agencies.

But before I run off and say that outreach campaigns don't work or that SEO, content creation, and inbound marketing is the holy grail, let me assure you of two things:

1. As a marketer with many companies under my belt, and having managed hundreds of millions of dollars in media spend, the single most effective and profitable customer acquisition strategy has always been outreach, i.e., email and social media messaging, coupled with traditional snail mails and occasional phone calls. Note that this does *not* involve cold-calling but is used when alerts from sales enablement tools like Outreach or Salesloft provide notifications that your prospect has opened emails several times, forwards them to team members within their organization, and/ or opened attached sales and marketing collateral more than xx times. These are all triggers indicating some interest, and only then is it the right time to efficiently call your prospect. Traditional cold-calling has been dead for a number of years (recall

how I told you in Chapter 1 how I, back in 2017, had to bite the bullet and let go of thirty-five hardworking loyal telemarketers because the ROI from cold-calling had simply deteriorated beyond profitability).

2. Most B2B, SaaS, and savvy marketing companies rely on outreach as their primary acquisition tool. Yes, they all complement this with digital ad campaigns, SEO, social media, and so forth, but they understand that the *engine* is outreach.

To support my notion, I also refer to a recent study conducted by McKinsey & Co. showing that *email marketing is forty times more effective* at reaching your target customers than social media.

When I run marketing campaigns for my own companies, I refer to outreach and paid search being the twelve-cylinder engine in my sports car. Social media campaigns, SEO, content creation, etc., are important in the equation, but they are merely the nice, shiny wax on that car. They make it look good, attractive, slick, and intriguing to engage with, but without the V12 engine, I ain't going anywhere!

The image on the following page is a survey result from SaaStr, the world's largest community for business software, regarding how inbound versus outbound contributes to the revenue generation of their members. The table shows the percentage of revenue in the left column and the percentage of responses in the right column.

SaaStr
22,716 followers
4d · 🌐

What percent of your revenue come from outbound sales?

What percent of your revenue comes from outbound?

The author can see how you vote. Learn more

0%. All inbound.	11%
10%. Mostly inbound.	18%
20%-30% ✔	18%
30%-50% + outbound.	53%

1,607 votes · 2d left · Undo

Case Study #1: 125–150 new clients per month at <$500 CPA

At this stage of our company, our growth had derived primarily from two quite rudimentary customer acquisition tactics. The primary driver was a predictive dialer solution (VanillaSoft) with features such as autodialing, voicemail drop, and smart caller ID. But other than this dialer technology, our sales approach was almost equivalent to my first outbound sales projects back in 1999!

The second main acquisition tactic was running Google Ads campaigns (known then as Google AdWords) on highly competitive exact-match keyword phrases like [google ads agency] or [free google ads audit] or [ppc agency]. They converted pretty well, but leads cost us upward of $500–$700 with a CPA per client of $1,500+. We spent hundreds of thousands of dollars some months and were in the red unless the client stayed with us for a minimum of six to seven months (break even).

So the objective in rolling out a more sophisticated outreach strategy was to generate more predictability, combat our stagnant growth (customer churn now equaled new client acquisitions), and support our otherwise struggling SDR team.

The current SDR efforts were quite siloed or one-dimensional, meaning that we predominantly engaged with prospects via cold-calling with little support from our marketing team. For lack of a better term, it was a "smile and dial" sales operation.

Here is the project plan that I developed and as written back in 2017:

Outreach 2.0—Project Description

Objective: With the launch of our new outreach project, we aim to unify all demand generation efforts and push in the same direction as follows:

1. **Our Data Entry Team** supports the sales process by expanding its contribution and post-lead assignment to create various performance status reports and information we can send out through email sequences (and LinkedIn Sales Navigator) to trigger a need to speak with one of our SDRs.

2. **Our Content Marketing Team** orchestrates and creates content (i.e., articles, white papers, ebooks, videos, and infographics) to be included in our email marketing outreach efforts that underline our thought leadership in PPC/SEO and educate prospective clients on the need to improve their current digital marketing strategy and to consider our solutions.

3. **Our Marketing Team** creates webinars and events aligned with the targeted vertical and geos selected by our CRO. Webinar recordings and event invitations will be used for our email outreach efforts.

4. **Our In-House PPC Campaign Manager** supports the outreach process by using the collected emails for SDRs to run customer match campaigns via Google AdWords, Facebook, LinkedIn, and Twitter. This effort, combined with email and cold-calling, will provide a 360-degree approach to our outreach efforts.

5. **Our SDRs continue to call out** simultaneously while we market to prospects and run various customer match and retargeting campaigns, all aligned in a sequence to improve our outreach process, consume fewer leads, and ultimately yield better call-to-appointment ratios.

Based on research into best practices for sales development and outreach campaigns provided by TOPO, we aim to launch the following multichannel outreach strategy with xx interactions over xx business days and leverage various content as attachments to our emails and LinkedIn messages. Simultaneously, while conducting outreach, we have enabled remarketing and customer match campaigns via Google AdWords, YouTube Ads, and Facebook to create a sense of familiarity with our brand *before* they receive an email, call, or LinkedIn message from us. The diagram on the following page illustrates the steps and timeline of the outreach sequence.

Direct Sales Outreach Sequence (18 steps over 48 days)

Day 1

✉ **Step 1** - Email - SEO optimizer report

in **Step 2** - LinkedIn connection request

Day 2

📞 **Step 3** - Call - no voicemail

Day 5

✉ **Step 4** - Email - local listing report

Day 6

in **Step 5** - LinkedIn InMail

Day 10

✉ **Step 6** - Email - test my site / Think with Google report

Day 11

📞 **Step 7** - Call - voicemail

Day 14

✉ **Step 8** - Email - credibility content

Day 17

in **Step 9** - LinkedIn - post comment

Day 20

✉ **Step 10** - Email - US Hispanic opportunity

Day 21

📞 **Step 11** - Call - no voicemail

Day 28

✉ **Step 12** - Email - Google Adwords ROI LTV calculator

in **Step 13** - LinkedIn - post comment

Day 32

✉ **Step 14** - Email - Bing Ads campaign expansion

Day 40

✉ **Step 15** - Email - case study (industry specific)

Day 45

in **Step 16** - LinkedIn - post comment

Day 47

✉ **Step 17** - Email - tech and digital indicators

Day 48

📞 **Step 18** - Call - voicemail

Content Examples for Outreach Sequences

(content to support each message in the sequence)

Email #1—SEOptimer Report (Targeting All Prospects)

Our Data Entry Team creates a report and downloads PDF using SEOptimer on all business leads (white labeled).

The report/PDF (see example in screenshot below) is to be sent to the business by the assigned SDR and include educational articles depending on which areas need attention, according to SEOptimer report.

Our Content Marketing Team writes content to support/educate the prospect on why the prospect should fix this issue, and the series of content be added to the email as support—for example, in this case, we'd write articles like:

- *How a High-Converting "Rainmaker Lead Gen Website" Can 10x Your Business*
- *Website User Experience: A Key Metric That Impacts Your Advertising Profitability*
- *Why Social Proof and Having Raving Fans Are Key for SMB Advertising Success*

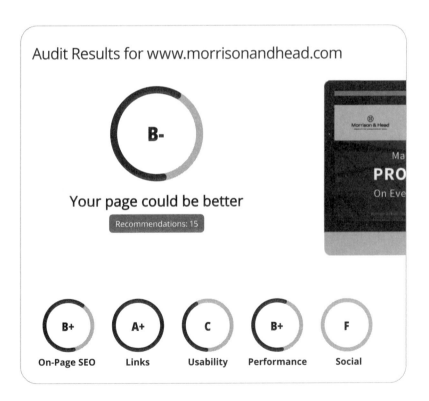

Email #2—Local Listings Report (Targeting All Prospects)

Our Data Entry Team creates a report and downloads PDF using our Yext white labeled "Local Listing Scanner Tool" on all our business leads.

The report/PDF is to be sent to the business by SDR and include educational articles highlighting the SEO value of having uniform local listings along with the need for reputation monitoring.

Our Content Marketing Team writes content to support/educate the prospect on why they should fix this issue, and the blog series will be added to the email as evidence—for example, in this case, we'd write articles like the examples below from Yext:

- *Capture Reviews from Customers and Feature Them on Your Own Website*
- *#FireUpYourFans to Improve Your Rating and Protect Your Brand's Online Reputation*
- *Respond to Negative Reviews and Convert Unsatisfied Customers to Brand Advocates*

46 Location Data Errors Detected

Paradise Dental
8351 S John Young Pkwy, Orlando, Florida 32819
(407) 370-4600

		Business Name	Address
G	Google	⚠ **Temporary problem scanning on this p** The publisher system is not responding to ou be fixed shortly.	
YAHOO!	Yahoo! view listing	Paradise Dental of Orlando	8351 S John Young Pkwy, Orlando, FL
▷	Bing view listing	Paradise Dental Group	8351 S John Young Pkwy, Orlando, FL
f	Facebook view listing	Paradise Dental of Orlando	8351 S John Young Pkwy, Orlando, FL 32819
			8351 S John

Email #3—Test My Site/Think with Google Report (Targeting All Prospects)

Complementary (or perhaps redundant but another source) to the SEOptimer report, our Data Entry Team creates a report and downloads PDF using Google's tool "Test My Site" on all business leads.

The report/PDF is to be sent to the business by the assigned SDR and include educational articles on the need for a mobile website strategy in today's business world, such as:

- *How Google's "Mobilegeddon" Algorithm Changed the Game for SMBs*
- *7 Reasons How You're Losing Money Without a Mobile Optimized Website*
- *How Mobile Is Changing the SMB Advertising Landscape in 2017*

Note: Supportive articles could also be written with reference to visual analytics tools and how they can help boost performance and, of course, mention how we *always* install Hotjar to measure and optimize conversion rates for our clients' sites and PPC landing pages.

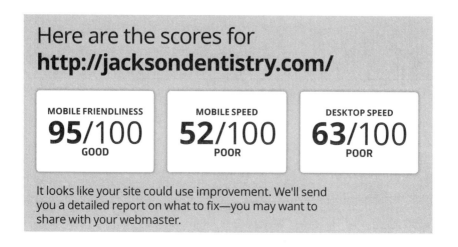

Email #4—Credibility Content (Targeting All Prospects)

During the outreach sequence, after an area of opportunity has been highlighted (via the various performance reports), our SDR follows up with a series of emails asking for an opportunity, earning their trust, and offering to help them solve the problem—just like the thousands of other businesses we have helped. Ideally, we'd aim to create more Google and Microsoft joint case studies to cover all possible customer scenarios. At a high level we grouped them in three categories covering most businesses (of course the more vertically specific we can get, the better):

1. Local Business Case Studies
2. National Business Case Studies
3. E-commerce Business Case Studies

An additional area of credibility could be sharing an appropriate Google lead warmer video and growing the video inventory as we expand to new targeted verticals.

Email #5—US Hispanic Opportunity (Targeting All Prospects in USH Geos)

Our Data Entry Team should enter the zip code of businesses that operate in USH high-density markets with our USH Zip Code Tool. It highlights the percentage of the population who are USH in the business's particular zip code. With this intel we would probe the question, *"Do you have a bilingual PPC/SEO campaign strategy in place?"*

These insights should be supported with our:

- *Various USH campaign-focused case studies and video testimonials*
- *Third-party articles regarding the explosive growth of USH demographic*
- *Our webinar recording with Google's Multicultural Team*

Email #6—Spyfu Report (Targeting Existing PPC Advertisers' Prospects)

Our Data Entry Team creates a report and downloads PDF using our Spyfu white labeled license on active Google AdWords business leads.

The report/PDF is to be sent to the business by the assigned SDR and include educational articles on PPC strategies. Our Content Marketing Team writes content to support/educate the prospect on why they would consider professional managed PPC services and highlight competitor research market intelligence such as:

- *How to Reverse Engineer Competitors' Keyword Selection and Out-compete Them*
- *How to Apply Pareto's Principle to Google AdWords Campaign Management*

- *How to Eliminate Wasted Ad Spend and Generate a Profitable AdWords Strategy*

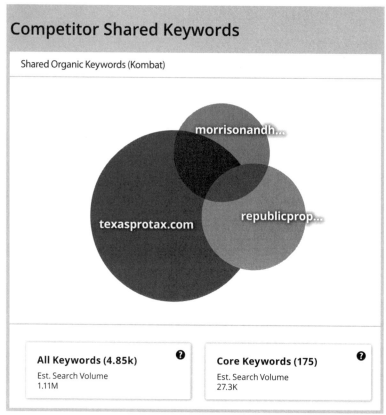

Email #7—Google AdWords ROI/LTV Calculator (Targeting Existing PPC Advertisers' Prospects)

When the leads have been identified as either an existing active Google AdWords (or paused) advertiser, the SDR should send out the email template where we probe the question in the headline, "[Name], Does YOUR

AdWords ROI Match Industry Benchmark?" In the body of the email we provide a small explanation how we, in conjunction with Google, created this ROI Campaign Calculator and probe the question of whether their AdWords campaigns are profitable. This email, with link to calculator, should also be supplemented with articles on call and conversion tracking, advanced bidding strategies, bid management software, and machine learning.

- *Three Google AdWords Metrics to Measure Your Advertising Performance*
- *What Is the Average ROAS by Industry for Google AdWords?*
- *Understanding ROAS/ROI of Your Google AdWords campaigns*

Email #8—Bing Ads Campaign Expansion (Targeting All Existing PPC Advertisers' Prospects)

When leads have been identified as existing AdWords advertisers, the assigned SDR shares some of our case studies of how often a better ROI can be expected with Bing Ads added to the equation, along with general market insights on search volume, market share, demographics, and average CPCs. Supportive content could be traffic and CPC data relevant to them using estimations found in the Bing Ads Intelligence tool. In the event their existing agency hasn't proposed this, we are in a great position to get our foot in the door with the objective of winning all their digital advertising business. The email should be supported with education content like:

- *1 out of 4 Search Queries in the US Happens on Bing. Are You Missing Out?*
- *Bing Ads vs. Google AdWords: The Pros and Cons of Each*
- *5 Ways Bing Ads Is Better for Your Business than Google AdWords*

And in the event that they already use Bing Ads (e.g., identified via BuiltWith), the assigned SDR instead offers a complimentary Bing Ads Evaluation referencing our proven track record with Bing Ads—for example,

1. Our Bing Ads joint case study for K9 business
2. Our Bing Ads joint case study for Siutse Hair Extensions
3. The webinar recording with Gary and Purna from Microsoft

In addition, we should include supportive educational content such as:

- *How We Use Kenshoo and Machine Learning to Boost ROI from Bing Ads*
- *How You Can Create a Profitable Bing Ads Campaign Using Google AdWords Insights*
- *Don't Compare Apples with Oranges: The Big Difference between Google AdWords and Bing Ads*

Email #9—Case Studies (Targeting All Prospects—Industry Specific)

When selecting and targeting popular verticals with high potential measured by the size of industry and resources (e.g., Legal or Dentistry), our assigned SDR should send out a series of videos and case studies to highlight our expertise in their particular vertical.

For example, when targeting Attorneys:

1. Google's Video Message Supporting Our Legal Marketing Expertise
2. The Longo Firm's Video Testimonial
3. The Written Case Study and ROI Calculation from the Longo Firm

Additionally, we can support with articles from our blog regarding our approach when managing PPC campaigns for Attorneys in different legal categories. A good example from another industry is the article, *"How We*

Generated Over 1,400 Calls from AdWords in Three Months to a Limo Company," written in-house, which I always use when speaking to Limo company prospects. Does the trick every time!

Note: As content for follow-up email(s), in this sequence, we can have our Data Entry Team insert the prospect's URL into the Google AdWords Keyword Planner and subsequently Google's Ad Preview Tool and thereby producing screenshots of suggested keywords, the traffic, and CPC estimations, for example, and subsequently how their competitors are currently ranking for the same relevant search queries.

Email #10—Tech and Digital Indicators (Targeting Existing Advertiser Prospects)

Using tools like Mixrank, Builtwith, or SimilarTech, we identify and select a series of web technologies and advertising platforms that indicate that the prospect is a potential good fit for our services.

For example, SMBs with Facebook Pixel (Facebook's conversion tracking), Bing Ads Conversion Tracking, our marketing automation technology like Pardot.

In these cases, our Data Entry Team inserts the prospect's URL into a tool like BuiltWith, as in the example you'll see below, and then looks for an email template we have written (I write these) plus supportive articles/content to "personalize the message" and speak to the relevance of considering our solutions.

For example, with Pardot/Salesforce users:

"Hi [Name],

I noticed that [Company name] is leveraging Pardot for marketing automation. I want to congratulate you on the sound decision of going with a sophisticated platform like Pardot!

On that note, I wanted to share this article with you on how Google AdWords can now integrate with Salesforce. Many of our customers have experienced significant growth in ROAS from Google AdWords after we optimize their keywords, ads, and campaigns according to revenue and profitability.

Do you have fifteen minutes tomorrow to discuss how you can track every penny spent with Google AdWords and boost your company's revenue?"

Another email template example, in this case for Facebook advertisers:

"Hi [Name],

I noticed that [Company name] is leveraging Facebook Ads to acquire new business. I want to congratulate you on the sound decision of promoting your business digitally!

On that note, I wanted to share this article with you on how Google AdWords can complement your Facebook campaigns considering that AdWords predominantly targets consumers with a commercial intent who are actively looking for your products/services, while Facebook usually is used for brand awareness and not-yet-engaged consumers.

Do you have fifteen minutes tomorrow to discuss how you can boost your revenue by adding Google AdWords to complement your Facebook advertising strategy?"

Note: And so we can continue writing email templates and content for various tech indicators like Google Analytics, HubSpot, AdRoll, Call Tracking, CrazyEgg, Kenshoo, Twitter Ads, etc.

Another route is pitching Google Shopping and our Kenshoo e-commerce strengths to e-commerce platforms we identify using Shopify or BigCommerce and that are compatible with Google Merchant Accounts and Google Shopping.

Case Study #2: 120+ reseller agency partners in <2 years

At this stage, we had pivoted to exclusively selling to resellers of other marketing solution providers in the United States. We began testing selling our solutions with some initial trial and error by some of our former top direct sales performers. It quickly became evident that this was an entirely different sales cycle where a high level of business and financial acumen was a requisite for deal success. So, once again, I found myself at the starting point exploring how to sell this solution at scale.

This time around I created a similar outreach strategy with an approach as follows:

1. Email sequences sent out with high levels of list segmentation (I'll expand on how momentarily).
2. LinkedIn connection requests and social selling. To do so we spent a great deal of time commenting on posts, extending congratulations for promotions, awards, or similar messages (I had my sales assistants and BDRs do much of this for me).
3. For select larger accounts where we sent a partnership proposal/agreement but they kept postponing the launch, we then sent out "snail mail" as a step in the outreach sequence. This consisted of a handwritten letter with a brochure attached and/or a pair of branded socks (in case they had gotten "cold feet"!). It may sound cheesy, but a little humor and a laugh can go a long way. The same goes for traditional snail mail vendors, especially in the SMB space, where adding this step to your outreach equation can be very effective.
4. Remarketing campaigns were rolled out using the email addresses of our agency prospects. We deployed what were then referred to as "Customer Match Campaigns" enabling us to

showcase ads on Google Search, display networks, YouTube, and Facebook/Instagram although they had never been in contact with us before or visited our website. In my opinion, remarketing is often the secret weapon that can act as a catalyst for your outreach campaigns. Once more, this emphasized why "Smarketing" —the effective collaboration between sales and marketing (described in Chapter 6)—is so important for your organization's success.

5. Additionally, I'd travel around the United States in areas with a high density of agencies and typically pair up my travel with an industry conference at the same time. This way, I'd invite a prospect for a cup of coffee or lunch. Many of the meetings and subsequent deals came about by *not* asking for an agreement outright in my copy but instead by just inviting them for lunch with the objective of "exploring partnership opportunities and trading some industry war stories."

6. Last, phone calls were mainly done when prospects opened documents, emails, or other collateral several times in a short time span (to support this, we used the sales enablement platform Outreach; more on this in Chapter 13).

The combination of these six steps turned out to be a slam dunk as we produced more revenue with just me as our sales rep than when having an entire sales team. The result? More partnerships than we could keep up with, revenue skyrocketing once again after having stagnated with direct sales, and EBITDA going from red to several million dollars in less than two years.

On the following page is a snapshot of the monthly performance and results of our outreach strategy after just twelve months, outperforming all previous sales models.

SPM Portfolio Revenue/Management Fees

What Is the Ideal Sequence for Your Business?

There are many opinions on what an ideal sales sequence looks like including how many touchpoints to include, the mixture of calls, emails, and social media, along with the frequency of touchpoints and overall timeline. It really depends on your industry and target audience, and even though best practices are good, I recommend keeping an open mind on this.

For example, I've read articles that feature the "Rule of 7" (seven touchpoints over seven days) or that you experience diminishing returns after nine touchpoints, but the fact of the matter is that it really depends on the creativity and effectiveness of your copywriting and supportive collateral. For example, if your sequences are just a traditional sequence of intro email, next resurface email, request for demo, resurface then add some credibility, resurface and then the infamous "breakup email," then sure. From my experience, by doing this, you're cutting corners and leaving a lot of money on the table because that's how the masses do outreach and your company will be just another predictable salesy email in their inbox— likely ignored.

Below is a sample outreach sequence I very successfully used for partnership propositions. It's a bit less aggressive than the example I used for direct selling, with more time between each interval and much more focus on relationship building and social selling. Quite often it would take two to three outreach sequences with three to four months between each before I landed a deal. Just because they acknowledged our solution was advantageous for them and they were convinced, a lot of other factors were often in play such as existing vendor agreements, software contracts still in term, or a larger in-house team that had to be downsized. These all took time, which is why patience and consistently staying on top of opportunities were key.

Channel Sales Outreach Sequence (10 steps over 40 days)

Day 1

Step 1 - Email - introduction / partnership proposition

Day 2

Step 2 - LinkedIn - connection request

Day 3

Step 3 - Call – voicemail

Day 10

Step 4 - Email - follow-up - threaded

Day 12

Step 5 - LinkedIn InMail

Day 17

Step 6 - Email - Partnership ROI calculation example

Day 25

Step 7 - Email partnership case study

Day 32

Step 8 - Email - partner portal demo video

Day 35

Step 9 - Email - sales enablement support / white label proposals

Day 40

Step 10 - Email - account growth recommendations

Channel Sales Outreach Sequence #2 (Continuation After 3 Months)

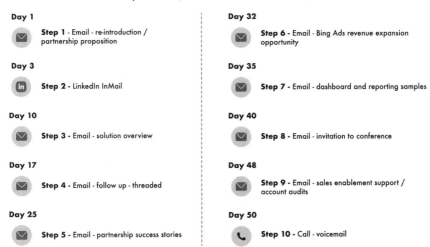

Day 1

Step 1 - Email - re-introduction / partnership proposition

Day 3

Step 2 - LinkedIn InMail

Day 10

Step 3 - Email - solution overview

Day 17

Step 4 - Email - follow up - threaded

Day 25

Step 5 - Email - partnership success stories

Day 32

Step 6 - Email - Bing Ads revenue expansion opportunity

Day 35

Step 7 - Email - dashboard and reporting samples

Day 40

Step 8 - Email - invitation to conference

Day 48

Step 9 - Email - sales enablement support / account audits

Day 50

Step 10 - Call - voicemail

Lead Enrichment on Steroids: The Holy Grail

Now let's talk about how to find leads, enrich, and segment them. From my experience, this is where most companies fail because they rely solely on purchasing data from a third-party lead provider and then take a "a one size fits all" sales approach by sending out more or less the same messages to all prospects. This is the *worst* you can do. Not only will you deter serious and highly qualified prospects from doing business with you, but you'll likely also be reported as spam by many because you ticked them off.

For all my outreach campaign projects, both in-house and ones developed for clients, I've always taken the following approach to lead list building and enrichment.

1. **Web Scraping:** Use web scraping technology such as Builtwith or MixRank to create lead lists based on technology lookup and thereby creating relevant narratives with hooks. For example, if you're selling software that is compatible with Facebook's API,

then leverage Builtwith to extract websites with Facebook Pixel Manager installed, and use that as your opening statement with an intro such as, *Hi [Name], I noticed that you're using Facebook for demand generation efforts. Congratulations! Many of our customers who also advertise on Facebook have experienced 2–3x ROAS by implementing our budget optimization solution. Can I show you how you can experience similar results?"*

2. **Directories:** Use industry-related directories to pull companies and websites. As well, we used sites such as PitchBook, Crunch-Base, or AngelList to find companies either seeking or already successfully raising capital (from pre-seed to IPO). The common denominator being that these companies are all eager to scale revenue and are likely to embrace your help if you can demonstrate how.

3. **LinkedIn Sales Navigator:** The best choice to enrich your lists with relevant up-to-date contacts and understand the prospect in better detail. Company and employee size nine times out of ten prove more accurate via LinkedIn than when purchasing the information through D&B Hoovers, ZoomInfo, or similar sites since it is updated on an ongoing basis by the company and employees rather than via surveys, website updates, and company filings.

4. **Lead Enrichment Tools:** Enrich lead data and uncover all relevant contact information using tools like Datanyze, Clearbit, Hunter.io, or FindEmails.com.

5. **Lead Inventory Depository:** Our in-house team of Data Enrichment Coordinators organized all of this information and updated it on an ongoing basis in our lead database. I personally like to hire for this role in-house to ensure high quality and accountability

throughout the lead enrichment process. Many companies outsource this to freelancers or specialized low-cost providers in the Philippines or India (more on this in Chapter 14) with the risk of having lower quality assurance over this critical resource for your sales success.

6. **Email Verification:** To mitigate high bounce rates and having your domain blocked, validate the emails collected using email verification tools like Warmup Inbox, BriteVerify, or Kickbox.

What worked really well for me regarding step 5 above was to create a commission system for my in-house Data Enrichment Coordinators located in Nicaragua. In fact, an increasing trend in the B2B, SaaS, and agency industry is to set up small satellite offices or outsourced teams in the Philippines, India, or Latin America for such data entry tasks. Their role is to ensure the data is accurate and organized properly—half the battle in sending out effective messages and closing deals en masse.

Often these employees are your lowest paid folks, but they hold the keys to whether you become profitable by creating a predictable and scalable revenue machine through your outreach efforts, thereby allowing you to downsize your marketing budget from a lead generation standpoint. Hence, why I'd often pay $100 commission per deal closed to Data Enrichment Coordinators if the deal came from a lead they had enriched. This may not sound like a lot, but if outsourced, this individual may earn only $500 per month, so they can quickly double or triple their salaries. In return you'll have a highly motivated Data Enrichment Team that aims to produce as much volume as possible while ensuring they get the information and data as accurately as possible.

On the following page is an example from my last agency venture targeting resellers, of how I segmented a lead list in a spreadsheet.

Account-Level Lead Info (The Company)

- Company Name
- Website
- Company LinkedIn Profile
- Instagram Profile
- Facebook Page
- Phone
- Street
- City
- Zip Code
- State
- Country
- Number of Employees
- Annual Revenue
- Year Founded
- Offer PPC (Yes/No)
- Other Services Offered (e.g., SEO, Website Dev, SMO, etc.)
- Google Partner (Yes/No)
- Microsoft Partner (Yes/No)
- Vertical Focus
- Vertical Case Studies
- Company Names from Case Studies

Lead-Level Info (Individuals at Company)

- First Name
- Last Name
- Job Title (usually either Founder, Partner, Owner, CEO, President, C-level, or select Directors)
- LinkedIn Profile (to connect and conduct social selling)
- Instagram Profile and/or Facebook Profile (some may find this

excessive, but here's where you can find good rapport-building info such as their recreational interests, hobbies, etc.)
- Prospect City and State (especially needed for the "I happen to be in town; can we grab a cup of coffee" messages, in case the account has several offices)
- Direct Office Number
- Cell Phone Number
- Prospect Email
- Email Tool Used to Find Info
- Email Verified (Yes/No)
- Lead Supplier
- Data Enrichment Coordinator
- Date Lead Last Updated

Guidelines for Effective Outbound Messaging and Emailing

By now I trust I've provided enough evidence to support my claim that a highly sophisticated outreach sequence to your target accounts combining emails, calls, social media connections, and interactions, as well as snail mail can be one of the most cost-effective approaches when conducting an account-based selling customer acquisition strategy.

However, nailing the right language, delivery method sequence, time frame of touchpoints, length of sequence, etc., requires much consideration and A/B split testing.

Furthermore, the adoption of new sales sequences hinges on having buy-in from your frontline reps. That's why I recommend you also probe your SDRs and AEs regarding what feedback they're getting from their prospects and then combine that feedback with the data, analytics, and intelligence gathered from your sales engagement platform reports. If you methodically review and optimize your sequences with such an approach, I can guarantee you that your new sales will skyrocket and become hyper-profitable.

Earlier in this chapter, I showed you some sample sequences and emails. However, since this varies greatly depending on your industry, the products you're offering, the size of companies you're targeting, and many other factors, let's cover some fundamentals to consider when crafting your copy for emails, both for your overall approach and your messaging.

Remember "The Six Principles of Persuasion" we covered in Chapter 2? These guidelines are fundamental when writing good persuasive copy for your sales sequences. But when I write my email sequences, there's a few other guidelines I keep in mind:

- **KISS.** Keep it short and simple. Who has time to sit and read your novel of an email in today's hectic business environment? Get to the point fast! A good rule of thumb is, if you can't read the email on your phone without scrolling, it's too long.
- **Your Customer Is the Focus.** Make your messaging completely about your customer: their pain points and/or value they can expect. No one cares about your company, stats, or reps. All that's going through your prospect's mind as they read your email is, *"What's in it for me?"*
- **Your Subject Line Is Key.** According to research done by market research firm Chadwick Martin Bailey, 64 percent of people open emails because of the subject line. Therefore, this is where you really want to juice up your creativity and include custom parameters such as names, numbers, stats, or refer to seasonality, upcoming events, introductions, or similar to create a sense of familiarity that intrigues your prospect to open the email. With that being said, never mislead or make promises you can't keep. What good

is a high email open rate if engagement is poor and requests to unsubscribe skyrockets?

- **Keep It Human.** Many sales folks, including yours truly early in my career, fall in love with using a lot of acronyms and industry jargon. Fact of the matter is that most people don't talk like that, which is why using simple day-to-day conversational language resonates better with most prospects. *Note:* There are of course cases, for example when addressing a CFO, that you can use financial acronyms and business language to demonstrate you know their wheelhouse well and are qualified, but avoid using big words to try to sound smarter.

- **Your Objective.** Each email should have a clear objective and a CTA. Don't write mystical copy assuming that your prospect reflects on it and gets back to you. Be clear with your messaging, what you're asking for and what the desired next step is.

- **One Thing at a Time.** Don't bundle all your benefits and value into one email. That's what your sequence of messages is for. This also enables you to enforce the KISS principle. Each email should add value, hit a different potential nerve, and be distinct from the other messages in your sequence.

- **Focus on Value.** Try to add value to each touchpoint but from a different angle. You never know what may trigger their interest and cause the reply and next conversation. The worst thing I see with novice email sequences is one email focused on value-add and then a series of "resurface emails" and "checking in to see if you got my initial message" ones. If they were interested the first time, they'd likely have replied then.

- **Always Be Testing.** Most sales engagement tools for managing your sales sequences allow you to do A/B split tests. I've used

Outreach for this in my last companies and tested everything from headline effectiveness, my opening paragraphs, amount of touchpoints in the sequence, to the time of day and day of the week for sending emails. I'm usually surprised how the data is different from my assumptions which is why my rule of thumb is always, always, always be testing, then analyze and optimize your outreach approach.

My Typical Guidelines for an Effective Sequence Are:

→ Sell benefits, NOT your features.

→ Your subject line will make it or break it!

→ Focus on value and limit writing about yourself.

→ Focus on credibility, scarcity, and social proof.

→ Incorporate facts, numbers, and statistics.

→ Create a detailed ICP/avatar and consider their pains and gains.

→ Segment the messaging (only 1-2 USPs per email).

→ A CTA is important, but a good question can be even more effective!

→ Continuously A/B test snippets, headlines, and CTAs.

Another effective principle to keep in mind when writing your sequences is the AIDA copywriting formula popularized by copywriting legend Gary Halbert.

If you're a sales nerd like myself, you may also recall AIDA from the classic ABC=Always-Be-Closing scene with Alec Baldwin in the 1992 movie *Glengarry Glen Ross* (slightly tweaked from Gary Halbert's version).

AIDA = *Attention. Interest. Desire. Action.*

Attention: For me, this is all about the email headline. You need to grab your reader's attention with an attractive headline that's relevant to your prospect's needs. Something that stands out and cuts through the noise of hundreds of emails your prospects likely receive daily. Something personal, relevant, and custom to them. This is an art, and the difference between a rainmaker outreach strategy and failure can be boiled down to a simple thing—the headline.

If it doesn't draw attention, you'll drown in the inbox and that's the end of your efforts. Hence why there's many articles written on this subject and why there's a series of subject line tester tools out there such as Test Subject by Zurb, Email Subject Line Analyzer by Attrock, and many more.

And for Pete's sake, don't use the shortcuts such as an artificial reply to scam your prospects to open the email. Is that how you want to begin your business relationship? What are the chances of you getting it after they quickly discover your ways?

Another hack, proven more effective, is inserting the prospect's name into the subject line as it draws their attention by calling them out.

The key metric to measure here is your email open rate. From my experience, you want to land somewhere between 25 percent and 35 percent.

Interest. Now they've opened your email. Terrific! But you must create continued interest right out of the gate so they keep reading. The objective is to create some strong, compelling opening paragraphs to pique their interest and nudge them to read through your entire email. The goal is to get them to (1) review attached collateral or (2) click through to your associated campaign landing page. Topics that have worked well for me here are (1) a brief description of their problem and our solution, (2) case studies, and (3) questions regarding challenges they're likely to experience.

The key metric to measure here is your email click-through rate. From my experience, you want to land somewhere between 10 percent and 15 percent.

Desire. Once interest has been established, you now have to dive directly into how your solution enriches your prospect's life and company results. There's a whole science to landing page architecture, structure, and messaging, but the main takeaway is that you must focus on value, benefits, and social proof, often with compelling visuals and bullet point copy.

The key metric to measure here is further engagement and email response rate, and from my experience, you want to land somewhere between 5 percent and 10 percent.

Action. The final step is action—loud and clear. A strong CTA is needed here, preferably with emotional hooks that trigger the prospect to either submit a form, schedule an appointment, make a call, or request a meeting. And voilà, just like that, it's now time for you to shine during a meeting after this, up until now, almost fully automated process of demand generation.

The key metric to measure here is your meeting scheduling rate (discovery or demo call), and from my experience, you want to land somewhere between 2 percent and 3 percent.

Note: If you do the math with fifty to one hundred emails sent out per day (my recommended volume limit to avoid ending up on spam filters or potentially getting your domain blocked) and by using my email funnel benchmarks described above, you are now able to calculate backward using other previously established sales metrics in mind—for example, ARPA, demo-to-close ratio, and so forth (as described in Chapter 6)—and then project the revenue outcome and ROI from your outreach campaign efforts.

I've now shone a light on how profitable a sophisticated outreach strategy can be if done correctly and covered all the fundamentals required for you to cut through the noise and get high reply and engagement rates. This is by no means an easy task but utterly worth every minute spent and can provide 100x ROI. The most successful B2B and SaaS companies predomininantly attribute their growth to getting this right.

In the next chapter, we'll discuss how your Marketing Team can support the effectiveness of these sequences along with other steps of your sales cycle by creating a series of sales enablement collateral that will wow your prospects and drive up your close rates.

10

PERCEIVED VALUE AND INFLUENCING DEAL SUCCESS RATES

Will ensure that you're putting in an equal effort to your sales and marketing value proposition so that it aligns with the actual quality of your product or solution.

C losing leads at a higher-than-usual rate and establishing a solid benchmark for deal success is one of highest ROI initiatives you can take on as a founder or sales leader within your organization.

Way too often, when hired to improve a company's sales processes, I find that the bar is just way too low when it comes to deal closing rates. In part, this is because (a) sales leaders prefer to overdeliver, and (b) reps at times build up a series of excuses to alleviate the pressure for closing deals at the highest possible rate.

There is by no means a silver bullet for influencing your deal success rates. Rather, there's layers of factors and processes to consider. A few stand out more than others and can make a strong impact on your top and bottom line if implemented. In this chapter, we'll touch on some of these best practices.

But before we do so, let's consider how much influence just impacting your closing rates can do for your organization.

If we assume that you're conducting an average of one hundred sales demos per month and currently closing 20 percent of these opportunities with an LTV of say $50,000, then increasing your closing rate by just 5 percent would mean an extra $250,000 in revenue generated. That kind of extra revenue should be able to buy you some additional marketing resources or sales support staff, wouldn't you agree?

So with this calculation in mind, let's review a few initiatives you can take to win these extra percentages.

MAKE YOUR SALES DEMOS ELECTRIFYING

Let's assume you've built a solid sales plan (as we discussed in Chapter 4) and baked out all of your sales processes accordingly. Now your sales demo effectiveness is probably the single element that can make the biggest difference in how your prospects perceive the value of your solution and how you can influence the closing rate of your opportunities.

You've already qualified the lead through your discovery call process, whether using BANT, MEDDIC, or another lead qualification methodology, and you know they are a fit for your solution and company.

And if they've accepted to see your solution demo, in nine out of ten cases they're not just snooping around. They're utterly curious as to whether your solution can help solve some of their problems or make their business better. So the ball is now 100 percent in your court.

So your sales reps should approach a sales demo the same way that Roger Federer enters center court at Wimbledon for the men's final tennis match.

Nothing is left to chance. You are fully prepared and have studied your opponent beforehand. You've warmed up, you know your strategy, your coach is on the sidelines cheering you on, and you have extra rackets strung just in case something fails. It's time to execute, perform a show, and win the match!

This sets the precedent for (a) how excited they'll walk away from your conversation and whether they strongly advocate for your solution internally, or (b) if instead they just politely accept your proposal and are already thinking of going with your competitor because they were able to convey a better value proposition during their presentation or demo.

When closing partnership agreements at my previous company, I made it a must to listen to my demo recordings afterward and refine my approach until I perfected the process. If the prospect didn't express how they were impressed with our solution, a high level of excitement, or explicitly began asking buying questions such as clarification on terms and conditions, discount options, or our onboarding process, then I considered my demo a failure. Even with a less emotional, introverted prospect, I needed to spark such a reaction.

There are many actions you can take to pique the interest of your prospects to the desired degree. I recommend implementing the following steps in your demo process (then practice, practice, and practice some more):

1. **Research Your Prospect in Great Detail.** This goes without saying and should already be done during the discovery call process. However, very often sales teams have SDRs take care of this part and then hand over the prospect to your AE if deemed qualified. It's important that your AE (or whoever is doing the

demo) conduct their *own* research on everything about the prospect. Besides the rudimentary business and factual information, this includes relevant PR, partnerships, awards or other recognition they have attained, noteworthy articles by the prospect, and relevant information from their social media. This arms you to a degree that can help you outflank your competition. Often the devil is in those little details when it comes to earning trust and landing the deal.

2. **Prepare Rigorously for Your Demo.** For me, this means mapping out everything important you want to cover during the call, what you want to highlight, and being prepared to discuss any feature your prospect may want to focus on. The same goes for showing up early, having all applications, tabs, videos, case studies, etc., pulled up on your screen and ready to rock 'n' roll! I like to tell my reps to be prepared as if their life depended on it. Maybe that's a tad exaggerated, but I'm trying to make a point. Remember, showcasing that you're properly prepared for the call and mindful of their needs often can be interpreted as you being excited to work with them and earn their business. This alone gives you a head start as I often find demos by reps nowadays are generic and almost robotic, covering only what they are expected to show, and not prepared for the unexpected.

3. **Make Them Feel Truly Unique and Keep It Human.** It doesn't matter how busy you are, how many rejections you received, or how your day is going so far— always pull yourself up and walk into the conversation being enthusiastic, energetic, and appreciative of the opportunity to earn their business. This may go without saying for many, but once again, I consider each demo as a tournament final match where you must show appropriate

levels of energy and charisma. Make sure to build rapport in a genuine fashion by asking thoughtful questions based on your research or past conversations. Remember that *"people buy from people they like"* still holds water in today's world.

4. **Set a Clear Agenda and Summarize Past Conversations.** Many reps are afraid to establish an agenda, worried that their prospects don't want to hear about select items you have to cover. But if your agenda is well thought out with a clear narrative that builds momentum, then you need to "stick to the script" while of course being adaptable. Don't be afraid to challenge your prospect with why something is important to cover or highlight how their competitors find it to be one of the more valuable features of your solution. And if there's consistent lack of interest or pushback, then it's back to the drawing board to revisit your demo pitch contents and flow. Point being that you must follow a process and stick to it. Otherwise, it's impossible to assess what's working and what's not so that you can optimize accordingly.

5. **Provide a *Custom* Solution That Aligns with Your Prospect's Needs.** This counters the otherwise robotic and generic demo approach I often encounter with reps. If your prospect has provided valuable intel about their pain points, current solution, or specific areas of interest, then showcase that you have paid attention and customize your demo accordingly. Likewise, make sure to mention these topics when setting your agenda at the beginning of the call. This gives your prospect peace of mind and cultivates patience so that you have the floor to present your case in the best way possible.

6. **Use a Pitch Deck but Keep It Interactive.** Many reps stick to their pitch deck and limit their demo to specifically showcasing

the standard solution features in detail. I prefer interactive product demos since they enable your prospect to experience live how your solution can solve their specific problems. Personally, I have dummy accounts set up when conducting demos showcasing our methodology in practice with real data and actual ROI calculations. This requires some degree of technical understanding, but you don't have to be a sales engineer to demonstrate at this level. It's just a matter of some study and rehearsal. Showcasing the experiences of real users and how you'll better manage expectations and mitigate customer churn, for example, can be powerful elements of a highly successful demo.

7. **Value Focus. The Why and Problem Solving. Sprinkle It with Storytelling.** How did you invent this solution of yours that you're offering? Was it a coincidence or some problem that kept coming up with your customers? Tell the origin story. People love storytelling. In fact, your pitch is significantly better remembered since research by the cognitive psychologist Jerome Bruner in *Actual Minds, Possible Worlds* shows that listeners remember stories up to twenty-two times better compared to hearing facts and figures alone. When you incorporate stories that have the customer's needs at the center, that's when you make home runs.

8. **Make Realistic Promises and Manage Expectations.** We covered earlier in Chapter 3 how devastating customer churn can be for your company's bottom line. Therefore, it's better to be 100 percent realistic with regard to your performance expectations—it's way better to risk losing a deal or two by underpromising and planning to overdeliver. And occasionally this may happen if the

competition outflanks you. When you have many reps, I recommend, when possible, to create an ROI calculator. You can use this to set the right expectations and subsequently as a supportive sales tool that post-demo can be shared with the prospect's CFO or other decision makers. Most Enterprise-focused players have incorporated this practice in their sales process. I've personally been persuaded effectively with this approach by Salesforce and HubSpot. Whether it's demonstrating ROI from their investment versus the expected increase in revenue, cost reduction, or increased efficiency, an ROI calculator can be extremely helpful to land the deal.

9. **Listen to Their Feedback and Agree on Next Steps.** A good B2B or SaaS sales rep never stops listening and recognizes that it's their opportunity to *learn* as much as possible about the prospect's needs and concerns. Embracing these questions, even after the discovery call and during the demo, empowers you to customize the demo even more to their specific needs, significantly increasing the likelihood of securing a deal. Don't stick to your script or demo outline if their questions reveal that another direction is more effective. The same goes with next steps as for when, who, what, and where. If you need to present the demo to another decision maker in the process, welcome the opportunity and adjust your approach according to their role and vendor procurement process.

10. **Send out a Summary Immediately and Attach Relevant Collateral.** If your reps are too busy to send out proposals, relevant collateral, and ROI calculations immediately after the call, then bite the bullet and hire sales support staff. Believe me, the impact will be tenfold, as deals won't be lost because of delays or

competitors beating you to the mark post-demo. You've already invested thousands of dollars by now generating interest via marketing and getting to this stage of the sales cycle, so make sure to get a compelling proposal in their laps immediately after your call or at the latest the next day.

The image on the following page is a sample screenshot of how I organized my bookmarks for a solution demo. I typically have twenty to twenty-five tabs open in my browser in a systematic and chronological order. I align them "organically" with my demo flow and they are supported by a pitch deck. I always open the tabs in the same order so that as questions arise from my prospect during the demo, I can navigate the tabs with my eyes closed to immediately demonstrate in great detail performance data, benchmarks, relevant case studies, etc.

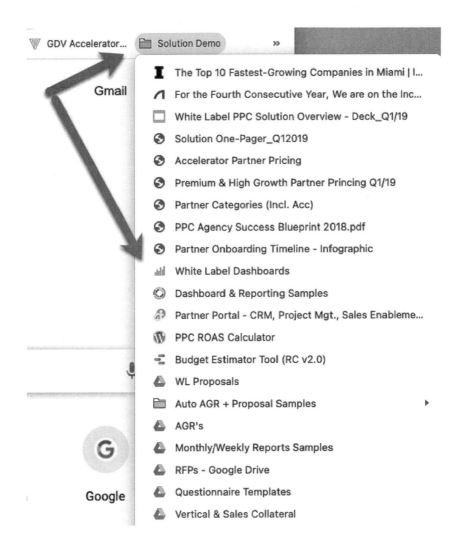

SALES ENABLEMENT COLLATERAL AND PROPOSALS

Before you skip this section thinking it's not your responsibility, that Marketing should take care of this, or that it's too much work to create such a strategy and collateral, then consider the following stats:

- According to Aberdeen Market Research firm, companies with a sales enablement strategy in place are 32 percent more likely to make their sales quota versus companies that don't.
- According to market research firm FocusVision, the average B2B buyer's journey involves consumption of thirteen pieces of content.
- According to Forrester, 90 percent of B2B sellers don't use their sales material because it's irrelevant, outdated, and difficult to locate and customize.
- According to Miller Heiman Group, companies that have implemented a sales enablement content strategy have increased their win rate by 27.1 percent.
- According to a study by CSO insights, only 51 percent of sales professionals felt that their sales enablement collateral met or exceeded their expectations and 54 percent said they didn't have enough content to help them move their prospects through the sales cycle effectively.

And if you do some further research on the subject, you'll learn that there are a hundred more compelling reasons why you should amp up your sales enablement strategy. In Chapter 13, I'll cover in depth the sales enablement tools and software that you can leverage to ramp up your sales. For now, let's talk about how you can help your sales initiatives today by cost-effectively beginning to create valuable collateral that can drive immediate incremental growth of your deal success rates and revenue.

But what exactly is sales enablement collateral? In summary, it's collateral that helps the seller build trust with prospects and demonstrates the value of their solutions. Below are twenty collateral examples I recommend adding to your "Smarketing Program Roadmap." They aren't necessarily in priority order, but you can develop them as you see fit once you and your team collectively gauge what makes the most impact for your sales.

Note that sales enablement collateral is a blend of both internal collateral designed to empower your reps when navigating complex sales conversations with prospects *and* collateral that can be shared with prospects during the sales cycle to enhance the deal process in your favor.

1. **White Papers:** An authoritative report or guide (usually ten to fifteen pages long) with an educational tone that informs your prospective clients about how to solve a potential problem or understand an opportunity to improve something within their organization. According to research by Demand Gen, White Papers are the second most popular content format after video.

2. **E-books:** A popular content format highly effective for B2B demand gen efforts. According to research by Content Marketing Institute, 51 percent of B2B businesses incorporate e-books into their content marketing strategy. They can be effective to fuel credibility and authority within your domain.

3. **Blog Posts:** A highly popular content format. It's important to keep quality over quantity in mind. They are key from an SEO perspective. Equally important is their use by sales reps to address questions prospects may have during the sales cycle. Their flexibility and focus easily allow reps to share them in their outreach sequences as they see fit.

4. **FAQs:** A must-have element in your sales enablement collateral. Not only can they be useful to display on your website or landing page to set correct expectations, they can demonstrate your expertise and instill trust with prospects at any stage in the sales cycle. Additionally it will increase the efficacy of your sales cycle by cutting down on unproductive questions from your prospects.

5. **Research Reports and Data Sheets:** Research and data on a subject in your marketplace can be very helpful as it aids data-driven observations. These can help facilitate better decision making for your prospects as well as validating your hypotheses. Here's an example of how to use such data during your sales process and how posting snippets on sites like LinkedIn can be effective in many ways.

 Gary Garth • You   **+ Follow**   •••
Founder of Great Dane Ventures, The Accelerator Platform a...
4yr • 🌐

Quote from Forbes.com article:

"As a small advertising agency in today's economy, if you aren't incorporating multicultural consumers into your work, you are hurting your agency's growth and your clients' growth. To put it bluntly, if you aren't doing multicultural marketing, you will not succeed. Consider the following reason:

• The Hispanic population is projected to increase by 115% by 2060, which will make up 29% of the U.S. population, according to a report by the U.S. Census Bureau.

#digitalmarketing #googleads #bingads #blueoceanstrategy #whitelabel #ushispanicmarket #whitelabelppc #multiculturalmarketing

U.S. Hispanic Campaign Expansion

> Receive support from WSM's fully bilingual staff to tap into the next media jackpot to reach the US Hispanics population performance.

> Leverage Hispanic-targeted campaigns for higher click-through and conversion rates while at lower costs.

> Benefit from a brand new keyword strategy and tailored ad copy to maximize your return on ad investments.

1M Colorado
2.1M Illinois
3.5M New York
14.4M California
1.6M New Jersey
1.9M Arizona
0.9M Georgia
1M New Mexico
4.4M Florida
9.8M Texas

6. **Competitor Scorecards:** A brief overview of how you stack up against your competition with key insights and pros and cons of features, pricing, terms, and conditions (obviously with the objective of positioning your solution advantageously).

7. **Product Explainers:** Especially in video format (the number one content format per "Demand Gen"), these are effective in giving your prospects a sneak peek of your solution and thereby pique their interest in getting a full solution demo.

8. **Demo Recordings:** An overview of your solution can be used during several stages of your sales process. This is especially true for B2B sales where often there are multiple decision makers, several vendor comparisons, and multiple procurement processes in place. Providing a demo recording helps you move deals forward faster and more effectively.

9. **Features and Benefits One-Pagers:** When your prospect is particularly interested in one or more features, these can be useful to move them from interest to the demo stage in your sales process. As well, you can circulate these after the demo process to reinforce the value of your solution for a particular benefit that sparked their excitement.

10. **Sales Pitch Decks:** It goes without saying these are a must-have element of your sales process. But they need to be refined to perfection, especially if meant to be shared with prospects after the demo process who then circulate internally within your prospect's company. You should create pitch decks for each customer segment and scenario. To demonstrate this, here's a screenshot of one I created in my last company, with help from Microsoft, *specifically* designed for the furniture vertical.

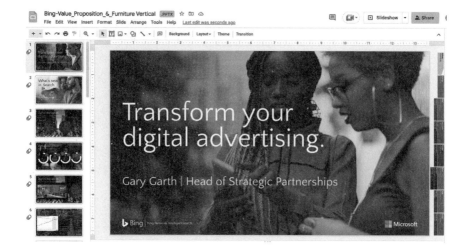

11. **Objection Handling Guidelines:** A cornerstone internal document of any successful sales organization. Even the best-fit prospect most likely has a series of objections that, if not answered effectively, can cause them to walk away from the table and select another vendor.

12. **Sales Playbooks:** Your one-stop resource for all the critical information that enables your sales reps to follow your best practices and maximize performance.

13. **Internal Success Videos:** Especially relevant when scaling your team. A lot of golden nuggets and useful practices get siloed up or lost in translation as you grow. Creating videos by your reps for other reps (and prospects) is very useful to demonstrate what worked well and why.

14. **ROI Calculators:** One of my absolute personal favorite pieces of collateral proven to shorten sales cycles and boost win rates. They can empower your sales teams with interactive ROI calculations

conducted either by your reps on calls or by prospects during the sales cycle.

15. **Pricing Calculators:** A must-have if your pricing structure is complex or difficult to understand. They can also be useful as lead capture elements when prospects visit your site while conducting research and inquiring about more information.

16. **Brochures and Booklets:** Useful because of their format and length and can be circulated as needed with prospects as a quick introductory overview of your company and solutions.

17. **Call Scripts or Pitch Guidelines:** Extremely helpful when onboarding new reps and scaling. Your pitch undoubtedly varies depending on your buyer persona, if the lead was sourced outbound versus inbound, or whether the conversation was triggered by an asset download or a marketing campaign. Crafting messaging that's customized for each scenario may be easy for the more experienced rep but not for newer reps within your company.

18. **Newsletters:** Helpful for prospects at any stage of your sales cycle by establishing trust and staying top of mind. The initiative also helps your brand reputation and forms a relationship with your prospects, regardless of how much interaction they have had to date with your sales team.

19. **Webinars:** A very common sales enablement strategy. They can serve as a scalable initiative for you to engage with leads and prospects at any stage. Very popular is to bring in subject matter experts from your partner networks and thereby tapping into their audience. Here's an example from my last company done together with Microsoft.

Gary Garth

Head of Strategic Partnerships
White Shark Media

Mauricio Orantes

Partner Manager for the Americas
Microsoft

20. **Podcasts:** Are becoming more popular than ever from a B2B sales perspective because you can establish partnerships, leads, connections, and long-term relationships by inviting relevant guests on your show. Podcasts also create deeper engagement compared to other avenues and are a great way to position your brand as a legitimate player in your space. Here's how I position my podcast that serves a lead gen tool for my Accelerator Platform and marketing agency but not directly branded as such. The target audience for either solution is entrepreneurs seeking growth—hence the podcast channel.

Common for all the above-mentioned types of sales enablement collateral is that they're proven to help your customer-facing employees, whether SDRs, AEs, or CSMs, to more effectively prepare and interact with prospects and customers. Think of it as a handyperson going to work and having a few tools in their toolbox versus a set of twenty that cover almost every scenario and with a few clicks can be added to the conversation to make the difference between an opportunity won or lost.

From a personal standpoint, I can't imagine running a sales organization without a heavy arsenal of such tools at my reps' disposal. The value of creating such content is exponential as it can be used 360 degrees within your organization.

First and foremost, it aids as great learning content when onboarding new reps. Implementing this step in your sales enablement collateral process further helps you to continuously audit and update your content so that it's always relevant—something many companies neglect once created.

Second, marketing can leverage much of the work in the demand generation process and marketing campaigns while also giving your reps strong ammunition to advance more and better conversations with prospects and ultimately close more deals.

Last, it promotes better collaboration between your teams, especially between sales and marketing but also finance and operations. They will be able to better understand what works well and possibly allocate more resources toward areas of growth potential.

Who, What, How, and Where?

There's a plethora of reasons why so many companies struggle with getting these highly valuable sales enablement initiatives deployed, despite the proven ROI. So let's instead focus on how you can effectively frame and roll out your sales enablement collateral strategy, and equally important, how to make it stick.

When I founded the reseller program of my last business and began onboarding many channel partners, I quickly discovered some of the challenges companies may face when attempting to roll out an effective sales enablement strategy that makes a true impact on revenue growth with a justifiable ROI.

Some of the questions and challenges I encountered were:

- *Which sales collateral is most needed? One thing is what our resellers ask for or desire, but another thing is what they actually need to close more deals.*
- *How do we make sure that all this collateral is accessible, organized properly, and easy to find so it's always at their fingertips in the heat of the moment with a prospect, and how do we make sure it's constantly updated?*

- Who should be responsible for the collateral ideation and creation process, how to distribute it effectively, and how to train stakeholders on it?
- How do we measure which sales collateral works best, which is and isn't adopted properly, and why that is?
- How do we measure the ROI of all this work associated with creation and distribution of sales enablement collateral?

Based on these experiences and after speaking with thousands of sales managers in my partner network and customer base regarding what worked or not, I created the following process I recommend you adopt if you want to experience the statistically validated and expected ROI described at the beginning of this chapter.

Step #1. Identify stakeholders of the project. Remember what Jim Collins, author of *Good to Great* said? *"First who, then what."* The same applies when assembling your team and deciding who is to take lead on this strategically important initiative. In fact, research conducted by IDC states that sales and marketing misalignment leading to decreased sales productivity and wasted marketing costs companies a whopping $1 trillion a year. My point here is that when you look to assemble your team, you want to at the very least get stakeholders from both sales leadership and marketing leadership involved. Ideally also adding leadership from sales operations and your customer success teams to the equation helps ensure 360-degree buy-in on the project.

Step #2. Define the objectives of your sales enablement collateral strategy. Since this initiative undoubtedly correlates with a needed investment in budget for tools, manpower, and focus diverted from elsewhere, you want to crystallize your objectives and establish an ROI for the project. As with everything else, but especially true for sales and marketing, "You get what you measure." Start by asking questions such as:

- *What is the purpose of creating this new sales enablement collateral?*
- *What steps do we need to take to ensure the adoption of sales collateral by our client-facing staff?*
- *What outcome are we expecting from this activity? And how do we measure the ROI?* If you did your homework in Chapter 6 and laid out all pertinent sales metrics, you can quickly establish quantifiable targets of improvement that your CFO and financial decision makers expect in order to allocate you the needed budget for this initiative.

Step #3. Take stock of what you already have in place. There's no need for you to reinvent the wheel if it already exists within your organization. Very often when I work with companies I conduct what I call "Sales Process Architecting Audits." In my experience, there's golden nuggets in the form of collateral hidden in departments you wouldn't expect. Because departments often work in a siloed fashion, they haven't shared this valuable content across departmental lines. For example, ROI calculators often sit in finance for analysis purposes that can be repurposed to use with clients. Customer Success Managers often have some stellar product explainer videos in stock that they use to secure solution adoption from clients that could serve tremendously well for new reps in training or for reps to share with prospects during the sales cycle.

Step #4. Gather feedback and data. Ask and you shall receive. Before you run out and begin creating new content, make sure to survey your entire salesforce and client-facing staff about their needs, what they like the most, what prospects and customers ask for most frequently, and of course, what works best. Furthermore, if you already have a Sales Enablement Platform in place that provides analytics on how prospects engage with content shared (e.g., open rates, time spent in documents, heat maps as for what they read the most, etc.), then make sure to incorporate this data in your overall assessment of the current structure and strategy for moving forward.

Step #5. Assess each asset. Now, before you discard certain content and assets, it's important that you consider if any underlying factors may have caused poor effectiveness and views by prospects. For example, ask yourself the following questions:

- *How did you organize this collateral previously and who had access to it? How frequently did it get shared, and was it during the appropriate time in your sales cycle that the rep shared it?*
- *Can select existent content be refurbished or updated for continued usage? For example, blog posts can be reinvigorated into usage by converting them into videos, and old fact sheets can be displayed more effectively as infographics.*
- *Can select collateral be merged or split up to increase efficiency? Look for redundancies or gaps in your sales process as to what is shared and when.*

Step #6. Mind the gaps and prioritize. I recommend assessing your current sales metrics here first. Where in the sales process are we lacking versus industry benchmarks? Is it when first engaging with prospects or during the discovery and demo process? What about during the lead nurturing process or reinforcing the value proposition, especially important with a longer sales cycle. The answers to these questions, along with data from sales metrics, help you make better decisions regarding what sales enablement collateral you need to prioritize to get the biggest bang for your buck right out of the gate (and possibly obtain more budget for the project faster by quickly demonstrating value). This is an important exercise to undergo since many have a tendency to create what I call "vanity collateral" that makes one feel good or proud about your solutions and company but doesn't make as good an impact as other more *needed* collateral. Your priority should always be selecting the collateral creation that facilitates the highest growth possible.

Step #7. Create a content creation roadmap and calendar. It goes without saying, but many organizations fall victim to constantly prioritizing the ongoing "urgent" requests that the salesforce unquestionably brings to the table by saying, *"If I just had this piece of content, I'd close this deal..."* It's in the nature of your typical sales rep profile (including yours truly) to be constantly distracted by the next shiny object they see. Instead, develop a content creation roadmap in line with your plan and strategy tied in with expected ROI and metrics improvement, of course with some degree of flexibility built in. For that, design (or download a template) a content calendar (also known as an editorial calendar) defining when and where you plan to distribute forthcoming content.

Step #8. Organize your sales enablement content. There are many ways to go about this. Most companies now use Google Drive, Folders, Docs, and Sheets to organize this because it enables easy collaboration (this book was written in Docs). From experience, I'd highly recommend investing in a Sales Collateral Management Platform. Outreach or HubSpot have this integrated into their platform, but you can choose other document management software like PandaDoc or Congo (much more on this in Chapter 13). The point is that you get organized and provide a good UX for your reps, clients, and partners to secure the adoption and correct usage of collateral that you have invested heavily in creating.

Step #9. Distribute your sales enablement collateral. Remember, this content can often be used both internally and externally, so make sure that you establish alignment in your different teams about when and how it's circulated, along with periodic updates and related messaging. You want to make sure that the messaging and collateral used during training aligns with what is used for marketing and sales execution and shared with clients.

Step #10. Train, measure adoption and effectiveness, then optimize. At my last company with a channel sales focus via resellers, we used Communities by Salesforce and also flirted with Allbound PRM. Common for both platforms was that they were incredibly valuable for segmenting content at either permission hierarchy (client or partner segments) or verticals/industries. They also provided analytics for what content got accessed by whom, when, and to what degree or frequency.

This proved to be incredibly valuable intel for optimizing our overall strategy and process. Very often we'd create a piece of absolutely pure gold collateral that didn't get any traction for a variety of reasons. Instead of discarding it, we learned with these tools that adoption subsequently developed by just creating more awareness for the new collateral and/or discovering that training was needed for it to be embraced and used effectively by our partners' reps.

On the following page is an example of how we organized sales enablement collateral for resellers in my last company. We made it easy to navigate with search, either by vertical or collateral type, and with notification capabilities each time new content was added.

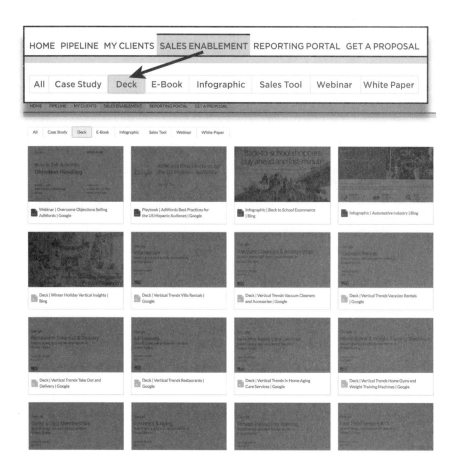

Testimonials and Case Studies

Your customers can undoubtedly become your best marketing ambassadors and rocket-fuel your growth if you structure the testimonial and case study request to your satisfied customers effectively.

Client endorsements of any kind, undoubtedly, increase the desirability of your solution and also lower price resistance, discount requests, concerns, and objections.

Additionally, your case studies can have multichannel usage from a sales and marketing standpoint by, for example, converting case studies into blog posts and publishing as content on social media and, of course, being listed on your website either on the home page or a specific case study section.

From personal experience, if you have a company that targets a horizontal segment of industries, you want to segment or categorize your testimonials and case studies in an industry index so that your sales reps and/or prospects can easily navigate to ones relevant for them. Usually, buyers want to know how you've helped someone like them in a similar industry. If you're a SaaS company hiring a marketing agency, what good is it that the agency has a killer case study for a manufacturing organization? It's not relevant for them. That's why in Chapter 3 I strongly advocate verticalization for most companies—it makes your marketing efforts far more targeted.

Another recommendation that worked well for me in my previous company was incentivizing our Account Managers and Customer Success Teams with bonuses and commissions for every case study they collected and with competitions for those who could collect the most. For one, it fosters an environment where clients should be satisfied and happy to the degree that they feel comfortable issuing an endorsement of you. In addition, internally, you create a sales-like environment fueling performance around obtaining a volume of case studies that in return yields ROI by influencing deal success rates.

Another positive element I encountered with these case study collection contests was that same-store growth per customer grew on average since an upsell or cross-sell initiative was low-hanging fruit for our reps because the client's approval of a case study was a clear indicator that they were satisfied.

Last, a good process to incorporate a culture of creating case studies is to implement online review tools like GatherUp (formerly GetFiveStars when I used them), Podium, or similar products. They automate the customer feedback process for collecting testimonials and suggest that these clients could serve as candidates for case study requests.

Below is an example of how I frequently used our case studies to publish on LinkedIn and share as a sales enablement collateral tool during my sales process.

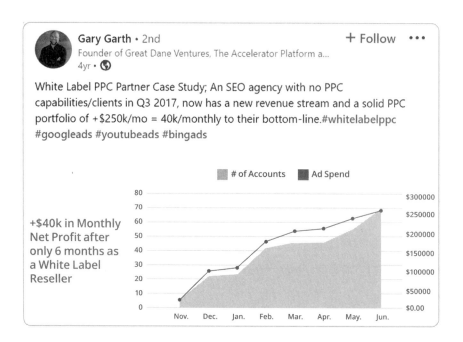

Rainmaker Proposals and Quick Turnaround Time

Let's be real here. If you're like most salespeople, you're not exactly stoked about spending countless hours creating a proposal, attempting to find the right combination of words, stats, and facts that convince your prospect you're the right person and company for the job. It's time consuming, dreadful, and requires a high level of attention to detail. Not a fun task, and that's why so many folks drop the ball at this step of the sales cycle. Hence why this is your opportunity to stand out, shine, and steal the deal at the finish line.

According to Dooly, 41 percent of a sales rep's workday is *not* spent selling, costing companies 38 percent in revenue every quarter. Now, admittedly this encompasses everything sales admin-wise (i.e., CRM updating, internal meetings, etc.), but issuing proposals and responding to RFPs is definitely a big time-consumer for most sales reps.

At my last company when surveying the sales management of our reseller network, I came to learn that most reps spent between four to six hours creating a proposal. And the larger the deal size was, usually the hours invested increased accordingly.

This lost sales time not only causes a negative impact on revenue but also leads to sales rep frustration because of the extra workload and frequent failure to hit quota. At the same time, you don't want your reps to speed through an RFP process and issue lower quality, just to meet the proposal demand timelines and fulfill the quantity to issue.

Most companies have adopted some sort of proposal technology, but still, just as with email sequences and messaging we previously discussed, the devil is in the details with proposals as well. So if you expect a high closing ratio while having a high efficiency in your proposal management process, I recommend you implement the following guidelines I picked up over the years, especially during my last venture where we issued hundreds of proposals for resellers in a white label format as a value-add to our partner program. The feedback from working with 200+ resellers who also had different preferences and insights as to how to structure a proposal was invaluable. And because we used proposal software, we were able to get data on what works best for engagement, what to exclude, and how to organize the narrative so that prospects actually read it.

1. **Preparation.** It goes without saying that you should create pro-posal templates. Taking things a step further to not reinvent the wheel for each scenario can not only minimize time spent in the process but also generate higher closing ratios for your team

overall. Creating various templates for different use cases, a snippet library for common scenarios, image libraries, etc., goes a long way allowing you to scale the process more effectively to justify adding a proposal creation team to your organization.

2. **KISS and Use Visuals.** Keep it short and simple. You want prospects to read it and notice the most important elements. If you add thirty pages to your proposals, which I see very often, bragging about all your awards, adding all possible services and case studies, is likely only to cause information overload and be counterproductive. If you have proposal software with heat maps and behavioral analytics already in place, you're likely to agree with my notion here. Another way to ensure your important content is absorbed properly is converting text to visuals when possible. Research from 3M Corporation shows that people are wired to process visuals 60,000 times faster than text. Leverage that in your proposal process to make sure you get your point across.

3. **Tell a Story.** This is where your creative juices should kick in and where to spend your valuable time (the rest should be boilerplate) by sprinkling storytelling with insights gathered through your sales conversations with the prospect. Then summarize why you are uniquely qualified to help them reach their financial and functional goals with a specific and well-defined strategy. Every sales cycle starts with a problem and your prospect looking for a solution. Explain this in a compelling and well argued way, and you have yourself a client soon thereafter.

4. **Personalization.** Most marketers know that personalization is everything when it comes to engagement. This doesn't mean just adding your prospect's logo on the cover and inserting their name here and there. You're selling your solution to a company, but

who's the person buying it on behalf of the company? Make sure to customize accordingly. If your pitch is directed to the Operations Manager, emphasize how your solution can drive operational efficiency and streamline processes. If your pitch is geared toward the IT Manager, perhaps elaborating more on the IT infrastructure optimization and its benefits is more likely to land you the deal.

5. **Numbers, data, and stats.** From my experience, the more you can back your pitch with stats, facts, and research demonstrating in numbers or percentages how you can support their company better than the competition, the more your odds of landing the deal increase. Numbers don't lie, and most marketers are often afraid to provide performance estimates, worried about the possible ramifications if they're not met. My two cents here is that although you may fail on expectations occasionally, you'll win more in the end by providing performance projections and detailing areas of improvement with data.

6. **Success Stories.** It goes without saying that adding client success stories to your proposals creates a sense of social proof and demonstrates your expertise as a solution provider. But are you selecting the right client success stories to include in your proposal? If you're pitching a B2B company, don't include a B2C e-commerce testimonial, for example. Ideally use a case study of another client in the same industry and similar size of company. The more your prospect can resonate with the pain solved and gains attained by your success story, the better suited you will be to get their business.

7. **Simplistic Pricing.** I recently underwent a mystery shopping process and collected twenty-five-plus B2B proposals for a client. Some of the pricing examples baffled me. They appeared to almost

be designed to create confusion with a blend of retainers, long pricing grids, à la carte options, and much fine print to make matters worse. They almost looked like a pharmaceutical company commercial with disclaimers and total confusion. It may be hard and won't always secure precise margins on deals, but make your pricing easy to understand and you'll land more deals and create better client satisfaction by ensuring there are no unexpected surprises regarding the cost.

8. **Next Steps/Client Onboarding Process.** What to expect, by when, and who does what? Answer all these questions, preferably supported by visuals, and you decrease the uncertainty of your prospect and stand out from the crowd of competition. You haven't even begun working for your client, but you're already highly organized and detailed about what they can expect from you. Your client is likely to think that if you're this meticulous before signing the deal, just imagine how good things will be once they become a client of yours. Again, this is a step many companies avoid detailing and another opportunity for you to outshine the competition.

9. **Agreement, T&Cs, and Collateral Support.** The company Proposify discovered that the most common winning proposal length is ten pages according to their audit of 1.6 million proposals. Again back to the notion of KISS, you want to keep these items separate from the proposal. You can always circulate these along with payment processing *after* they accept your proposal. People never read 100 percent of your content, which is why you just want to provide an overview of the client's goals, the solution, and what sets your company apart from the crowd.

10. **Ongoing Optimization.** Like everything else in your sales process,

THE ZERO TO 100 MILLION SALES BLUEPRINT

remember to measure, analyze, and optimize on an ongoing basis. Look for patterns, assess your closing ratios, which pages do prospects skip or spend the most time on. Leverage the analytics of your proposal software to customize your proposal content accordingly. Don't be afraid to exclude content and elements that you otherwise consider mandatory in a proposal if they aren't consumed properly. The goal is better closing ratios and the ability to subsequently deliver according to client expectations.

The Groundwork of a High-Converting Proposal

So what details should you include in your B2B proposal? As mentioned above, you want to keep it concise, consider who you're pitching, and focus on the most valuable aspects of them doing business with you. Certain information may be better to circulate after the proposal has been issued. For example, in most of my companies, we have a "proposal email sequence" where we check in with the prospect with regard to our issued proposal in a nonintrusive way and with days in between each email. Common for every email is that we attach some relevant and valuable content as a reinforcement for why they should choose our solution.

Therefore, don't make the mistake of throwing everything at them at once. Less is more at times. But these fundamentals should be considered best practices and included in your proposals:

1. **Proposal cover and an executive summary.** This is your summarized pitch on steroids which should be crisp, personalized, and evidence-based, fueling the prospect with excitement to continue reading.
2. **Problem statement and your solution.** How can you help them? Have you understood their pain point(s), their exact challenges,

and how this can help their company? Make sure to spell this out in detail with metrics of improvement and ROI calculations as much as possible.

3. **Project deliverables and milestones.** What's included exactly? If something they expect isn't, make sure to be up front about it. Who will be assigned to get the job done? How will you attack the project? What resources will be assigned and by when will you get each milestone completed? You want to convey clarity and transparency here to avoid future misunderstandings.

4. **Pricing and terms.** Keep it precise, easy to understand, and aligned with their budget as much as possible. Research from Proposify shows that proposals with interactive pricing have a close rate 12.6 percent higher than those with static pricing.

5. **Your team and social proof.** Illustrate your team's expertise and how you have crushed it for other similar clients. There's nothing worse for me than speaking with an eloquent sales rep and then being assigned some junior rep who is new on the job to get the work done after I signed the deal. Make sure to introduce the full team they can expect to work with from the beginning. Highlight their experience in the domain, projects they have delivered great results with, and why they're a terrific match for their company and this specific project.

Below is a screenshot of the digital proposal structure I implemented in my last company and offered to 200+ resellers. Using proposal technology like Conga and with a dedicated team to facilitate the high volume of RFPs, this became one of the most popular sales enablement support features offered to resellers since it drastically reduced hours of sales administrative time for our partners' reps. Plus it was proven to convert higher than standard proposals (~45 percent RFP win rate). The result was that the proposal you see below was almost cut in half content-wise because we discovered certain sections weren't even read. Our partners' closing ratios skyrocketed as a result of that alone.

How to Negotiate Deals
(Like an FBI Hostage Negotiator)

You're almost at the finish line now. For months you've been soliciting, pitching, probing, and demoing your way up the decision chain through countless conversations with multiple stakeholders in the prospect's company.

Finally they come around, acknowledging your value proposition, and adding you to the short list of possible vendors under consideration. Next, you spend hours creating ROI calculations and a compelling proposal, feeling confident that it's only a matter of time now before they sign on the dotted line.

And then...Boom! They hit you with an unexpected curveball requesting a ridiculous amount of extra value or lowered price beyond your permitted discount parameters. What to do? You've already invested hundreds of hours landing this deal. Desperation kicks in, to say the least.

There are lots of good books on negotiation strategy to guide you in this type of situation. Among the most well known is *Getting to Yes: Negotiating Agreement without Giving In*. Its problem-solving approach was developed at the Harvard Business School over twenty years ago.

However, one of the most compelling recent approaches to negotiation that's influenced my style is Chris Voss's book *Never Split the Difference: Negotiating as if Your Life Depended on It*. It's a departure from *Getting to Yes* in many innovative ways, all developed through years of practical experience as the FBI's lead hostage negotiator.

Unlike the *Getting to Yes* model, Voss firmly believes most negotiations are irrational and emotionally driven. Approaching them from a rational perspective often results in failure. You must understand the counterpart's underlying psychology and apply your emotional intelligence to take control of the conversation. Active listening is critical. Then it's not so much what you say; it's how you say it. And often that is mostly with carefully probing questions delivered in empathic ways.

There are many intriguing principles and tactics set out in his book that have proven highly effective in hostage negotiations but also apply to business negotiations. Among them, several stand out:

- **Maintain Self-Control and Emotional Regulation:** Don't deny your emotions or ignore those of others. Instead, identify and influence them. Your counterparts are neither fully rational nor completely selfish. They want to feel safe, to feel in control, to be understood, and to be accepted. Knowing how to identify and influence emotions instead of denying or ignoring them is key. The negotiation relationship between you and your counterpart can be viewed as a therapeutic one. Active listening to your counterpart is central to understanding their problems. Techniques include the following. The desired outcome is to hear your counterpart say, "That's right" at each step of the process:
  » Mirroring their responses to lead to a change in their behavior
  » Effective pauses to keep your counterpart talking
  » Minimal encouragers to provoke your counterpart to reveal more
  » Labeling to identify and name what your counterpart is feeling
  » Paraphrasing by repeating what your counterpart is saying in their words
  » Summarizing: using both labeling and paraphrasing
- **Tactical Empathy:** View your counterpart as your partner rather than your adversary. Seek to understand the feelings and mindset of your counterpart. This does not mean agreeing with them. Seek to understand why their actions make sense to them and what might move them to change their position.
- **Calibrated Questions:** These are a range of open-ended questions designed to do a number of things such as:
  » To gently say no, in response to no
  » To provide the illusion of control
  » To unearth deal-killing issues
  » To identify behind-the-table deal killers

- **Beware of "Yes," Master "No":** Many back away from "No," fearing rejection, but negotiators should strive to elicit "No" from their counterparts. It enables the negotiator to determine what their counterpart wants by eliminating what they don't want. "No" is usually a temporary decision, used to maintain the status quo. Hearing "No" may actually mean a variety of important things for the negotiator to then work with, including:
  - » I'm not ready to agree.
  - » You're making me uncomfortable.
  - » I don't understand.
  - » I can't afford it.
  - » I want something else.
  - » I need more information.
  - » I want to talk this through with someone else.
- **Black Swans:** A hidden, unexpected piece of information that can completely upend a negotiation dynamic. Information regarding an "unknown unknown" can lead to dramatic breakthroughs in the negotiation, especially by shifting leverage. It's important to not let what you do know obscure what you don't know. There are usually at least three, and it's critical to learn to recognize them.

My 11 Golden Rules of Negotiation

Although negotiations certainly are a psychological game of chess in many ways, as Chris Voss spells out, and there are many strategies and tactics on how to play it most effectively (more on that in a bit), I live by and recommend my 11 Golden Rules for making deals in the business world. Some of these apply to both parties in a negotiation, whereas others may apply to either the buyer or the seller.

1. **Create a mutually beneficial agreement.** A truly successful negotiation is all about coming to where both parties walk away satisfied with the feeling they are extracting satisfactory value.

2. **Give and take proportionally and don't give away things for free.** Ask for something in return, even if minuscule and not a deal breaker. Salespeople have a tendency to give it all away for fear of losing any kind of deal, often devaluing themselves and their solutions. In the big picture, it's better to stand your ground and lose a deal or two, rather than discount disproportionately, since that often sets the stage for future discount requests.

3. **Don't lay it out all at once.** Very often good negotiators aim for partial agreements before asking for additional conditions. The likelihood of you landing a deal by making several big asks regarding price reductions and term changes all at once are slim to none. Know what to ask and when during the negotiation process.

4. **Start low and work up.** As a buyer, I've made thousands of deals in Latin America over the last decade, and especially in this region, I recommend offering as low as possible (almost to the extent they laugh at you or get insulted) and work your way up from there.

5. **Summarize terms agreed on *during* the process.** Especially with larger, more complex deals, this helps to avoid going backward at any point because of what was agreed on previously during the negotiations.

6. **Avoid negotiating with an intermediary.** If at all possible, find a rationale to talk directly with the decision maker(s).

7. **Be respectful of others' time, capacity, and priorities.** If you're dealing with a vendor who's successful and in high demand to work with, understand that they have the ball in their court and

are in a superior position to set terms. You can bend it a little, but asking too much won't lead to anything but frustration and annoyance.

8. **Prioritize.** As the seller, you may be losing another good deal because you're giving too much attention to a high-demand prospect with constant asks. Better to prioritize daily and focus on deals with the highest likelihood and potential to close.

9. **Don't be an asshole, rude, or slam the door.** Karma's a bitch and will kick you in the butt eventually.

10. **Don't be afraid to walk away.** If the terms of the agreement have become so undesirable for you, then it's better to respectfully pass on the offer. Very often, that can lead to your counterpart coming back and loosening their terms (assuming they truly are interested in working with you).

11. **Timing.** This can be everything in the art of negotiation. From a micro perspective and as a seller, it can be something as little as who speaks first after you throw out your proposed price. And from a macro standpoint, as a buyer, I like to circle back with sellers on the last day of each quarter since larger companies often book revenue by the quarter and are often inclined to extend additional discounts to land the deal with you to help "save the quarter."

In this chapter, we have covered the many ways you can drive incremental revenue gains by investing thoughtfully in a sales enablement collateral strategy. If there's just one takeaway from this section of the book, it's to stimulate productive conversations between your sales and marketing team—around what content should be created for your company over the next six to twelve months, how to measure its effectiveness, and which joint ROI targets to establish that will foster better cross-departmental collaboration. Finally, I set out some effective guidelines for approaching negotiations as a seller and buyer.

In the next chapter, we are going to cover some of my all-time favorite growth strategies with the highest possible associated ROI: upselling, cross-selling, and business referrals.

11

THE LOW-HANGING FRUIT

Will show you how to get more bang for your buck and solidify long-term relationships with your customers by extracting the full potential and mutual value of your relationship.

The name of the game for company growth is revenue optimization, and there are a number of factors at play to accomplish this that sales and marketing in particular need to consider. The diagram on the following page illustrates the relationships between these.

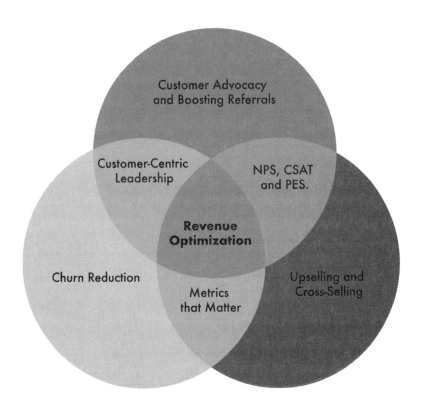

Often I hear, "Hey, Gary. Quick question for you":

- *What are your most effective methods to drive revenue optimization?*
- *Who within our team should conduct upsells and cross-sales? Is it the Account Executive who landed that specific customer initially five months ago or the assigned Account Manager who has been having the ongoing weekly conversations with the customer ever since?*
- *At what point should we roll out our upselling and cross-selling initiatives, and how do we identify exactly when is the ideal time to bring up this conversation with clients?*
- *When exactly during the sales cycle and customer journey should we ask our customers for referral(s)? Is it immediately after they sign up*

for our service, after the onboarding process, or is it better for us to wait
for some sort of indicator that they're satisfied with our solution and
service levels?

- *Which tools can we use to automate our revenue optimization processes*
  and create a company-wide framework of references?

These are just a few of the most common questions I get from my consulting clients aiming to boost revenue. Frankly, I get quite excited when I hear these because it clearly indicates my client has the right mindset when it comes to effectively optimizing their revenue strategy by picking low-hanging fruit.

After all, according to the Customer Service Institute, on average 65 percent of a company's revenue comes from its repeat customers. In other words, your customer's revenue potential doesn't stop at the initial point of sale. On the contrary, there are many ways for you to grow revenue per customer beyond the initial transaction value. Mastering the art of upselling and cross-selling is one of the best ways to expand revenue per customer and boost your company's profitability.

So if your business isn't meeting, or ideally exceeding, this benchmark, then perhaps it's time to evaluate what you're doing currently and aim to foster more customer advocacy and brand loyalty.

Why? Because it's significantly more expensive and difficult to acquire a new customer than to grow an existing relationship and its associated revenue.

Another key reason I like to remind folks is that if your customer is growing their business with you, then it's very unlikely they're about to cancel and walk away.

So here are a couple of questions to ask within your organization to promote the account growth of your existing customer base:

- *Are your customers satisfied and engaged enough with your products or services? Are you leveraging tools like CSAT (Customer Satisfaction), NPS (Net Promoter Score), or PES (Product Engagement Score) to measure customer satisfaction and product adoption?*
- *Do you have solid revenue optimization processes in place in your business for remarketing, cross-selling, and upselling, and are the efforts aligned with product updates and promotional offers broadcast by your marketing team?*
- *Are you checking in with all of your customers on an ongoing basis either via newsletters, social media, special events, or holidays? And if you're operating in the B2B sector, are you and your customers conducting quarterly annual business reviews to collaborate on your mutual growth and success?*
- *Last, consider whether your marketing team are all-in when it comes to promoting your customer success stories by engaging with your existing client base and distributing the message via case studies, testimonials, reviews, and press releases.*

Tell Me More, Tell Me More

Lifetime value, CAC-to-LTV ratio, customer churn, cross- and upsell rates are all key metrics to monitor and optimize to positively influence your company's growth trajectory. However, all of these are severely impacted by the mother of all metrics.

Your customer satisfaction.

A phenomenal customer experience (CX) is typically linked with incremental revenue gains for companies. However, I've come to learn that most companies in the B2B sector are severely lacking an adequate CX when compared to the B2C market.

Statistically speaking, according to McKinsey & Company, most B2C companies' typical CX scores are between 65 percent and 85 percent, while B2B companies average less than 50 percent.

Hence before you begin discussing sales and cross-sales strategies, the very first thing on your agenda should be whether you have appropriate feedback loops (i.e., CSAT, NPS, PES, QBRs, etc.) to survey whether your customers are satisfied with your work. Otherwise, you'll be shooting yourself in the foot trying to ask for more business when they're not satisfied with the current state of business with you!

In other words, your customer experience is not only a brand differentiator—it's also a catalyst of your revenue optimization strategy. In fact, a survey by Walker Research shows that a whopping 86 percent of buyers are willing to pay more for an outstanding customer experience.

So how can you tap into these customer experience insights to boost your revenue? In many ways actually. For example, with a justifiable higher pricing strategy, decreased customer churn, increased volume of upsells and cross-sells, as well as a boost in customer advocacy and referrals.

With this in mind, let's now review the most common methodologies used to survey your customers' satisfaction rates.

Customer Satisfaction Score

CSAT is a survey tool used by many companies to measure customer satisfaction levels. In my previous company we circulated surveys roughly quarterly, and I saw that our partners, Google and Microsoft, did the same with us as their clients/partners.

However, there's no one size fits all for CSAT processes. You can choose to circulate as frequently as you see fit or as I often recommend, after the following touchpoints during the customer journey:

- When the purchase is made or agreement/contract is signed
- After the client onboarding process
- On a monthly basis typically after your AM has engaged with your customer during their recurring monthly meetings
- A month or so before your agreement/contract expires and prior to that negotiation and renewal

Normally, you'll want to ask a couple of questions regarding your service levels or interactions with your client-facing staff such as:

- *On a scale of 1 to 5, how satisfied are you with our solution?*
- *What's working for you and why?*
- *How can we improve your experience with our company?*
- *Is there anything our team members can do better?*
- *How likely are you to recommend our solution to others?*

And you can ask as many questions as you want; however, if you are to prompt a good survey response rate, I recommend that you keep it to a few essential questions and never more than five.

Sometimes I receive surveys from vendors with ten-plus questions. My question to them is, who the hell has time to do that? I'm busy running a business here!

Here's another recommendation to consider. If you want a fair sample size of CSAT survey respondents and statistical validation of the data for improvement, create a survey outreach sequence (a combination of emails and calls) sent "personally" by the assigned AM or CSM in order to prompt more responses.

From my experience, if you just send out a generic survey blast from Marketing across your entire customer base with no follow-ups, your response rate is likely to be in the low-end single digits and responses primarily will be from your unhappy customers.

You want to get a good sample size of what's working and not. Especially for upsells, cross-sells, and referral purposes, you want to collect a good portion of positive feedback as well and not just use the CSAT surveys to *reactively* solve problems with unsatisfied customers.

Net Promoter Score

Another powerful way to measure your customer engagement, and one of my favorite methods, is the NPS, where you gather feedback from your customers with one simple question such as:

"On a scale from 1 to 10, how likely are you to recommend our solution to others?"

Depending on the score, you usually categorize your customers into brackets as *Passives, Detractors,* or *Promoters.* And having an abundance of the last is what makes a business grow and thrive!

Additionally, the feedback collected from your negative scores—that is, the Detractors—can serve as extremely valuable input to improve potential gaps in your solution and your overall process management.

I recommend having a CSM (Customer Success Manager) facilitate the survey administration and responses. In my experience, just like with CSAT surveys albeit in a shorter format, few customers, especially the Passives or Promoters, bother to fill out responses unless politely reminded to do so a few times.

In that case, a personalized check-in phone call can significantly increase the volume of answers and help collect feedback by asking questions like:

1. *What is the primary reason for your score?*
2. *How can we improve your experience moving forward?*

3. *Which product/service feature of ours do you value the most?*

4. *What was missing or disappointing in your experience with us?*

5. *What can we do to make you a 100 percent satisfied customer?*

An interesting fact, and perhaps the motivation you need to roll out your own NPS initiative, is that Bain & Company research has established a strong link between organic growth and a company's NPS. Their research revealed many interesting facts. Most relevant for me is that, on average, an industry's Net Promoter leader outgrew its competitors by a factor greater than two times!

What Is Net Promoter Score?

Net Promoter Score (NPS) is a customer loyalty and satisfaction measurement metric gathered by asking customers the question: "On a scale from 0-10, how likely are you to recommend [company] to others?"

○ Promoters (score 9-10) are loyal enthusiasts who will keep buying and refer to others, fueling growth.
○ Passives (score 7-8) are satisfied but unenthusiastic customers who are vulnerable to competitive offerings.
○ Detractors (score 0-6) are unhappy customers who can damage your brand and impede growth through negative word-of-mouth.

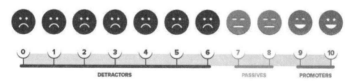

% PROMOTERS - % DETRACTORS = NPS (NET PROMOTER SCORE)

Product Engagement Score

I work with many SaaS players and have operated in that space for many years. Although NPS is a significantly important tool for B2B and consumer brands, the mother of all metrics when it comes to SaaS players is PES.

$$PES = (Adoption + Stickiness + Growth)/3$$

However, to properly measure and optimize your PES, you need to have a collection of tools, systems, and processes in place (along with a mindset to challenge the status quo). As with everything else, it all starts with data, which is why configuring a solid product analytics platform is key to your success.

Tools I've worked with and can recommend are Heap and MixPanel. Both enable you to track user activity across your entire SaaS business.

And with data now leading the analysis, you can begin identifying areas of improvement, aiming to optimize the user flow of your product features and processes. Essentially, you want to fix all areas within your SaaS solution that can help optimize the adoption of features and engage your users at a higher level.

A few tips to further improve product engagement are:

- *Improve your overall UX and make it as seamless as possible to navigate*
- *Promote features for a more advantageous UX within your platform/app*
- *Give your users the aha moment as soon as possible to secure their buy-in with continued engagement and feature adoption*

If your business falls into this category, I recommend that you read up on PES best practices from Pendo, the company that introduced PES to the SaaS business landscape in the first place. Your objective should be to provide a singular, quantitative, business metric to measure the overall engagement of a product with the goal of quickly diagnosing how your product is performing.

How to Calculate Product Engagement Score (PES)

The product engagement score (PES) is a key metric to optimize in order to lower churn, improve retention, and increase your product engagement. It is a composite score made up of three elements: adoption, stickiness, and growth.

Calculating your product engagement score is actually pretty easy:

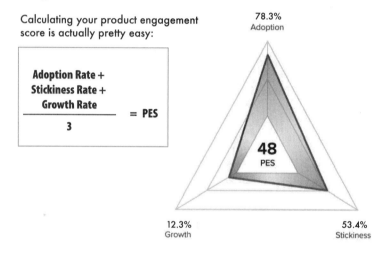

$$\frac{\text{Adoption Rate} + \text{Stickiness Rate} + \text{Growth Rate}}{3} = PES$$

Upsells, Cross-sells, Renewals, and Referrals

"The odds of going to the store for a loaf of bread and coming out with ONLY a loaf of bread are three billion to one."

—ERMA BOMBECK

The idea here is simple. Maximize the longevity and potential of each and every customer for mutual satisfactory results. In some events the low-hanging fruit can be an upsell—for example, adding more users/licenses to your agreement—or moving the customer to a larger package—for example, from Pro to Premium. In other scenarios it can be cross-selling customers—that is, selling them additional related products to their existing agreement with you.

Either strategy works and can vary from customer to customer. Very often upselling is directly tied up with your customer's budget and capacity for growth, so not always within your control (e.g., if your offering is a SaaS solution and an upsell is directly tied up with the amount of employees).

But in many other scenarios where your goals are tied up with marketing results, cost-saving tactics, or growth of revenue, customers are usually very interested in investing more if the associated ROI can be justified.

How to Foster a Culture of Upselling

Below is an example of how I launched an upselling initiative at my last company, in collaboration with Google, for all client-facing staff but predominantly AMs and AEs. The concept is simple. Make upselling *as easy as possible* by demonstrating potential incremental revenue gains, leading the pitch with data and ROI projections.

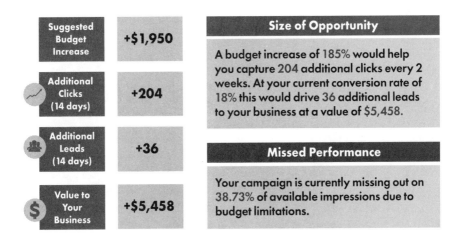

		Size of Opportunity
Suggested Budget Increase	+$1,950	A budget increase of 185% would help you capture 204 additional clicks every 2 weeks. At your current conversion rate of 18% this would drive 36 additional leads to your business at a value of $5,458.
Additional Clicks (14 days)	+204	
Additional Leads (14 days)	+36	**Missed Performance**
Value to Your Business	+$5,458	Your campaign is currently missing out on 38.73% of available impressions due to budget limitations.

Often, opportunities and low-hanging fruit don't get picked up by sales organizations because they don't have an easy streamlined approach to asking for more budget. Complicating matters with the complex administrative hassle of creating new proposals each time is a showstopper. The same goes for pitching without visual support and documentation. The key to success lies in a healthy balance for your reps between speed, ease of customization, and effectiveness in pitch.

In the scenario above, to foster collaboration between the Account Managers (asking for extra budget and upsell) and the Account Strategists (implementing and managing the account) we:

- Fostered cross-departmental collaboration by creating a joint commission structure and upsell KPIs
- Created a framework that ensured campaign goals were identified and documented in our CRM to identify when they were suited to try and upsell
- Created a streamlined process supported by task creation in the CRM and a sales pitch outline for every scenario

Below is another way to create an upselling narrative where packages were presented with low, medium, and high price points and with the incremental new customer gains expected.

📅 **Lead Projection**		CPC	CVR*	CPA
Your plan can get **6 conversions** for **$4k**		$44.05	6.98%	$631.09

	Low **$4,000**	Medium **$8,000**	High **$12,000**
Clicks per month	91	182	272
Conversions per month*	6	13	19

What about Cross-selling?

In scenarios, like the one described above, there's no opportunity to grow your revenue per customer because of certain uncontrollable limitations in the clients' business. In many of these cases, however, a cross-sell can be pursued.

For example, in my last company, our primary offerings were Google Ads (Search, Display, and YouTube), Microsoft Ads, and Search Engine Optimization (SEO). If a client already was maxed out on budget in one category—for example, Google Search Ads—yet overall was satisfied with our work but not yet leveraging a network such as Microsoft Ads, in that event we would instead demonstrate why, how, and what to expect (possible in nine out of ten cases) and pursue a cross-sell. Other cross-sell avenues could also be landing pages for a campaign, a new website redesign, or a complementary SEO strategy.

The point is that there's usually always an opportunity to pursue additional revenue. The question is whether your clients are satisfied in the first place, if you've established enough trust with them to be open to your suggestions, and then whether you've implemented an internal process to identify and facilitate these low-hanging revenue opportunities.

Here's an example illustrating how simple it can be. Our Account Strategist created some quick custom talking points with concise recommendations for an existing customer who had deployed a Google Ads campaign. We suggested they invest an additional $2,500/month for Bing Ads. This may not be a visually compelling pitch deck, but the key here is to make it simple, easy to roll out, and yet with convincing arguments for why they should invest additional budget with your company.

We were careful to not result in revenue cannibalization (e.g., deferring budget from one channel to another, giving you no additional revenue gains, just extra work). Remember, if they're already an existing customer and you have established trust with them, they are expecting you to drive performance and ROI for them—not spend time on flashy presentations trying to sell them extra features. So a quick evidence-based note format like that below can sometimes be enough to get your point across and generate $2,500 monthly in revenue.

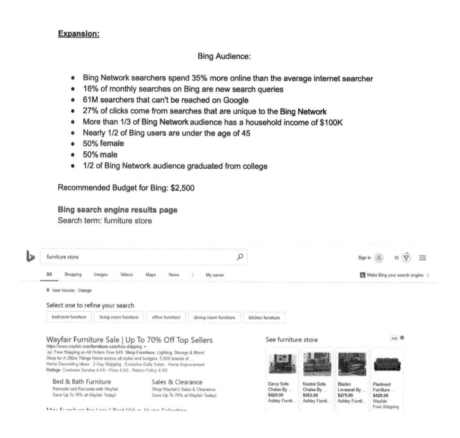

The point here is to illustrate that upselling and cross-selling isn't always straightforward and is a difficult subject to master. It demands the right combination of timing and awareness of the customer's situation and needs. Required also is a healthy balance between selling extras while ensuring you can actually meet expectations so that it doesn't backfire and cause unexpected customer churn. There's no boiler room template for it or a silver bullet that can drive success. However, significant revenue gains can be expected here with low-hanging fruit for the reaping that you must harvest to fully exploit your company's growth potential.

Creating a Referral Engine

Nine out of ten companies I come across in my agency or Accelerator Platform don't have a referral strategy in place. If they do, it's a strategy that severely lacks execution and the results are practically nonexistent. If you're brutally honest, you can probably relate to this. If not, congratulations. Go ahead and skip this section.

But before you do so, consider the following statements:

- *According to Forbes, 78 percent of B2B marketers believe that B2B customer referral programs are a source of high-quality leads.*
- *According to Capterra, 88 percent of B2B decision makers rely on word of mouth (online and offline) for "information and advice."*
- *According to Annex Cloud, referral marketing generates 3–5x higher conversion rates than any other marketing channel.*
- *According to Marketo, 10.99 percent of sales referrals convert while only 0.9 percent of regular sales prospects turn into customers.*

There are many compelling statistics motivating why you ought to roll out a referral strategy, but there is an equal amount of white noise out there about them. Many companies and salespeople give up on the initiative because of a few failed attempts.

I have tried referral programs of all shapes and sizes over the last twenty years in six different companies. The results? Here are ten quick and easy-to-implement guidelines for you to roll out with your team and send out. Remember, referrals aren't complex—it's just about getting it right, not complicating the process, and doing it consistently!

1. **Timing:** The best time to ask for referrals is immediately after the initial purchase is made. I call it the "honeymoon phase." The customer is still floating on a bubbly sky envisioning what the true potential looks like that they can realize from the agreement. Leverage this and ask for referrals immediately after the contract is signed.

2. **Paradigm Shift:** Many sales reps position their asks for referrals as the buyer doing them a favor. Flip it around. You just helped them with your solution to drive growth and ROI. How can *they* return the favor to you? It's all about tone of voice, confidence, and what you believe in your soul to be true.

3. **Who Else?** Scan your book of business for 5-star reviews online, customer testimonials, positive feedback from your CSAT surveys, and customers who have been with you a long time. These are obvious referral sourcing candidates that undoubtedly have a few warm leads just burning in their pockets for the taking.

4. **How Much?** You don't necessarily have to offer your customers anything in return for the referrals. Most don't. I'd argue otherwise. If, for example, your customer acquisition cost (CAC) is $1,500 and your lifetime value (LTV) is $5,000, then why be cheap and offer a $100 gift certificate or similar? You're still winning massively if you offer a $500–$1,000 bonus per referral that converts. This way, you may actually create some consistent referral ambassadors for your company.

5. **How To?** Don't just ask for referrals and sit and wait for them

to circle back. Be assertive, schedule a quick ten-minute call if needed. And be proactive by taking a look at their LinkedIn contacts to scan for any suitable prospects you preferably want them to introduce you to.

6. **Make It Easy:** If needed, using KISS, write up a draft email for your customer and instruct them that all they have to do is copy-paste, send, and cc you. Easy peasy.

7. **Quid Pro Quo:** If a prospect is pounding you for discounts, don't just give in to get the sale. Make it a requirement for them to provide two to three referrals once the contract is signed.

8. **Make it a habit.** When walking prospects through our ninety-day onboarding process and campaign rollout, a standard phrase of mine in every explanation would be, *"Mr. Customer, at this point, once we meet our established targets, I expect you to make a few introductions to peers within your network that could find equal value as you with our solution. Fair enough?"* Say it with a smile, of course, and also remind them of it during monthly check-ins when you're ahead of the curve performance-wise. No need to disguise that you are a sales rep eager to earn new business.

9. **Contest:** I have rarely heard of this elsewhere, but what has worked well for me is launching sales incentives and contests with a focus on client testimonials and referrals that convert. For one, it gets your entire organization aligned with what the only objective is—performance and satisfied customers. And second, it can be the best ROI of any sales bonus you have ever issued before.

10. **Technology:** Once you experience the true potential of a referral program and want to scale it next, you'll want to implement some referral software programs to manage it appropriately.

VIP Customer Appreciation Events and Programs

While working with Google and Microsoft as a reseller, I witnessed how they rolled out hundreds of new customer acquisition events—a common practice for any company looking to scale growth via channel sales programs.

It could be everything from hosting a dinner for select prospects in their city, to renting a hotel conference room and inviting business owners for a "digital breakfast." Usually there would be a hook such as a special offer and a guest subject matter expert speaker in a category of high interest or demand.

The goal with these events was crystal clear—drive net new customers and revenue with an expected ROI of 8–14x. Most often this would be feasible, hence why such marketing stunts are still highly used.

However, in line with the notion of the low-hanging fruit and optimizing revenue by decreasing churn and facilitating same-store growth, I also witnessed another interesting approach to revenue optimization strategies and that is "VIP Customer Events" also called "Customer Appreciation Events." Most larger B2B and B2C companies have Customer Loyalty Programs in place, and I bet you're already a member of one or more.

I experienced firsthand the increased ROI from motivating our $100,000/ month clients to stick with us for the long haul and often give us extra business because of the appreciation. My recommendation is to perhaps prioritize such events from a sales and marketing budget perspective, over allocating most dollars toward net new customers—as most SMB companies do.

Don't wait until you become a bigger company with this initiative. Do it as soon as possible. It may be the foundation needed in your customer base to take things to the next level. It takes a lot of new sales to replace that one $100,000/month account whom you neglected while chasing down new business. In other words, don't step over dollars to pick up pennies!

Launching a customer appreciation program within your revenue optimization strategy may become a vital factor in the success of your business. Here are some benefits you can expect to gain:

- **Increased Profitability.** As mentioned earlier, research shows that acquiring a new customer can cost five times more than retaining an existing customer and that increasing your customer retention rates by just 5 percent can increase profits from 25 percent to 95 percent. The concept for this is simple, especially since CAC is usually high in B2B sales and an extended LTV yield increases profits per customer. The key here is to make your client feel important, like a VIP (even though they aren't necessarily) and getting them to stick for a longer time with an increased probability to purchase more via upsells and cross-selling initiatives.
- **Elevate Your Market Position.** Online reviews and feedback are the do-or-die of any company. You cannot get away with having a large volume of unsatisfied customers. It leads to lower closing ratios, deals lost, and an out-of-control spiral effect of more negative reviews that essentially can take you out of business. Ensuring that you build a solid foundation of truly satisfied customers leads to better reviews across media and sites. This gives you a competitive advantage in the market when prospective buyers are conducting research on possible vendors and comparing you with your competition's digital footprint in reviews.
- **Clients for Life.** I'm still friends with some of my former best customers. Once you have created truly loyal customers who appreciate the lengths you have gone to in making their business successful, they will never dream of doing business with someone else, even if their price is more favorable than yours. You have to utterly

f**k things up to make them leave. Hence why your customer appreciation strategy is a critical ingredient to increasing the number of loyal customers and giving you a solid foundation to scale your business and revenue.

We have now highlighted the importance of customer satisfaction as the centerpiece for revenue optimization. And with an understanding of key metrics such as CSAT, NPS, and PES, you are now well positioned to develop a more effective strategy for driving upsells, cross-sales, renewals, and referrals.

In the next chapter, we are going to focus on how you can get things organized, structured, and streamlined to establish the groundwork for effective scaling. We will also cover some of the important ingredients of that equation including process creation, CRM implementation, and developing a Sales Ops team to execute everything.

12

WITH ORGANIZATION COMES EMPOWERMENT

The do-or-die element in order to take your company from a small business to become a significant player in your category by creating the right systems—the only way you can scale your team and organization.

Sales has evolved *a lot* since I rolled out my first sales teams back in the early 2000s. The first company, ITNETBIZ A/S, had approximately twenty sales reps, and all we had was an old-school landline dial phone, a call list printed out on paper, along with a call script and rebuttal library. That's it. When a sale was made, the rep would fill out a form by hand that would be given to our sales admin, Stine. She'd fax out an order form to be signed, followed by an invoice.

And lead management was so rudimentary that our reps would be calling on each other's leads (and clients) with daily infighting about who was the true owner of a lead or a sale in the making. At times I'd have to puff up my chest, slam my fist on the table, and use my 6' 5", 230 lbs. size to go out on the sales floor and practically break up a fistfight in the making. Intense.

Nowadays, a modern sales organization is 180 degrees the opposite. No longer would Stine, my good old sales admin I had back then, be able to juggle the suite of sophisticated sales technology most savvy companies use, integrate cloud-based applications with process management, leverage big data, analytics, and provide a structured overview of everything via KPI and Sales Metrics reporting.

Now Stine's role has evolved to Sales Operations—the backbone of any successful sales organization.

Ready for Scale? Build an A+ Sales Ops Team

There's no way around it. In order to scale your shop, make sure you bring on board an organized, structured, and meticulously data-driven Sales Operations Manager early in your build phase.

Believe me, it's better done sooner than later *before* discovering that your lead inventory is a mess with zero organization and that your leads and accounts are blended in one big mix. Then it's too late, and you'll wish you had taken my advice and hired for this role within year one of setting up your shop.

Not only will the right candidate help you get things set up correctly and document all processes from A to Z; they'll also subsequently ensure that your sales machine is always running on all cylinders.

From my personal experience, this is one of the most important roles in a successful sales organization.

You need someone disciplined, methodical, intelligent, creative, hard-working, and able to juggle systems, process compliance, and KPIs, along with strong interpersonal skills to be able to interact effectively with your sales reps.

Every Sales Ops superstar I've hired within the last decade (Karen Hite, Emily Arbizu, or Elizabeth Navas come to mind) have all had the skillset to run an entire department or even their own company like clockwork.

My point here is that this is probably *the most* important hire for your company revenue-wise with the exception of your sales leader. But even the best sales leaders, including yours truly, *need* Elizabeth, Emily, or Karen to make shit happen!

What did they all have in common—that is, what are the required attributes of your future superstar Sales Operations Manager? Let's break it down in detail.

- **Process Oriented.** To scale, you'll need a systematic Six Sigma-like approach to strategize, plan, hire, onboard, execute, manage, and report—hence why your Sales Ops Manager should eat, breathe, and live process management.
- **Business Minded.** You need to ensure at all cost that your sales initiatives and focus are aligned with your business objectives. This includes cross-departmental alignment for client onboarding, fulfillment, billing, and maximizing your ARPA via upselling and cross-selling when possible. Your Sales Ops Team ensures no one drops the ball during the entire customer journey, and if they do, they're ready to assess and create a process to improve.
- **Organizational Skills.** Reports to sales leadership, marketing, and finance. Feedback and hiring requests to HR, facilitating contracts, or ensuring customer success via onboarding and post-sales support vehicles are all critical functions. The list of tasks is long, which is why no Sales Ops person can survive in this role without being a close candidate to the most organized person in the world!

- **Emotional Intelligence.** They are expected to interact daily with multiple personality types, from pushy, high-energy sales reps asking for more leads, to your CFO requesting data for financial analysis, or your Sales Manager who wants everything done yesterday. This role requires a high degree of emotional intelligence to balance all of these personalities.

- **Ability to Work under Pressure and Tight Timelines.** The name of the game in sales is emotional pressure, stretch targets, and highly demanding employees and clients—while upper management decides to roll out a new product, enter a new market, or change the sales compensation structure. Juggling it all and making sure priorities are set straight and met calls for an individual who can manage a great deal of work at once and get the job done.

- **Curious and Creative.** There's no way around it. With the pace of evolution in new technology, constant changes in market conditions, and the need to constantly aim to innovate and optimize, you need a curious soul at the helm of your Sales Operations always looking for new and better ways to do things.

- **Results Oriented.** Performance is needed. Yesterday, today, and tomorrow. Daily targets. Monthly and quarterly goals. KPIs to hit and metrics to improve. You need someone who keeps their eyes on the prize constantly and who loves it!

- **Program Management.** Direct Sales, Channel Sales, Affiliates, and referral programs. Or territory management and lead management for SMB or Enterprise sales teams structured along vertically focused sales initiatives. There are many programs to manage, and you need a Sales Ops Manager to have this capacity.

- **Analytical and Data Driven.** Remember Chapter 6 In God We Trust, Everyone Else Brings Data, and the twenty-five sales metrics to measure, analyze, and optimize next? Well, at the forefront of this mission critical element for success is your Sales Ops Goddess (yes, usually Goddess) extracting data, pulling reports, configuring dashboards, and trying to make some sense of all the madness going on at once. This requires some degree of mastery in data analysis and an understanding of how the data connects.

- **Technologically Savvy.** Sales enablement tools, CRM, BI, data reporting, scheduling tools, and proposal software are just a few of the sales technologies today's savvy sales departments leverage to scale efficiently. In my experience, most often this involves ten-plus tools for the sales tech alone and seventy-five technologies across an entire company according to research by ZoomInfo. Needless to say, you need a Sales Ops Manager who's at least a part-time techie.

- **Financial Acumen.** Your Sales Ops Manager has to navigate commission structures and systems, adjust contract language including financial terms in collaboration with legal, and provide ongoing communication and reports to your CFO or finance team.

- **Strong People Management Skills.** From my experience, managing a large sales team is as difficult as it gets. At times they are irrational, emotional, and highly demanding individuals who need motivational support, policing, and at times just a hug. Your Sales Ops Manager should be a strong extension to your HR and Head of Sales to ensure everyone is managed optimally for the benefit of your company and culture.

- **Relationship Builder.** They must be able to interact well with clients, partners, vendors, consultants, reps, admin, finance, fulfillment, and many other internal departments. You want a people person who can be objective, professional yet friendly with the objective of establishing strong relationships and ties across all stakeholders in your organization.

Below is a snapshot of some of the characteristics to look for when hiring your Sales Operations Manager. And yes, hiring a good one is almost like finding a needle in a haystack, so start looking today if the role isn't currently fulfilled satisfactorily in your organization.

Sales Operation Manager's Required Skillsets

1. Process-oriented
2. Business-minded
3. Organizational skills
4. Emotional intelligence
5. Ability to work under pressure
6. Curiosity and creativity
7. Results-oriented
8. Project management
9. Analytical and data-driven
10. Technology savvy
11. Financial acumen
12. People management skills
13. Relationship builder

So What Is Sales Operations Exactly?

At its core, the sales operations role is to support and enable your sales team to sell more efficiently and effectively by providing structure, systems, and organization related to everything and anything related to your sales department.

Just think of your new sales rep onboarding criteria for success discussed in Chapter 7. They need proper induction, onboarding, training, ongoing monitoring, evaluation, and support if they are to have just a slim chance of success. Your sales manager should be busy with coaching, strategizing, and bringing in revenue collectively with your team. So who's gonna dot all the i's and cross the t's with regard to scaling up new reps? Sales Operations.

Or what ensures that clients are onboarded in a systematically superb fashion always? Or that CRM data and updates are in compliance? Or that all your sales processes are aligned with your tech stack setup and configuration? Or that you don't run out of leads or that they're distributed effectively among your team for optimal efficiency and that they're categorized for reporting purposes? Who pulls the data for KPI reporting and supports internal sales meetings with metrics and slides?

Your Sales Operations Team. And the list goes on.

In summary, the four main pillars of your Sales Operations Team are:

1. **Strategy.** Strategy is a word loosely thrown around when it comes to sales. Your C-suite may request the achievement of xyz KPI and meeting annual targets. But if there's no tangible strategy to support those objectives, then you can forget all about increased sales, profits, or market share. Your Sales Ops Manager has to, in conjunction with your Sales leadership, understand what resources are needed to meet targets and how to get forecasts within a 10

percent range of those topic targets to ensure that budgets are realistic and that profitability is optimized. This requires strategy 101 and then some.

2. **Operations.** To ensure revenue and performance is always at an optimal level and with few hiccups, you need well-oiled machinery. As mentioned earlier, it's not a matter of just facilitating contracts, data entry, and regular sales administrative tasks. You need to make sure that operations from A to Z are streamlined. The list is simply too long for me to begin mentioning examples. The best way to explain the burden of responsibilities on Sales Ops is to look at your customer journey and zoom in on every task, process, and technology needed to make this flow seamlessly and understand that your Sales Ops Manager is the one holding things together.

3. **Technology.** Overseeing the ongoing needs analysis, management, and implementation of sales technologies is a massive responsibility on its own. There are new players constantly entering the market and categories being added to this domain. I dig deeper into the massiveness of this subject in the next chapter, but just for some context, at the time of writing this book, according to a report by Future Market Insights, the sales platforms software market is expected to expand from $71.5 billion in 2022 to $193 billion in 2032. $193 billion! That's more than the GDP of Panama, Luxembourg, and Costa Rica *combined*.

4. **Performance.** Measuring KPIs, revenue targets, sales metrics, and ensuring that at the end, the sales department has the resources and processes in place to hit those targets is the ultimate responsibility of Sales Ops. If everything is done properly, i.e. overseeing the sales funnel, streamlining operations, hiring, and

training—then performance will be enabled and your company can celebrate more wins than losses with growth to follow.

Here are the functions a Sales Ops team oversees and an overview of the four main pillars: strategy, performance, operations, and technology.

The Four Main Pillars of Sales Operations

- Sales Process Architecting
- Sales Tech Design
- Sales Channels & Methodology
- Goal Setting & Sales Forecasting
- Sales Planning Process

- Opportunity & Pipeline Management
- Compensation Management
- "Smarketing" & Sales Enablement
- Measurement of KPIs & Metrics
- Workflow Process Management

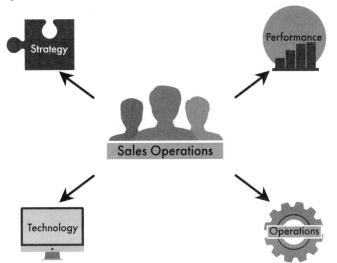

- Technology Evaluation & Roadmap
- Technology & Tool Integration
- Adoption of Sales Technologies
- Data Management & Enrichment
- CRM/Tech Manuals & Compliance

- Product Training
- Cross-Departmental Collaboration
- Proposals, Contracts & SLAs
- Talent & Skills Development
- Hiring & Onboarding

ABD—Always Be Documenting

According to a study by McKinsey & Company, the average knowledge worker spends 19 percent of their time searching for and gathering information. That's more than two whole working months!

And as we dive into the next chapter and cover everything related to sales tech from Sales Readiness Platforms to CRMs, hopefully you'll understand the necessity of documenting everything—otherwise you'll run your head against the wall with all the extra expenses, complete chaos, and poor tech adoption that will entail.

The first time I encountered the need for documentation at scale was in the early days of my last company. We had reached about one hundred employees. I was CEO while running sales simultaneously, and my former partner, Andrew Lolk, was spearheading the product fulfillment team with Google AdWords solutions for SMBs.

As the sales team had quickly grown from me and one SDR a year ago to now nearly thirty SDRs and AEs combined, I was experiencing many challenges in sales such as getting SDRs to write proper notes in our CRM.

Proper note-taking included how to set follow-ups with headlines or which lead statuses applied to various call outcome scenarios. Simple stuff one would think, but without documentation of exactly how to do this, it was very ambiguous and left things to unnecessary interpretation. This challenged me a lot when skimming through the CRM because everyone had their own way of doing things.

Other examples were best practices of how to prepare for a sales call or the call approach. I found that despite the fact that I coached the team daily, played recordings of successful calls, and discussed the strategy minute by minute, the sales reps (and especially the newer ones) had too much bias with their opinions of how they thought things could be done better. Besides many headaches and frustrations, the result meant longer learning curves and high attrition rates.

The tipping point, however, was when one month we hit 20 percent in customer churn (that's like *bleeding* money compared to the industry standard of 3 percent).

There was a huge misalignment between sales and fulfillment regarding setting expectations for performance, establishing an appropriate media budget, or just explaining next steps of the customer onboarding process. Too many of our established processes were left for interpretation. The best way I can explain it was that the sales reps saw the glass as half-full always, and the fulfillment team as half-empty.

The solution? Andrew came to me one day and had taken the initiative of creating our Sales Wikipedia, or just "The 'Wiki" as it quickly got named, and also wrote up the first couple of articles of documentation.

We wrote down everything we could think of, creating more than 250 articles, including scenarios such as:

- Playbooks for different kinds of account audit scenarios
- How to follow up and when to follow up
- A CRM manual with explanations from A to Z
- Onboarding process in detail, including an FAQ and timeline for the first ninety days of the customer journey and client deliverables
- How to sign up a client and mandatory "next steps" information that had to be explained verbally. Each of these were reviewed by our Sales Q&A team (now replaced by AI apps)
- How to handle a customer cancellation request
- Counterpitches for most of our closest competitors (later this evolved into our competitor scorecard)

- RFP process. Turnaround times. How aggressive or conservative we could be in promising performance gains—for example, for lead gen campaigns where an opportunity for improvement was identified
- Call scripts, rebuttals, demo processes, questions, and much more

The result? It wasn't easy. But within just a couple of months, our customer churn rate dropped to 5–6 percent while sales actually went up because of all the extra collateral that now was at the fingertips for every rep. Things I previously was saying to our reps verbally up to one hundred times a day, yet never fully stuck, were now being followed and applied.

The rule of thumb at the end became, "*If it's not in the Wiki, it doesn't exist,*" and that sparked a process of ABD—Always Be Documenting!

Here is the best way to explain before and after the development of our "Sales Wiki":

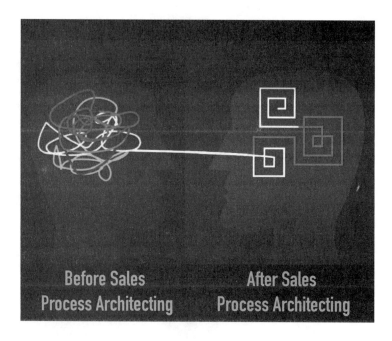

Before Sales Process Architecting   After Sales Process Architecting

Weekly Sales Meetings Done Effectively

And even though it's highly recommended to document in writing every process from A to Z in your Wiki or similar knowledge database, don't forget that you're running a sales team here.

Energy is better transferred through verbal communication than written, and you need to engage with your team and get feedback ongoing. That's why establishing an organized process, in collaboration with your Sales Ops Team, with regard to sales meeting preparation, meeting summaries, and action items is equally important to creating your Wiki or written knowledge sharing database.

According to research by HubSpot, salespeople spend 12 percent of their time attending internal meetings. That equates to over nineteen hours per month. Personally, there's *nothing* I hate more than meetings for the sake of meetings, especially ones without a clear agenda.

A complete waste of everyone's time! We are here to sell and make money. Don't take away our valuable selling time, I have thought to myself hundreds of times throughout my career when having to attend meetings with partners or other departments.

From my perspective, consistency in meeting frequency, the structure, and the messaging is more important than lengthy meetings and everything should be able to get covered in two forty-five-minute meetings per week. That's how I run my sales meetings. Get down to the essence of business and create a standardized agenda that covers the most important points—precisely, effectively, and swiftly.

My Weekly Sales Meeting Agenda:

1. **KPI and Metrics Review.** Create dashboards that include all pertinent KPIs and metrics that everyone has access to and that are continuously updated.

2. **Pipeline Updates.** Have your team members prepare for the meeting with their own brief overview and with reports pulled by Ops. Ask if any new interesting deals are surfacing you haven't picked up on. The idea is also to make your reps self-aware of where they stand month to date so that they can allocate extra focus/time as needed to catch up or ask for help before it's too late.

3. **Roadblocks.** Share new challenges, collateral needs, competitor initiatives that are taking a bite out of your deals, prospect objections, or feedback. Make sure to give your reps the microphone as well to voice subjects that may need attention or additional support from you to solve.

4. **Action Items.** A quick summary of action items addressed during the meeting is highly recommended to get your reps engaged during the meetings. This way, they know it's only forty-five minutes, but there's value to extract and important items or challenges they're facing will get addressed and prioritized. You're there to help!

5. **Wins.** Motivation and knowledge sharing is the objective here. It can be as simple as having just a few select reps share details on their recent win. They'll love "taking the stage" while being celebrated, and the rest of the team either learn and/or crave to be the center of attention at the next meeting.

Non-negotiable:
Get a CRM and Configure Correctly, Yesterday

I'm hiring for a new company as I'm writing this book. For one of the key positions, I've managed to headhunt a skilled industry veteran who's willing to transition despite earning very good six-figure annual compensation and being a department head at her current employer.

During the interview process she explained that the company she currently works for doesn't have a CRM. She said they use project management software for client deliverables but nothing with regard to prospecting, sales, and customer relationship management. You can imagine my reaction. Needless to say, it was an easy sell when I explained just how quickly we'd likely outgrow her current employer in both customers and revenue. She realized there's likely a greater future ahead for her at my newly founded company. I believe this was a big factor in her taking my offer.

This example is by far an anomaly. Research from HubSpot reveals that 40 percent of companies still don't have a CRM and rely solely on spreadsheets and emails to manage their customer relationships. This blows my mind, but then again, no wonder why 80 percent of new businesses have to close their shop within two years after launch.

In the next chapter, we'll dive into the plethora of sales technologies available today, including CRMs—impossible to cover in one book alone since there are *thousands* of systems available in the market led by multibillion-dollar companies such as Salesforce, Microsoft, and Oracle.

And CRM companies aren't just software firms any longer. Back in 2016, I attended Dreamforce in San Francisco, Salesforce's annual event. Nearly 200,000 people from all around the world flew in to participate and learn all the latest and greatest trends in CRM and business.

The keynote speaker was Tony Robbins, and will.i.am from the Black Eyed Peas performed. It was more of a rock concert than a business conference from my perspective. I'd say that it's probably best described as a culture with raving fans who brand themselves "Trailblazers" and live and breathe Salesforce. Many pay thousands of dollars to become certified in various Salesforce system pathways—either as in-house resources for a company using Salesforce or as external consultants for companies aiming to implement and configure Salesforce to their needs.

However, don't think that Salesforce, the number one CRM company in the world which, as of 2022, employs 75,000+ people and has a market capitalization of $181 billion, is doing all of this because of pure good and their slogan *"We bring companies and customers together."*

Salesforce, like most other CRM players, knows that the number one killer of success with CRM implementation and usage, and therefore lost recurring revenue to Salesforce, is low CRM adoption by its customers' employees.

After all, how beneficial is a CRM system for a company in terms of productivity and efficiency gains, if everyone isn't using it or using it the wrong way?

It won't matter how well configured your CRM system is and how many cool features it has. If your employees don't use it, it lacks data, or is inaccurate, you might as well save tens of thousands of dollars and continue using Sheets and email.

Just kidding! There's no excuse for not having a CRM in your company from day one of your launch. There's zero to slim chance that without one you can implement the best practices described in previous chapters regarding revenue optimization processes, lead management, upselling and cross-selling, or monitoring the most important sales metrics that can move the needle of your organization in the right direction.

It's a no-brainer investment for your organization. Data from Nucleus Research in 2014 revealed that the average ROI on CRM investments for companies is $8.71 for every dollar spent. In fact, Dynamic Consultants commented on the evolution of the CRM market in 2021 and calculated that the ROI likely has now increased to $30.48 for every dollar spent.

You may be asking yourself, "So how does one measure ROI from a CRM perspective?"

I have purchased *many* CRMs over my career and have experienced that many leading CRM players such as Salesforce, Microsoft, or HubSpot all use dynamic pricing tied up with ROI calculators to attempt to predict the ROI you can expect from the software investment. They probe you with a series of questions designed to demonstrate the financial gains expected by you improving various sales metrics due to your new CRM capacity.

In the event you purchased a CRM elsewhere and you want to do your own CRM ROI analysis, or just better frame expectations internally before acquiring your next CRM, here is my list of recommended questions for you to consider:

- **Sales volume and size of deals.** Have the number of sales you've closed per month/quarter/year increased? And what about the initial deal size?
- **Sales cycle length.** Are opportunities converting into sales quicker since you implemented the CRM? That is, have you been able to shorten your sales cycle?
- **Marketing and sales collaboration.** Are you converting more MQLs to SQLs and consequently closing more of these opportunities after your CRM implementation?
- **Sales admin tasks.** Has the administrative time of your reps decreased? Can your reps now spend more time interacting with prospects and selling versus doing tedious admin tasks?
- **Feedback loops.** Have you been able to optimize your media spend and resource allocation from a demand gen standpoint? In other words, are you keeping track of which channel's leads are originating from and their corresponding conversion rates?
- **New market categories.** Have you been able to sell into new market categories such as new verticals, geographies, or company

sizes as a result of implementing your CRM and having a more structured approach and follow-up?

- **ARPA.** Have you been able to upsell or cross-sell to more of your customers following your CRM implementation?
- **Churn and LTV.** Last but not least, have you been able to retain more customers as a result of rolling out your new CRM? And how has that affected your LTV per customer and thereby profitability?

How to Get High Adoption and ROI from Your CRM

I think we now can agree that the question isn't whether you'll install a CRM or not—it being the bedrock of your sales tech stack—but rather, how do you ensure that it's the *right* CRM for your organization, that its user-friendly, shows accurate updated info, and has a super-high adoption rate by your team members?

Many CRM providers, especially the low-price tiered solutions in the market targeting SMBs, are very much DIY solutions offering free trials and educational content on how to set up, configure, and launch their CRM software.

But wait! Don't drop this book, run off investigating CRMs, and sign up for free trials right and left. Instead, you'd be wise to diligently absorb the next section explained in detail as it's aligned with all the best sales process practices explained to this point.

- **First, create and test processes.** A major advantage in implementing a CRM is that you can streamline your sales processes: everything from lead acquisition, enrichment, prospecting, selling, and subsequently managing the relationship throughout the customer life cycle. But your CRM will only be as good as the processes you architect in the first place. It is highly counterproductive to implement a CRM if you haven't already established optimized processes for your entire sales cycle.

- **Accompany the customer journey.** The CRM system doesn't stop at the point of initial purchase. Make sure that you have mapped out the touchpoints and interactions throughout your *entire* customer journey so that your CRM can be configured accordingly. Go back to Chapter 3 with regard to mapping your customer journey, and then include processes and workflows from A to Z, particularly covering important steps such as upselling and cross-selling or how to manage a cancellation request.

- **Foster interdepartmental cooperation.** I can speak from experience how painful it can be to invest hundreds of thousands of dollars in a CRM (Salesforce) only to not have thought of how the software, if configured the right way, can foster interdepartmental cooperation. Get it right from the beginning. It's often highly expensive to reconfigure a CRM setup. It's even more costly if the configuration lacks interdepartmental collaboration, essentially also becoming a pain point for customers frustrated with your ineffective workflows and ultimately leading to customer churn.

- **Configure the CRM with a sales rep first approach.** The number one success factor of your new CRM investment is if your sales reps and client-facing staff find it useful, time-saving, adds value to their work requirements, and actually enhances their performance. This is your top priority since otherwise, low adoption becomes a very high risk factor. For starters, don't worry about reports, leadership, KPIs, etc. The data will be lacking and insufficient anyway if your reps aren't finding it relevant and using it.

- **Make your CRM the center of gravity.** This is where carefully selecting the *right* CRM is key for your company. If, like me, you use many other sales enablement apps and tools, make sure that the integrations with your selected CRM are available and preferably are native integrations. You don't want people having to jump from one app to another all the time. Your CRM should be the cornerstone of your entire sales tech stack.

- **Extensive training and manuals.** I can't stress this enough since the best CRM in the world essentially is worthless if your teams don't know how to use it properly. Just like a Ferrari is for a person who doesn't know how to drive. Don't cut corners with this as many companies mistakenly do. Trying to save money on training and implementation will eventually cost you 10x the price in the end. You want to create step-by-step manuals, have internal champions of the product, continuously measure adoption, and teach people shortcuts and automation functionality so that they embrace the tool.

- **Rigidity in setup or lack of funds for continued configuration.** There's rarely a one-size-fits-all solution when it comes to companies' internal processes. And they undoubtedly evolve over time. You won't experience high adoption success if it's a generic configuration, nor will it stick if you don't have the resources to configure the system as your needs and processes evolve over time.

- **Get the data right from the start.** Duplicate records, multiple account owners, inconsistent naming conventions, inaccurate information, or inadequate lead enrichment processes—these are just a few of the rookie mistakes many companies make when first rolling out a CRM that result in frustration for both staff and customers. And they'll lead to lost revenue opportunities. Combat this from the get-go by creating rules and processes around CRM data entry and put in place CRM data naming protocols. I recommend creating a complete handbook for data entry processes alone and training your team in CRM data management.

- **Automate, automate, and then automate more.** This is where the rubber meets the road for CRM adoption and typically yields a strong ROI as a result. Automating time-consuming sales administrative tasks makes your reps truly see the value in the tool and take things to the next level. Not only does it reduce the likelihood of manual errors, but your reps will free up valuable time to do what they like the most—selling.

By following these best practices for Sales Ops, documentation, and CRM adoption, you will empower your sales and marketing teams' abilities to succeed and attain the ROI and efficiency gains expected from your CRM investment.

And with that being done, you're now ready to level up your game and add complementary sales tools and technology to the equation. In other words, selecting and putting together a sales tech stack that supercharges your sales and revenue growth.

In the next chapter, I'll examine the complex sales technology landscape with the objective of navigating you safely through the tens of thousands of tools and software available to build the optimal sales tech stack for your company.

13

THE SIGNIFICANCE
OF TECHNOLOGY
FOR SCALE

Will unveil how today's fastest growing companies supercharge their growth by leveraging a suite of sales enablement technologies and growth acceleration tools.

A few important business principles that have stuck with me during my business journey come from the book by Jim Collins, *Good to Great: Why Some Companies Make the Leap...and Others Don't.*

This is a business bestseller that has sold more than 4 million copies to date. In it, Jim analyzes data from 1,400 companies that had been in business in the United States for at least fifteen years. He identified some common denominators that made a small number of select companies go from being *good* to becoming *great*.

One of the more interesting principles Jim points out is the "technology accelerators" concept. The *great* companies were really disciplined when it came to adopting new technology and only did so when it could accelerate the growth of their core business.

I recognize the same today when it comes to sales organizations selecting the right set of tools and technology to help amplify their sales strategy and processes.

Ten to fifteen years ago my sales teams solely relied on outbound phone calls and emails in order to move prospects down the sales funnel. Today, however, the common denominator of winning sales teams is that they all leverage and stack together a series of sales enablement, data, analytics, and automation tools to gain a competitive edge through predictive revenue programs.

In fact, if done right, this can be a significant catalyst for your growth. I've witnessed firsthand time and again how, when done right, it can catapult your business into the big leagues. As a sales dude myself, after seeing how effective it can be, I've become a huge Sales Tech (Sales Technology) and Mar Tech (Marketing Technology) enthusiast and spend as much time as possible investigating tools, reading reviews, interviewing peers, and viewing demos.

In my opinion, having a "near-perfect" sales stack isn't just a nice-to-have any longer; it's essential for you to stand a chance to survive in today's highly competitive globalized marketplace.

WHAT IS A SALES TECH STACK?

But first things first. For the reader who may still be unfamiliar with all of this, let's take a step back and define what exactly is a tech stack and how it can support your company's growth.

Essentially a sales tech stack is a set of sales-specific software solutions and tools used by your sales team to fulfill their job responsibilities and optimize their processes. That can be everything from where to find leads, store the contact data, send out email sequences, conduct demos, share collateral, build proposals, get signatures, onboard new reps, gauge customer satisfaction, and the list goes on as new tools regularly come to market.

More specifically, when stringing together the *right* prioritized collection of sales tools, you can optimize your team's workflows and processes and help your team spend less time on admin tasks by automating them, giving your team more time to focus on selling your offerings.

Why is this so important?

According to Salesforce's "State of Sales" report fourth edition, sales reps spend 66 percent of their time on nonselling activities. Not surprisingly then why, on average, only one out of three sales reps meet their quotas, right?

And the same Salesforce report shows that high-performing sales teams use three times more sales tech stack tools than underperforming teams. If you couple these findings with a recent McKinsey & Company report showing that companies with a >10 percent CAGR (Compound Annual Growth Rate) are 62 percent more effective in using digital sales tools, I'd argue that we have compelling enough reasons to take the selection of a sales tech tack quite seriously. Wouldn't you agree?

A 2019 study from Miller Heiman showed that on average, sales organizations now use more than ten sales technology tools and plan to add four more in the next year.

Now, that's a lot of technology to keep up to par with! And the sales tech trends keep evolving with new players entering the market almost daily, new features being added to existing software solutions, and categories morphing under competitive pressure. Frankly, keeping up with sales tech is almost a full-time job and requires a lot of attention to detail.

From the time I began writing this book until now, changes in technology, new automation software, and the growth of AI have exploded. Hence why it's more important than ever to look at this category from the lens of the learnings from *Good to Great* and cautiously select sales tech that act as an accelerator.

Align Your Tech Stack with
Your Company's Needs and Objectives

It goes without saying, you wouldn't even entertain delving into this chapter unless you've paid close attention to the previous chapters, where I set out everything from process creation and management, ICP definition, lead list building criteria, lead data enrichment parameters to know what problems to solve for prospects, or measuring performance with the right KPIs.

If things aren't properly structured within your sales organization, then just imagine the *ragnarok* (End of the World) events occurring after you add ten to fifteen tools to the equation! The confusion and inefficiencies will only propel your company out of control.

Therefore, mapping out everything and understanding your workflows, sales methodology, and processes in great detail is critical for your success. In other words, *architecting* your stack with the end goal in mind and then after its implementation continuously monitoring efficiency gains, instead of just incrementally adding the latest shiny pieces of software to your stack every time something new comes up or is recommended.

And just like with CRM implementation, the cornerstone of your sales tech stack is to *build everything around your sales reps' needs*, to benefit their sales efficiency and make it user-friendly.

A way to get started with this process is to ask the following questions:

1. ***Whom are you looking to sell to and why?*** Depending on your ICP, your offering, and the prospect's situation, you can use a variety

of tools to build your lead list, append the leads, and engage with them. For example, you may use CrunchBase to identify companies that recently have raised funds and are looking to grow, or leverage a tool like BuiltWith to pitch your solution to companies that have technology in place which your solution serves well.

2. ***How and where can you engage with them?*** And contingent on your outreach strategy, channels, and lead sources, there's a large collection of tools at your disposal to drive prospect engagement. Whether for building systematic multi-touchpoint sequences with sales engagement software like Outreach or SalesLoft for emailing, calling, and social selling, or to optimize inbound lead routing aiming for higher closing rates with scheduling tools like Chili Piper, you can easily drown in the vast sea of tech stack options in this category alone.

3. ***Why should they talk with you and how can they benefit from that?*** Demonstrating value, cutting through the noise, and differentiating your company value from the rising competition is, for most industries, only becoming more fierce. But thankfully, for the benefit of tech-savvy sales marketers, there are many tools being launched that can help drive your point across more effectively with prospects. Sales pros now have many more tools in their arsenal to communicate their message, and your reps can use them to convey the value of your proposed solution. Whether by designing quick, personalized, and interactive product demos to wow your prospects using software like Walnut, or by creating value-demonstrating ROI calculators with The ROI Shop, there is a plethora of choices.

4. ***How to close deals and onboard customers?*** It's now easier than ever to get prospect data and company information organized

in a structured fashion with ease of access at any point in the sales cycle. There are hundreds of multifaceted CRM solutions available for any company size. And the big players like Salesforce and HubSpot have native API integrations with a range of complementary tools and apps that allow you to optimize your sales processes, land more deals, and onboard a high volume of customers more easily than ever before. Additionally, proposal software like Proposify or PandaDoc amplifies the speed of deal success rates and potential volume of new customers your company can secure.

5. ***How to upsell, cross-sell, and renew customer agreements?***
   As covered earlier, these are areas with tremendous growth potential for most companies. It's not easy to develop the right framework to grow accounts and/or mitigate cancellations. But with the right groundwork in place, tools like ChurnZero can help companies more effectively onboard new customers, leading to higher CSAT rates, improved management of your renewal processes, and providing analytics that can help mitigate customer churn. Furthermore, there is software like Upsales that can help you spot account growth opportunities within your book of business more easily and apps like Recurly to ensure you can grow your recurring revenue without things falling through the cracks.

6. ***How to onboard, train, manage, coach, and compensate sales reps?***
   And last, with conversational intelligence and call analytics tools like Gong.io, or sales readiness platforms like Brainshark and MindTickle, getting new reps onboarded, trained, and coached for quota attainment has never been easier than before (if of course the underlying foundation has been designed and vetted).

THE ZERO TO 100 MILLION SALES BLUEPRINT

And with software like Ambition or Highspot to help you coach, develop your reps, and improve their productivity while sharing best practices across your teams, companies are now better than ever able to equip their reps to crush targets.

Safe to say that there are many options and technologies ready to earn your business, all with quite compelling reasons. Of course, this is dependent on your assessment of company needs outlined earlier in this chapter. Based on your decisions of where you need the most assistance, you can better allocate where to devote your budget and to which sales technology providers.

But another important consideration is understanding where you are in your company's life cycle. By this I mean where are you with regard to team size, growth targets, your burn rate, and the size of your budget?

Statistically speaking, the majority of startups cease to exist within a few years for many reasons but mainly lack of sales, profitability, and running out of cash. So if you're an SMB startup, you will have a different set of priorities with regard to your tech stack selection versus if you're considered a mature company that has reached consistent profitability and financial stability.

Or perhaps you're in an aggressive growth mode trying to grow xx percent market share by xx timeline. In that case, your selection priorities would be different because the budget may be less relevant and you add more lead list building and enrichment tools than other use cases. My point is that building your sales tech stack is more complex than just purchasing a collection of tools based on generic recommendations. You have to make sure your tech stack aligns with your overall objectives, processes in place, company size, and budget along with the level of tech savviness of your team.

To make this sink in easier, I've summarized this as follows:

	Startup Company	Growth-Mode Company	Mature Company
Budget	Constrained	Available if ROI positive	Large. Long-term view
Sales Team	Small/ Understaffed	Growing. New roles	Large/ Interdepartmental
Main KPIs	> Leads & Demos > Deals Closed = Breakeven/ profits	> Percent YoY Growth > MQL & SQLs > Deals & Revenue	> ARPA & LTV < CAC < Churn
Focus Areas	Proof of Concept	Growth & Market Share	Increase Efficiency & Profits

The Sales Tech Landscape Overview

A quote that stuck with me when conducting research on sales technologies is from Jill Rowley, a seasoned B2B/SaaS sales and marketing technology expert, who said, *"A fool with a tool is still a fool. A fool with lots of tools is an even bigger fool."*

And the landscape of sales technology is overwhelmingly big. Not as large as marketing technology, but the dynamics behind this explosion of sales tools are the same with consolidating platforms, new categories, and players emerging right and left, with expanding app ecosystems around them. And the big players continue to grow massively achieving multibillion-dollar valuations.

As an example, Outreach, one of the longtime tools in my own sales tech stack, raised another $200 million in 2021 in their series G round at a $4.2 billion valuation.

Another tool preference of mine, Apollo, raised $110 million in 2022 at a $790 million valuation led by Sequoia Capital, investors in some of the greatest startups including YouTube, Google, PayPal, and more.

In summary, Sales Tech is hotter than ever before!

And ambitious companies aren't shying away from acquiring sales tech to fuel their growth. In fact, the 2021 *Revenue Operations and Customer Acquisition Benchmark Report* by ringDNA and RevOps Squared revealed that 38 percent of the companies surveyed are spending $400 or more per sales rep per month.

So the only question left now is the million-dollar one—that is, which sales tech tools does *your* company need the most and which tool providers to select among the many hundreds represented in Sales Tech categories?

My Tech Stack Suggestions

It's *very* tricky to provide specific recommendations for a company's tech stack. Thousands of sales tools are available that market with different price ranges, features, user experiences, popularity, and available integrations. Plus, there are constant changes with new applications or company mergers. I found after interviewing twenty-plus subject matter experts in the field that *everyone* has a different viewpoint and preference.

Furthermore, as we discussed earlier, recommendations should be based on *your* company's needs, preference, and stage of development. It's a constantly evolving task from what I see in my own companies and the clients I work with.

One thing I can say for certain. Your B2B or SaaS company will never gain any traction in today's business environment if you don't give this task of building your revenue machine the attention it deserves. The best way to sum it up is that a sales professional without appropriate sales tools is like a carpenter without a hammer and nails.

In summary, if you collect the right set of tools and configure/implement them appropriately, your sales tech stack will:

- Amplify the process of how your reps find sales-qualified leads
- Automate tedious administrative low-value but necessary tasks
- Most importantly, track the most effective sales strategies across all mediums and channels

so that your team can spend more time on speaking with prospects, closing deals, and other revenue-generating tasks.

With that in mind, see below my recommendations for some of my favorite tools to consider in your sales tech stack as of 2022:

Tech Stack Recommendations (2022)

Category	Product	Comments
Lead List/ List Building	Apollo	Global lead list with verified emails and company data
		Works for all company sizes and very affordable pricing
		Also good for email sequences and sales engagement
Lead List/ List Building	Crunchbase	Great for event-based lead list building and monitoring
		Overview of investors, funding, and mergers and acquisitions
		Find contacts and data for sophisticated ICP targeting

Category	Product	Comments
Lead List/ List Building	ZoomInfo	Very comprehensive company and contact database Usually a high accuracy of correct phone numbers Require higher investment versus alternatives. Not SMB-friendly
Lead List/ List Building	Builtwith	Provides website technology identifiersby scraping Build list based on technology, the competition, or executives Spark intelligent sales conversations based on tech usage
Lead List/ List Building	Clearbit	Great tool to enrich/append your leads with needed data Identify your website visitors, collect data, and next engage Extensive company/lead database across good B2Bs
Lead List/ List Building	LinkedIn Sales Navigator	My number one go-to lead database. Most valuable and comprehensive Most accurate since updated by users and companies Build detailed list, filters, statuses, and inmail messaging
Email Warmup	Warmup Inbox	Helps you reach more leads and prospects with sequences Avoid spam folders, blacklists, and protects sender reputation Increase the deliverability of your email sequences

Category	Product	Comments
Email Warmup	Mailwarm	Like Warmup Inbox but programmatic and more expensive Increased reach since manually removes emails from spam High email deliverability since marking emails as important
Email Sending	Instantly	Scale your email outreach campaigns via unlimited senders Can manage multiple domains and send using Round Robin Includes tool to avoid spam and improves sender reputation
LinkedIn	Expandi	Tool for LinkedIn sequences and campaign automation Analytics on engagement of sequences and performance Many other similar tools but higher risk of getting blocked
LinkedIn	Dux Soup	Another Linkedin sequence and automation tool like Expandi Also offers features like follow-up sequencing, LinkedIn scraping, connection request, and profile visit automations
Scheduling/ Lead Routing	Chili Piper	B2B appointment scheduling software on steroids Great for inbound lead conversion rate optimization Lead sourcing to AEs/SDRs based on rules, performance, conversion rates, areas of specialization, etc.

Category	Product	Comments
Chat Tool	LiveChat	AI chatbot solution balanced with human agent capabilities Helps generate leads, create tickets, chat across channels Drive down your CPL and capture leads otherwise not
CRM	Salesforce	The leader in the CRM space. Solutions for all company sizes Massive app ecosystem. Ease of integrations. UX clunky Costly compared to other CRMs because of configuration needs
CRM	HubSpot	Another CRM leader, perhaps better for startups than Salesforce Trumps Salesforce with UX, price, and ease of getting started Doesn't have same customization possibilities as Salesforce
CRM	Close	Good solution. A mix of CRM and Sales Engagement in one Has many sequence features like Outreach and SalesLoft Offers snippets, reporting, dialing, reporting at a low price
Skills Development	BrainShark	Sales enablement and readiness platform to onboard new reps Assess effectiveness of sales coaching and product know-how Video, training courses, role-play options, and score cards

Category	Product	Comments
Sales Engagement	Salesloft	End-to-end sales engagement platform with mobile app Multi-touchpoint sequences: emails, calls, video, SMS, and LinkedIn. Schedule, reporting, and conversational intelligence
Sales Engagement	Outreach	The market-leading sales engagement platform (SE) Similar to SalesLoft. If SalesLoft is the Lamborghini of SE tools, then Outreach is the Ferrari! Very similar and great
Sales Enablement	Highspot	Sales enablement to help identify and share best practices Playbooks, processes, and collateral for reps in one place Includes frameworks for methodologies as Challenger and Sandler
Content Experience	Walnut	Create custom personalized interactive product demos Analytics and performance insights on demo performance Demo samples/templates for AEs, CSMs, or Marketing
Value Selling & ROI	The ROI Shop	Great tool to capture lead interest from your website Used throughout sales cycle to demonstrate value/ROI Sales tool to pitch cost savings, performance gains, etc.

Category	Product	Comments
Conversation Intelligence	Gong	The leader in conversation and revenue Intelligence software
		Great to coach reps at scale, provide feedback, and optimize
		Analyze interactions, create alerts for risks and opportunities
Proposals/ Contracts	Proposify	Helps streamline your proposal and closing process
		Smarketing process-friendly, template libraries, and insights
		Significantly reduces time on creating pro-looking proposals
Proposals/ Contracts	PandaDoc	Alternative to Proposify with more CMR integration options
		More suited for contract management, signatures, payments, etc.
		Includes features like renewals notifications and e-signature
E-signing	DocuSign	Although many good alternatives, DocuSign is the leader in e-signing
		Viewed more secure since recipient's authentication required
		Price of DocuSign higher than alternatives SignNow or HelloSign
Subscription Management	Recurly	Subscription and billing solution for MRR business models
		Great for scaling and eliminating typical involuntary churn
		Configure trials, plans, pricing, promotions, or support levels

Category	Product	Comments
Customer Success	ChurnZero	Churn mitigation analytics for your CSMs to react proactively Customer onboarding solutions to secure a higher CSAT Renewal and ARPA growth management notifications
Performance Management	Ambition	Sales coaching platform for recurring coaching programs Toolsets for accountability, amplification, and encouragement $1,000+/mo, so best suited for when ready for scaling
Compensation Management	QuotaPath	Automated accurate commission tracking with rep visibility Provide transparency and motivate your reps with carrot effect Integrates with CRMs like Salesforce, HubSpot, and Close
Channel Management	Allbound	The leading Partner Relationship Management (PRM) tool Partner onboarding, enablement, and marketing collaboration Integrations with most relevant channel tool stack options

> *For a more comprehensive overview of*
>
> **200+ Sales Tech tools and software,**
>
> *go to www.0to100million.com and get your free copy.*

I trust that with this chapter you have come to realize just how significant the impact can be of selecting the right sales technology tools for your organization. If done right, it can become an amazing asset for your company that will automate time-consuming sales admin tasks while empowering your reps to do things more effectively across the board.

Another key strategy of mine has been to outsource many roles and functions overseas to gain a competitive advantage. Typically, this is viewed as a cost-saving initiative for most companies. However, I have found that by looking overseas, it is possible to acquire talented people with a high degree of motivation to learn, improve, and develop a career, when compared with similar professionals in the United States. But this does not necessarily apply to all sales roles. In the next chapter, I will delve into the specifics of this topic.

14

OUTSOURCE AND DELEGATE BUT NEVER THE HEAVY LIFTING

A set of tools, best practices, and recommendations on how to leverage the globally outsourced world we live in.

My last company was basically an outsourcing company. We had 100 percent of our staff, nearly 300 employees at the peak of our growth, located in Managua, Nicaragua in Central America. Ninety-five percent of our staff was fully bilingual as we only targeted clients in the United States.

The initial reason we set up shop in Nicaragua was due to a Danish government program for Danish entrepreneurs where they could receive an investment subsidy of $700,000 or more over a three- to five-year period. To qualify, companies had to export their services or products to Nicaragua (or other select third world countries such as Afghanistan, Ghana, or Somalia) with the objective that the investment subsidy would translate into job creation and innovation for the country. I'm proud to say we made that happen.

What I learned in my nearly ten years in Nicaragua was that it was a good country, despite what the international media with a political agenda might broadcast. More importantly, there were a great deal of young, underemployed, and highly talented bilingual professionals with business administration or marketing degrees. Many ended up working at call centers simply because the local economy wasn't fueled to pay them adequately according to their skillset and education. The many call centers situated in Nicaragua largely worked as customer service extensions for big consumer brands in the United States, which is why they could pay these young professionals more than local Nicaraguan companies.

Furthermore, when launching our reseller program and speaking with thousands of other marketing agencies in the United States about their business, product fulfillment, and particularly sales processes were the key areas that our partners struggled or sought assistance. I learned just how common it is for companies to outsource many tasks to freelancers overseas, typically in India, the Philippines, or Latin American countries.

With that being said, I managed to win a lot of business from agencies that either outsourced to other countries or had their own teams in place overseas. How? you may ask. Well, there's several pros and cons to outsourcing to different regions.

EAST, WEST, OR SOUTH—WHERE AND HOW TO OUTSOURCE?

In today's globalized economy, more and more companies in the United States are seeking ways to continuously increase profits and cut costs. In fact, as of 2022, more than 300,000 US jobs are outsourced each year! And 66 percent of businesses in the United States outsource at least one department with the objective of cutting costs.

This begs the question of what tasks to outsource and where. Let's start with the latter.

From a sales admin support perspective, the following countries are usually mentioned when I speak to B2B sales organizations and marketing agencies that outsource.

1. **India** (offshore): India is undoubtedly the largest outsourcing player, whether it's 24/7 chat support options, data entry, or from my own experience, the many marketing agencies that outsource SEO (Search Engine Optimization). One thing that Indian out-sourcing companies have going for them is that they're often quite good technically and their fees are incredibly cheap by North American standards. However, the flip side, and something to strongly consider, is that despite promoting themselves as strong in English proficiency, there are some language and grammar bar-riers you will likely encounter. They write/speak British English usually, which is something to consider if they're writing content for you. Another possible obstacle are the cultural challenges. It can be hard for an agent in Bangalore, India to resonate with US business priorities or expectations, and that can sometimes cre-ate confusion and frustration. Last, there's a ten-and-a-half-hour time difference to consider if you, like me, are operating in Central Standard Time (CST). And if clients have urgent matters or there are changes required to project deliverables, often they have to wait until the next working day.

2. **Philippines** (offshore): I recommend the Philippines over India in most cases because the culture is more westernized and the cost of labor is very affordable with good quality work. Data entry, lead enrichment, website development, and paid search

campaign management are common tasks that get outsourced there. However, there's an even more significant time challenge with the Philippines being thirteen hours ahead of CST. In my last agency reseller company, I managed to win several large deals with US-based agencies, who prior to working with us, had their own satellite offices in the Philippines, but because of us being nearshore (Nicaragua), we were able to provide higher service levels for ad hoc customer needs and urgent matters.

3 **Central America and Mexico** (nearshore): Despite being more expensive than both India and the Philippines, there are many tasks I prefer outsourcing here, especially anything related to client-facing work, lead gen efforts, copywriting, or campaign management. For example, my former staff in Nicaragua were better accustomed to American culture and the level of English was higher than in both India and the Philippines. In fact, many of our employees were young Nicaraguans who had lived and studied in the United States but eventually chose to move back to be with their family and childhood friends.

There was already a large business process outsourcing (BPO) industry in place in Nicaragua when my former partners Alexander and Andrew and I arrived there in 2010. This included big call center players like Sitel and Convergys having tens of thousands agents there, but digital marketing outsourcing work was unknown upon our arrival. This quickly changed as we grew our agency and many others started as a result of our success. Now there's hundreds of marketing agencies in Nicaragua that outsource or service clients in the United States. A major challenge to consider here, as with most other countries you outsource to, is your ability to adapt to local customs and culture. For example,

Nicaragua is very big on holidays, and you won't be popular by forcing your staff to work during Semana Santa (Holy Week).

Preparing for Success with Outsourcing

For your outsourcing projects to be successful, you need to align the interests of both parties as much as possible. A win-win approach is required and it's important to think things through from end to end. For example, your outsourcing partner may benefit by a boost in leads and sales if your agreement is performance based. But if it comes with the expense of burning leads and opportunities or negatively impacting your brand in any way, there's a huge misalignment and downside for your company.

Also, don't try to bargain too much if you're setting up a performance-based model. Just because it's outsourced and expected to be low cost, you need to be prepared to make the rewards generous if you create a risk-reward environment. Let your outsourcing partners earn more than usual if you experience mutual victories.

In addition, I strongly recommend the following mission critical factors for success with outsourcing:

- **Reviews.** When hiring outsourcing partners, make sure to check reviews if possible (not always available especially if they're a white label provider), but at the very least, demand names and numbers for other companies in your category/market and make the calls to each and every one to get their feedback about your prospective outsource partner. Be specific in your questions. Also, make sure that a few of the referrals have preferably worked with your outsource partner for several years. You want a partner who thinks of long-term success.

- **Compensation structure and other related details.** How many revisions are included if it's design work for your sales collateral? Or how do they tackle inaccurate data in reports or lead lists if you've made an hourly payment agreement? Think things through and make detailed agreements up front. However, I do recommend you always pilot outsource partners with a time-limited agreement at a small scale before rolling out the master agreement.

- **Expectations.** Set the right expectations that are twice as detailed as you would otherwise do with employees or domestic outsourcing/contracting. Why? If you're outsourcing to India or the Philippines for example, it's an *entirely* different culture and business standard, so you should never assume that certain things that you consider standard are given. Create detailed processes for everything and clarify exactly what the expected outcome is and how long each task should take on average. Personally, I like to do things in-house first, time the task, create a process for it, and then screen-record the workflow. That way, no processes are left to chance and the expected quality of work is clearly demonstrated.

- **Agreements, NDA, and confidentiality.** This aspect can be tricky to navigate from my experience. How are you going to pursue litigation with an outsource company in India? I can only say from experience "good luck with that." The way I have mitigated such risk is by (a) not passing over too many tasks or client data that you consider confidential and (b) making a delayed payment structure. In other words, a sixty- to ninety-day payment schedule, so that you always have some leverage with your outsource partner in case they breach the agreed terms with you. With that said, although difficult, in fact almost impossible to legally enforce, you always need to create a formal legal contract according to the laws of *your* country.

Sales-Related Tasks You Should Outsource

Once again, let me emphasize that after twenty years in the business with a lot of trial and error, I don't recommend you outsource all your sales efforts. Sales, as pointed out in Chapter 1, is the heart and soul of your business. It's what makes it or breaks it. Don't entrust others with this responsibility.

However, there are several tasks in your sales framework that can be outsourced in order to maximize your internal resources and cost efficiency. Here are my recommendations from personal experience regarding which tasks you can outsource with a strong probability for success:

- **List Building and Lead Enrichment.** There's already a big existing outsourcing industry built around this part of your sales process. I have previously hired great team members in the Philippines and Nicaragua for these roles. Very often you can shorten their learning curve significantly because they are already acquainted with many data enrichment tools and know how to build lead lists ready for upload to your CRM. I would have them work with tools like Builtwith, import.io, or Datanyze and extract data from websites and directories targeted for our sales approach.
- **Graphic Design Work.** Very relevant for many SMBs, especially if you're bootstrapped or just starting up. We discussed in Chapter 10 how you need a robust sales enablement collateral strategy to ramp up your outreach strategy and demand gen efforts. Don't

try to cook something up yourself or have your nephew do the graphic work required only to come across as an amateur. You need graphics, illustrations, and artwork that elevate your proposals, pitch decks, white papers, etc., to a level that fosters trust and engagement with prospects and customers.

- **Competitive Research.** Although you may have the skills and resources in-house to execute on this, it can be beneficial to outsource for several reasons. For one, if it is tied up with a mystery shopping exercise, as described in Chapter 3, it provides you with an unbiased outside perspective versus using in-house team members for the project who, undoubtedly, will be biased and have their preferences regarding where to focus. Also, it's a rather rudimentary task that is often more cost effective to outsource.

- **Sales Process Architecting.** Although I have always considered myself among the best when it comes to sales, I have often hired subject matter experts either as advisors or consultants when entering a new category or market. Why try to reinvent the wheel if someone already has the expertise? Although it may be costly hiring consultants to provide a sales blueprint for you or help implement the right tool stack for your business, it often saves you tens of thousands of dollars in the end. You wouldn't outsource day-to-day work at the sales managerial level, but outsourcing for knowledge acquisition to shorten the learning curve can be priceless.

- **Data Entry Tasks and Quality Assurance.** Whether compiling data from leads and sales, verifying accuracy or sorting information to prepare source data for reports, these tasks are pretty straightforward and many companies hire overseas for them. Other similar tasks would be quality assurance of data, listening through calls to tag them appropriately in your CRM, or lead generation campaigns for clients to better determine ROI and areas of improvement. These are tedious time-consuming tasks but with tremendous value if done right and therefore are worth outsourcing.

- **Live Chat.** This is a big one for lead gen-focused B2B companies. You can even hire on a cost-per-lead basis. Personally I prefer having a real agent on standby over the AI chat robot approach many companies take. From my experience, people want to speak with a real person. Exchanging info and asking questions with a real chat agent on a website is less intrusive and your future client will be more inclined to give up info this way (and become a lead) than only having a form submission or call option on your site. Companies such as Apex chat or Juvo Leads specialize in this service with 24/7 attentiveness to your prospects.

What *Not* to Outsource

Let me repeat it. *Never ever* should you outsource your sales entirely nor the below-mentioned functions in your sales framework. Any business, in order to be successful, *needs* to be in direct contact with its customers and the market it serves. Strategy, framework design, and implementation can be outsourced, but the day-to-day core operation and most of the sales team must be in-house.

- **SDRs and AEs** I do not recommend outsourcing, perhaps with the exception if you operate in select verticals with a low price tag for your services or if you *severely* lack the skills and resources to do it in-house. But long term, if you want to scale things properly and sustain a certain level of quality, you want to have in-house training processes in place, career trajectories for motivational purposes, and most importantly build a unique culture! That's nearly impossible to do when outsourcing the key drivers of your salesforce.

- **Lead Generation and Social Selling.** Again, take it from someone who previously had *very* aggressive company growth targets (60 percent YoY) who, despite having sixty in-house SDRs, needed more volume and therefore interviewed and partnered with lead generation companies right and left. Let me tell you, it's *very* difficult to ensure a high quality level and the possible ramifications for your brand can be devastating with regard to bad reviews and your online reputation. This is why I do not recommend you risk your brand by outsourcing this to third parties.

- **Appointment Setting.** Same goes as for lead generation. Many entrepreneurs get tempted to outsource this brutal piece of the puzzle with regard to selling, especially when solicited by companies that offer appointment setting services with a "no cure, no pay" proposition. But again, your brand is at stake, and these companies, from my own learnings, burn through your leads quickly and surely, only focusing on getting the next appointment no matter the cost. It may work for Verizon, Quicken Loans, or similar companies with a large addressable market, but unless you're playing in this league, then steer away from the temptation of outsourcing appointment setting.

- **Sales Management.** This is an easy one, but I need to reinforce it since I often encounter companies that, as a result of (a) several failed attempts with hiring suitable sales management and (b) combined with falling in love with external sales coaches or consultants, entertain the idea of engaging with these external service providers at the next level to compensate for the lack of internal sales management. Having covered all the legwork that you need to do in the previous chapters in order to scale your sales and revenue effectively, it goes without saying that this is not a recommended long-term option. Helping with hiring, architecting, or "training the trainer," yes. But otherwise it will never be sustainable.

- **Recruitment.** Having tried it many times before, I do not recommend outsourcing talent acquisition efforts even if you are desperate to grow and struggling to find any sales superstars to join your organization. Recruiters are performance based and likely source the best candidate in their network to the highest paying client. Instead, as mentioned in Chapter 7, invest your money in building a sales talent "farming system" that benefits your organization in the long term. Also, from my experience, you can get the same results or better than recruiters by just getting a LinkedIn Premium subscription and soliciting the talent you want to employ in a sophisticated nondirect way via InMail. Acknowledge their success, share your job description, and ask if they know anyone of their caliber who might be interested in the opportunity. Many will reply being interested in the job themselves and others may recommend suitable candidates.

How to Quickly Get Started with Outsourcing Experimentation

There are many freelance platforms out there to choose from—all with some twist, specialization, or better approach for select work tasks, price ranges, or countries. Below are a few I can recommend for you to explore and get started with outsourcing.

99designs is a great platform where you can access designers from all over the world to help with creating logo and brand designs, artwork for social media, brochures, and much more. In fact, the cover of this book was designed using 99designs! What I also like is that you get many options because you can start a design contest and will often receive hundreds of designs to choose from, while you only have to pay for the winner of the design contest at a fixed pre-agreed-on price.

Upwork is also a valuable platform to consider that covers most freelance categories. At the time of writing this book, they're the biggest player. Think of it as an alternative to hiring through conventional recruitment platforms like Monster or Indeed. I have hired everything from copywriting to translation work and also sourced my Philippines-based data entry hires through Upwork. The platform is also geared well for businesses by having terms in place such as only paying for approved work, being able to scan for ideal hires by reviewing portfolios, requesting sample work, and having tools such as time tracking and payment tracking.

Fiverr I would only recommend Fiverr if your budget is very limited or for low-cost gigs. I have tried it for simple things such as HTML configuration of email signatures, design work, and data entry but have found it's a hit or miss. Even with 5-star reviews on freelancers and sample work looking satisfactory, many times I've specified my requirements, but in return they sent me a cookie-cutter templated approach of work that was unsatisfactory, and I had to go back and forth with the freelancer endlessly to get things as I expected them to be. Again, it's very affordable, but the risk of low-quality work is high. With that being said, since I last used them, they have rolled out Fiverr Business with features and support better suited for the needs of businesses hiring freelancers.

Toptal is at the other end of the scale by targeting companies that are aiming for higher quality freelancers and specialists. For that reason, the cost is significantly higher than the above-mentioned platforms, but as I like to say, sometimes being cheap ends up being more expensive. According to their website, Toptal is very exclusive about which freelancers can join their platform and offer their services. Of the 100,000 freelancer applications Toptal gets each year, apparently only 3 percent gets accepted. I have tried them for project management tasks, tech stack configuration, and financial modeling with satisfactory results despite the high price tag.

In-house Marketing Team versus Outsourcing to Agency

Another common service to outsource is marketing and demand generation. This is a touchy subject for me since I owned a marketing agency for over ten years and recently opened a new one, Elev8.io. I'm biased here obviously and don't necessarily advocate *against* outsourcing this mission critical element of your company's success, but I caution that a marketing agency is probably as important a hire as your Co-founder, VP of Sales, or Sales Ops Manager. Finding the *right* one, or worse selecting the wrong one, can mean the difference between thriving and bankruptcy. Perhaps you think I'm exaggerating. If so, I invite you to go back and read the sections in Chapter 6 about Smarketing—that is, Sales and Marketing collaboration.

Trust me. I lived in this world for ten-plus years and partnered with hundreds of agencies that subcontracted our services. I know firsthand that there are *many* really good agencies out there, but there are an equal number or maybe even more bad apples in the basket. And for the inexperienced eye, it's very hard to tell them apart.

So why is it so difficult to find a good agency? Well, understand that in the United States alone, there are over 150,000 independent marketing service contractors, advertising and creative agencies. Selecting the right agency for your company with the skillsets you need the most, let alone ensuring that the best employees from that agency (i.e., not just an inexperienced junior rep or college intern) are assigned to your company, is often like finding a needle in a haystack for many companies.

The experienced employees at agencies are often spread thin across multiple clients, campaigns, and responsibilities, significantly limiting their bandwidth and creative capacity to do effective work for you. All this while having time constraints regarding work done for you, since their agency/employer dictates and monitors the maximum amount of hours per client allowed to match their retainer and target profit margins.

These factors all significantly impact your probability of success when engaging with a marketing agency. I have found that partnering with a smaller specialized agency, preferably with a strong industry focus and with access to leadership, significantly increases the likelihood for driving results for your company. Often when an agency scales and becomes a big player, their pitch may sound good and they have many testimonials, but overall the quality of work, service levels, employee skillsets, and standards begin declining.

The graphic on the next page illustrates a common scenario and something to carefully examine when hiring your next marketing agency—the inverse relationship between agency size and the unique benefits per customer when it comes to quality and performance.

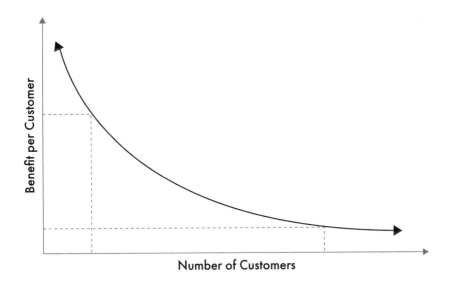

Another well-known fact about most marketing agency's models is that they rarely are subject matter experts across all required marketing categories. Inspect in detail what they actually do very well. If your company needs MQLs produced at high volume, then it serves you little if the agency's core competency is brand building and publicity.

Most commonly, agencies have in-house expertise in only two or three marketing categories and therefore subcontract all the additional services requested by the client. This is especially true since most clients nowadays prefer a "one-stop shop" solution from a marketing standpoint versus having multiple vendors/agencies on record. Hence they look for an agency that can fulfill all of its marketing needs to ensure that their strategy, objectives, messaging, promotions, campaigns, and overall execution are in complete alignment and consistent across the board. Makes sense, but be conscious whether it's something they can deliver on or if they just subcontract it to the Philippines, mark up the cost 3x, and cross their fingers that it works on your behalf.

The above-mentioned factors, along with the recent explosive growth in marketing agencies, digital nomads, and overall global outsourcing post-COVID, have caused a spike in overseas subcontracted marketing services to providers in countries like India, the Philippines, and Nicaragua.

Below is the result of Wordstream's "2020 State of the Agency" report asking agency owners whether they outsource and which services, if any. Notably, 59 percent *do* outsource.

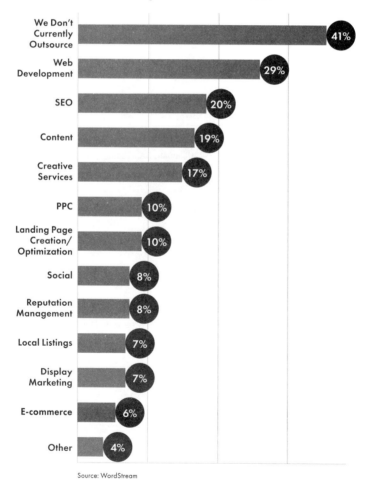

Do You Outsource Any of These Services?

Source: WordStream

THE ZERO TO 100 MILLION SALES BLUEPRINT

So what do you do? Marketing and sales go hand in hand and the alignment of these are vital for your success. This is not a book on marketing—that requires many more pages and a different focus. But understanding this domain greatly and to ensure that your sales and revenue generation efforts get the best support possible, let me at least give you a few pointers on what to look for and directions to take, depending on your criteria.

1. **You Have Marketing Expertise.** Going back to Chapter 5, you may not need an agency. And perhaps you're better off building out an in-house marketing team, if either you or your partners have prior experience with B2B and SaaS demand generation and marketing. Last, if you're in doubt on whether you have the appropriate internal resources, hire an external advisor to consult where your strengths and weaknesses are to ensure you hire an agency or team members with the right skills to get the job done.

2. **Growth Objectives and Requirements.** How aggressive are your growth targets? Is there a race with competition to capture valuable market share? And what is your burn rate? If you need an immediate catalyst for your marketing efforts, an agency is likely the route for you to take. This way, you don't have to recruit a team with diverse skillsets and expertise but instead hit the ground running with an agency that has the expertise and all the resources already in place.

3. **Your Budget and Resources.** Depending on your company's marketing strategy, you'll likely need a diverse set of marketing and demand generation skillsets. Everything from website development, landing pages, content creation and assets, SEO, Pay per Click advertising, social media management, email marketing,

and more. And *very* rarely does one marketing professional, at least at a decent cost, know how to master all of those subjects. Therefore, with a limited budget or when starting up, you may be better off working with an agency coupled with a few freelancers. Keeping strategies, messaging, and campaign execution in sync across several freelancers can, however, pose a challenge, which is why many companies default to a full-service agency when possible.

4. **You Can't Afford Mistakes.** Although many marketing agencies talk the talk and don't necessarily walk the walk, there are many great agencies out there. If you cautiously recruit the right agency for your company, in the end you're buying into subject matter expertise that almost certainly ensures you'll get marketing done right. I've seen many cases where folks hire a Marketing Director (with one or two skillsets) and complement them with freelancers only for it to go catastrophically wrong because of misalignment, wrong strategies, or not being on top of the latest trends. A good agency significantly mitigates the risk of you making marketing-related errors.

5. **Tools and Technology.** Analytics and BI platforms, call tracking, campaign management software, reporting technology, research tools, you name it. The Mar Tech space is even bigger than Sales Tech, which is why getting the whole suite of marketing tools to effectively run your demand generation efforts can be a costly affair at the initial phases of your business maturity. Agencies likely have the entire tech stack required for your success and furthermore, because of the volume of clients, get better rates than you can, despite them marking it up when adding to your services. It's economies of scale 101.

In summary, if you take the agency route, make sure to dedicate adequate time and patience to recruit, screen, and hire a full-service agency team. Last, my recommendation is to also pay the extra dime or two and get an advisor to help you with this. Hiring the wrong agency for your company can have a devastating impact on your company.

As we have seen in this chapter, there are many roles and responsibilities that can be beneficial for you to outsource: lead list building, data entry work, graphic design of sales collateral, support with architecting your sales framework, tech stack design, and of course, marketing-related tasks.

Finally, you have arrived. It's time to roll up your sleeves, get to work, crank up your sales machine, and go from zero to 100 million! In the next chapter, I'll provide a brief summary of what I've presented in this book and give you a few pointers of where you can go from here.

CONCLUSION

GET RID OF YOUR BLIND SPOTS; TAKE ACTION NOW

Unless you can tick all the main checkboxes from Chapters 1 to 14, you'll know your homework. Go find the right partner resources or employees to get everything you need done.

So let's recap. If you've read all chapters until now, you know we've covered these key topics:

1. How to research the entire market in depth, understand your future customers down to a science, create a compelling offer, and test launch your MVP.
2. You now also understand the different go-to-market strategies possible, the business segments, differences between sales channels, together with the resources required for either direction.

3. You have also scoped out your sales approach, the framework, and designed a winning sales plan for your company, giving you better insights regarding what resources, partner, co-founders, or employees you need to acquire in order to complement your skillsets and launch a high-growth business.

4. And by mapping out your entire customer journey, defining your pricing strategy, and understanding the value of your customer life cycle, you're now equipped with a complete understanding of the metrics and KPIs to monitor and optimize religiously and continuously.

5. Understanding the dynamics of hiring, you also created career path trajectories for your reps, onboarding plans, training vehicles, and built out an entire sales management framework for your sales management team to hire, retain, and develop sales superstars who ignite the growth of your company's revenue.

6. And by doing the heavy lifting of proper research, defining your ICP, their pain points, and understanding your value prop, you can now create compelling, value-driven, and high-converting messaging and collateral that supports the deal-making process.

7. We have also covered the required steps taken to measure and optimize your client satisfaction levels and establish a framework for leveraging that intelligence to extend your LTV and drive incremental revenue through existing resources.

8. And by understanding the significance of processes, systems, getting organized, and documenting everything from A to Z, you've also prepared your organization to rocket-fuel your growth by adding the right suite of tools and technology that can amplify your best practices even further.

THE ZERO TO 100 MILLION SALES BLUEPRINT

9. And whether you took the route of supporting your internal talent development process by developing outside partnerships, getting marketing support, or establishing a freelancer network, you now have all the tools and resources required to scale things by 100x!

10. The last and final step, a mission critical one, is whether you follow the guidelines and principles outlined in the book or just put it back on your bookshelf. Let me rephrase that because the real question that matters now is whether you want to become (a) a thriving business owner or (b) just a business operator.

You see, the expected outcome from applying these learnings is growth. Growth of clients, revenue, employees, and profitability but also *problems*.

Therefore, a few last recommendations for you to consider as you embark on this journey of creating your own $100 million company:

1. **Sales Process Architecting.** Get outside support wherever your blind spots may be. As Albert Einstein said, "Insanity is doing the same thing over and over again and expecting different results." If you need help with sales and what you tried hasn't worked, dig into your savings and get the expertise on board or hire consultants/advisors to change the status quo. With revenue comes growth, flexibility, added resources, and profits.

   Suggested Next Steps: go to www.garygarth.com/sales-accelerator and fill out the questionnaire. I'll personally assess your response if you reference my book, and if my team can't help you within the budget range or scope of service required, rest assured I'll point you in the right direction to someone who can make it happen.

2. **Accelerator Platform.** And if you have sales down to a tee, perhaps you're struggling with other aspects of your business.

As pointed out in Chapter 5, very few founders have all the skillsets and resources required to succeed in business. Our Accelerator Platform helps companies go to market, scale, and become profitable via a comprehensive playbook tested and curated by subject matter experts across multiple industries. You'll find everything from educational content, explainer videos, tools, and templates for 150+ critical tasks for successful business building such as financial modeling, investor pitch decks, sales and hiring forecasts, employee stock option agreements, SOPs, checklists, and much more.

Secure the success of your startup with our all-in-one accelerator program

ACCELERATOR™
SECURE THE SUCCESS OF YOUR STARTUP

Our Accelerator program helps startups go to market, scale, and become profitable via a comprehensive playbook tested and curated by subject-matter experts across multiple industries.

- An end-to-end operating system for your business
- 50+ startups and VCs use our accelerator platform
- Mitigate the risk of failure and streamline your execution

Suggested Next Steps: go to www.acceleratorplatform.io, request a demo, and speak with a business growth specialist to learn how our business Accelerator Program and weekly coaching sessions might just be the one thing you and your company have been missing to level up your revenue and growth.

3. **Goals, Grit, and Greatness Planner.** Take it from one who has been there and done that several times over. Once you've applied all of the steps outlined above you'll better your financial situation and in the eyes of many attain "success." But as one of my mentors, Tony Robbins, points out, "*Achievement without fulfillment is the ultimate failure.*" This is a phrase that has stuck with me because it's so true. And many successful entrepreneurs and founders agree with me. I trust you may join them.

Over the years, especially during the tough times when I was going through "the valleys" of entrepreneurship, a series of tools, when stacked together in the right sequence and meaning, made a tremendous difference to my life and happiness, regardless of the stress levels I was undergoing.

So I created a life planner where I included all of the exercises that worked for me. All are proven to foster a better mindset and include:

- Self-assessment
- Gratitude
- Affirmations
- Visualization
- Goal setting
- Ritual building
- Weekly planning
- Daily planning
- Prioritization
- Reflection
- And more

Stay on track with your goals, boost productivity, and improve your work-life balance

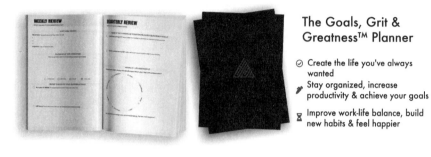

The Goals, Grit & Greatness™ Planner

- Create the life you've always wanted
- Stay organized, increase productivity & achieve your goals
- Improve work-life balance, build new habits & feel happier

Everything you need to achieve your goals

| ANNUAL GOALS | DAILY PAGES | WEEKLY PLANNER | QUARTERLY REVIEW | DAILY RITUALS | LEARNING MATERIALS |

Suggested Next Steps: go to www.goalsgritandgreatness.com and purchase your copy of the planner. Apply the coupon code "0to100million" and receive a 20 percent discount on your purchase.

4. **Free Sales Resources.** Last but not least, as we have covered many subjects throughout the book, you'll find a great collection of free resources accessible on our website that can help fuel your sales and growth optimization journey. You'll find tools such as sales plan templates, email sequence samples, lead inventory depository templates, marketing audit sheets, sales training templates, and more.

Suggested Next Steps: go to www.0to100million.com and access a series of free sales tools, templates, and recommendations for you to apply to your business immediately. I wish you well on your journey!

GLOSSARY

Key terms or acronyms, not otherwise defined in the text.

Affiliate Marketing: Partnerships where a company establishes referral agreements with third-party companies who in return get a commission for referring your solution.

ARPA: Average Revenue per Account. A profitability measure that assesses a company's revenue per customer account.

B2B: Business-to-Business. A sales model between businesses.

B2C: Business-to-Consumer. A sales model in which products and services are sold directly between a company and consumer.

BI: Business Intelligence. Combines business analytics, data mining, data visualization, data tools and infrastructure, and best practices to help organizations make more data-driven decisions.

Channel Sales: Sales conducted through a third-party partner who then sells to either a consumer or business.

Churn Rate: The rate at which customers stop doing business with a company over a given period of time.

CPA: Cost Per Acquisition. A marketing metric that measures the aggregate cost to acquire one paying customer on a campaign or channel level.

CRM: Customer Relationship Management. Technology for managing all of a company's relationships and interactions with customers and potential customers.

Cross-selling: The practice of selling additional products to existing customers.

CSAT: Customer Satisfaction Score. A metric that acts as a key performance indicator for customer service and product quality.

CX: Customer Experience. Encompasses every aspect of a company's offering—primarily the quality of customer care but also advertising, packaging, product and service features, ease of use, and reliability.

Direct Sales: The practice of selling directly to end customers and not through partners.

Elevator Pitch: A brief way of introducing your value proposition.

Google AdWords (now Google Ads): Google displays ads in Google Search and Maps and its partner sites when people search for similar products or services.

Horizontal Content Marketing: A strategy that appeals to potential customers who share some common characteristics but are distributed across a range of industries.

KPI: Key Performance Indicator. A measurable value that demonstrates how effectively a company is achieving key business objectives.

LTV: Lifetime Value. An estimate of the average revenue that a customer will generate throughout their life span as a customer.

MQLs: Marketing Qualified Leads. A lead that has indicated an interest in what a brand has to offer based on marketing efforts or is otherwise more likely to become a customer than other leads.

MRR: Monthly Recurring Revenue. The predictable total revenue generated by a business from all the active subscriptions in a particular month.

MVP: Minimum Viable Product. A product with enough features to attract early-adopter customers and validate a product idea early in the product development cycle.

Mystery Shopping: A method used to gather and measure specific information about competitors' products and services.

NPS: Net Promoter Score. Measures customer experience and predicts business growth.

PES: Product Engagement Score. Measures how users interact with a product typically focused on three key metrics—product adoption, stickiness (i.e., repeated usage), and growth.

PPC: Pay Per Click. A model of digital advertising where the advertiser pays a fee each time one of their ads is clicked.

QBR and ABR: Quarterly and Annual Business Reviews. A regularly recurring conversation with the customer around the value the vendor is delivering and, if used right, can ensure a smooth renewal process. a quarterly touchpoint with your customer where the intention is to review the impact of your product on the customer's business

SaaS: Software as a Service. A software distribution model in which a cloud provider hosts applications and makes them available to end users over the internet.

SEM: Search Engine Marketing. A digital marketing strategy is used to increase the visibility of a website in search engine results pages (SERPs).

SEO: Search Engine Optimization. The process of improving a website to increase its visibility when people search for products or services related to a business in Google, Bing, and other search engines.

SLA: Service Level Agreement. Defines the level of service a customer expects from a vendor, laying out the metrics by which service is measured, as well as remedies or penalties should agreed-on service levels not be achieved.

SMB: Small and Medium-sized Business. Small businesses are usually defined as organizations with fewer than 100 employees; medium-sized businesses are those organizations with 100–999 employees.

Tech Stack: The combination of technologies a company uses to build and run its sales and marketing activities.

Upselling: A sales technique that encourages customers to spend more money by purchasing an upgraded or premium version of the product they originally intended to buy.

USP: Unique Selling Proposition. The essence of what makes your product or service better than competitors'.

Value Proposition: A concise statement of the benefits that a company is delivering to customers who buy its products or services. It serves as a declaration of intent, both inside the company and in the marketplace.

VAR: Value-Added Reseller. An organization that is part of a sales channel for an original equipment manufacturer (OEM) and resells a product or service to the end-customer.

Vertical Content Marketing: A strategy targeted at a niche audience for a business in a specific demographic or industry.

White Label Partnership: Often called private label, where a reseller offers your solutions under their own brand to their customers.

ACKNOWLEDGMENTS

First and foremost thank you to every one of my readers. Thank you for your purchase, your interest, your support, and for allowing me to help you and your business grow.

I want to give a big shout-out and thanks to a number of folks behind the scenes who have contributed positively toward my success and the publication of this book—either many years ago in an indirect but very supportive fashion or, more recently, by helping with all the heavy lifting of getting this book in your hands today.

A tremendous thanks to my entire family for their continuous support and love. My beloved daughter, Belinda, for being my beacon of light and motivation whenever things looked the darkest. She reminded me indirectly to always take responsibility and set a good example for her and others around me in need of positive influence.

Thanks to my mother, Beth, who from a distance never failed to support me, love me, and believe in my far-reaching projects. And thanks to my entire family and friends in Denmark—I miss you beyond words and more often than you can imagine.

A big thanks to my brother Pax and family, Jackie, Kross, and Sydney, who've been a tremendous rock for me to lean on during my most difficult times. To my father, Michael, who passed away many years ago, for being a big motivating driver to realize my potential. And thanks to Maritza Rivas. the mother of my daughter, for her support as a great parent and teammate always.

And most recently, thanks to my editor and book coach Graham Barker, for always cheering me on and encouraging and instilling confidence in me that I had a book to share with the world. And kudos to Ben Tyson for pushing me to write this book many years back, kindly writing the Foreword, and never hesitating to help with my projects.

Also, a tremendous thanks to Elizabeth Navas, my first team member in Colombia who helped me get everything organized while launching Great Dane Ventures, Elev8.io, and my Accelerator Platform and for playing a supportive role in the realization of this book. Similarly, a big thanks to Sebastian Sepulveda, my graphic designer, who created all the outstanding graphics for this book and related projects.

Thank you to all my former partners over the years, most recently Alexander Nygart and Andrew Lolk, as well as the many great team members and superstar performers.

Above all, thank you to my many clients and business partners of all types and sizes without whom this book could certainly never have taken the shape it has and who fueled me with the many learnings I have shared with you in these pages.

Last, thanks to the terrific publishing team at Scribe Media for their flexibility, support, and belief in helping me share my stories in hopes of making a small impact in the world.

And if I have overlooked any of my many friends, other family members, business partners, or associates, then please remember that you all have played a big role in this enriching journey. I thank you deeply for your support, hard work, love, patience, and especially constructive criticism to help me raise my standards and motivate me to become a better person and professional. Your example has taught me to always begin with the end in mind. I trust this book will inspire you to do so as well.